WORTH IT ALL

Books by Jim Wright

You and Your Congressman
The Coming Water Famine
Of Swords and Plowshares
Congress and Conscience (with others)
Reflections of a Public Man

WORTH IT ALL

MY WAR FOR PEACE

JIM WRIGHT
Former Speaker of the House of Representatives

BRASSEY'S (US)
A Maxwell Macmillan Company
Washington · New York · London

Brassey's (US)

Editorial Offices
Brassey's (US)
8000 Westpark Drive
First Floor
McLean, Virginia 22102

Order Department
Brassey's Book Orders
c/o Macmillan Publishing Co.
100 Front Street, Box 500
Riverside, New Jersey 08075

Brassey's (US) is a Maxwell Macmillan Company. Brassey's books are available
at special discounts for bulk purchases for sales promotions, premiums,
fund-raising, or educational use through the Special Sales Director, Macmillan
Publishing Company, 866 Third Avenue, New York, New York 10022.

Library of Congress Cataloging-in-Publication Data
Wright, Jim, 1922–
      Worth It All : My War for Peace / Jim Wright.
          p.   cm.
      Includes index.
      ISBN 0-02-881075-9
      1. Central America—Relations—United States.   2. United States—
Relations—Central America.   3. United States—Politics and
government—1981–1989.   4. United States—Politics and
government—1989–1993.   5. Counterrevolutions—Nicaragua.
6. Military assistance, American—Nicaragua.   7. Wright, Jim, 1922– .
I. Title.
F1436.8.U6W75   1993
327.730728—dc20   93-17287
                                                              CIP

10   9   8   7   6   5   4   3   2   1

Printed in the United States of America

To Oscar Arias and Jimmy Carter,
men of peace . . .
and to the memory of
José Napoleón Duarte

Contents

Preface

This is the story of my journey through the political minefields of official Washington in the 1980s, when Central American wars divided our nation's policymakers like nothing else has since the war in Vietnam. I have written this book because the history of that turbulent time would not be complete without this particular insight from Capitol Hill.

Without intending to do so, I became a focal point of major controversy and the target of vicious attacks when I undertook to help end the Central American wars. I was accused of meddling in foreign affairs by the administration that brought us the Iran/Contra scandal. The domestic political opposition singled me out for attacks on my patriotism and my personal character. On May 31, 1989, I became a figure unique to history when I stood in the well of the House of Representatives and resigned as Speaker. To hold onto that post would only have prolonged the acrimony and divisiveness that plagued our government over this issue. I had done all that I could. By then I had helped stop the bloodshed. An honorable peace and democracy were on the horizon. That struggle ended my thirty-four year career, but from my perspective it was worth it all.

I had spent a lifetime supporting the bipartisan foreign policy objectives of nine Democrat and Republican presidents since 1943 when I was twenty years old and flying combat missions in the South Pacific. In the 1980s I became reluctantly convinced that a secret coterie of ideologues in the administration were violating this country's laws and lying about it to Congress and the public. I did not want to believe this, but it was agonizingly clear. As the chief Constitutional officer of Congress, I had a responsibility, and I tried my best to discharge it.

Invited by the besieged Reagan administration in 1987 to join a bipartisan call for peace, I wrote what came to be known as the Wright-Reagan peace plan. When it evoked a sympathetic response from Latin American leaders and began to work, administration spokesmen denounced me for trying to play secretary of state.

For my efforts, I was accused by Elliott Abrams of the State Department and a right-wing cabal of leaking classified information when I spoke privately of secret activities aimed at wrecking the peace talks in Nicaragua. Representative Newt Gingrich, Republican from Georgia, and other partisan activists hounded me for more than a year with charges that I had violated House rules. But I had broken no law nor intentionally breached any rule of the House. I probably paid too little attention to my personal affairs while driving, perhaps too persistently, to prod Congress into a more dynamic role in both domestic and foreign policy. For whatever errors of judgment may be laid to me, I assume full responsibility.

This book is my personal story of a painful effort to create a positive bipartisan policy toward Central America. It is also the story of a peace plan that came into being despite determined opposition at very high levels of government. Once implemented, though imperfectly, that plan stopped the killing in El Salvador and Nicaragua where savage guerrilla wars had claimed approximately 100,000 lives in the decade of the 1980s. The plan and its derivative agreements, elections, and internal reforms may yet set into motion sweeping changes in the area. If built upon intelligently, they may also bring about longterm changes in our relations with our nearest neighbors.

This is a story of contrasting visions of America's role in the post-cold war world—and of what positive things we can do to influence events in this hemisphere to the lasting advantage of ourselves as well as that of its people who have been so long denied.

This story is also about Congress and the very human ways in which that institution functions. Congress is not a symposium of saints and Olympian prophets but a collection of ordinary men and women grappling with extraordinary problems. That goes for its leadership in which I had the privilege to serve for twelve years. Whatever may be said of my congressional colleagues, they do work hard, and most of them, Republicans and Democrats alike, try their best to do what is right for the country. I hope readers will see this as they walk with me through these pages.

I have tried to write this book in a way that its story will be readable and its facts reliable. I vouch for the personal conversations that appear throughout. Wherever something is quoted from a news periodical, I have endeavored to give the source in the text rather than breaking up the continuity with footnotes. I didn't want this to read like a legal brief or an academic dissertation.

For many of the facts in chapters four and five, some of which were unknown to any of us in Congress at the time they occurred, I am indebted to information gleaned from subsequent congressional hearings and from four very informative books: *Banana Diplomacy:The Making of American Policy in Nicaragua, 1981 to 1987* by Roy Gutman; *Veil: The Secret Wars of the CIA, 1981 to 1987* by Bob Woodward; *Crossroads: Congress, the Reagan Administration, and Central America* by Cynthia J. Arnson; and *Sleepwalking Through History: America Through the Reagan Years* by Haynes Johnson.

In another attempt to make my recording of the sometimes acrimonious 1980s as factually accurate as possible, I have included in an appendix key documents from my personal files. I felt it important that those readers and scholars who wish to review the precise words would have available the agreements I made on behalf of the House of Representatives with leaders of the executive branch. Perhaps the most interesting are the letters and notes I sent to and received from President Reagan, Secretaries of State George Shultz and Jim Baker, Daniel Ortega, Oscar Arias, and other officials of Central America.

Anybody who has served in public office is indebted to many more people than he or she can ever hope to name. And I could no wise adequately thank those loyalists like Marshall Lynam, Kathy Mitchell, Jimmie Bodiford, and the late Craig Raupe, who was even more fiercely supportive on occasions when he thought I was wrong. Numerous congressional colleagues and others unmentioned in this manuscript contributed in ways that were indispensable to the mission it describes as well as to the book's completion.

Many of the details recited here would have been lost in the fog of indistinct memory had it not been for several key people. Dr. Ben Procter of Texas Christian University directed an oral history project, audiotaping my impressions of people and events throughout the 1980s on a frequent, sometimes daily, basis while meetings and conversations remained vivid in my mind. Wilson Morris, my foreign policy aide, kept detailed notes of my meetings with colleagues and

representatives of foreign governments. Congressman David Bonior
of Michigan and Richard Peña, my personal emissary to the Esquipulas meetings, both kept journals that they have shared with me.
Finally, I must express my appreciation to Dr. Robert Pastor, associate of former President Jimmy Carter and director of the Latin
American and Caribbean program at the Carter Center at Emory
University, for reading this manuscript while it was in process, discussing it with me on various occasions, and giving me many helpful
suggestions.

Norma Ritchson, Ora Beth McMullen, and my sister, Mary Connell, have helped me with research and preparing the manuscript. I
thank Frank Margiotta of Brassey's for believing in this book, Vicki
Chamlee for her patience as I strained to meet deadlines, and Con-
stance Buchanan for pruning a lot of my redundant prose and making this a better book. Two business associates, Bernard Rapoport
and Johnny Vinson, deserve my special appreciation for their tolerance of my time-consuming preoccupation with this manuscript.

Above all, I am indebted to my wife Betty, who puts the luster in
my life.

WORTH IT ALL

CHAPTER 1

Collision Course

Brothers, each one of you is one of us. We are the same people. The campesinos you kill are your own brothers and sisters.

—Archbishop Oscar Romero
shortly before his martyrdom in March 1980

"Damn it, Sergio," I exploded in exasperation, "I'm telling you for the fifth time that the United States is *not* going to invade your country! We're *not* trying to overthrow your government!"

"Your nation's weapons are killing our people," Sergio Ramírez answered coolly on behalf of the Nicaraguan government. "Your mines are blowing up our bridges. Your bombs destroy water tanks and leave our villages without water—"

"Yes," interrupted Nicaraguan cabinet member Jaime Wheelock, "and the former Somoza guardsmen who now carry your guns are boasting that they'll be in Managua in six months to put their old crowd back in power! The United States is paying them. Your country is paying in dollars and the Nicaraguan people are paying in blood."

A huge portrait of Augusto César Sandino dominated the sparsely

1

furnished room. So austere were the long wooden table and folding chairs in this chamber that my eyes were drawn back involuntarily to the oversized painting with its idealized version of the young revolutionary. There he stood, a study in innocence, bandolier slung over his right shoulder and on his head a tall Western hat. It was a hat of the William S. Hart or Tom Mix era, not a short-crowned Roy Rogers hat. On the youthful face was the ingenuous appeal of a young James Dean.

I sighed. These people have actually begun to believe their own rhetoric, I thought. It was April 12, 1982. Managua had undergone a striking metamorphosis in the months since my last visit. Then, in 1980, hope had reigned. Leaders in the business community were relieved to be rid of Somoza. Violeta Chamorro and Alfonso Robelo, who had just resigned from the original Sandinista junta, were sure that a new friendship with the United States could take root and flourish, based on equality rather than subservience. Enrique Dreyfus, president of COSEP (the Superior Council of Private Enterprise), a sort of national chamber of commerce, was speaking of a mixed economy and pluralistic society. Everywhere I'd looked in 1980, official slogans glorified health and learning. Billboards proclaimed: *Alfabetizacion es la Liberacion!* (Literacy is liberty!)

Now, in 1982, those same billboards glowered with an artist's portrayal of huge U.S. tanks trampling Nicaraguan terrain as shirtless, brown-skinned Nicaraguans fought them off with rifles. The printing trumpeted: *Triunfaramos Sobre los Yanquis, Imperialistas!* (We shall triumph over the Yankee imperialists!)

Was this a cynical manipulation of the public, a blatant appeal to patriotism as the historic excuse for surrendering liberties to police-state controls? The government, pointing to the fear of a U.S. invasion, had just enacted the Emergency Law suspending thirteen articles of the constitution and putting the country on a wartime footing. Several Nicaraguans, including Enrique Dreyfus, had been jailed. Or could these benighted leaders be so hypnotized by their own slogans that they actually believed the United States was trying to overthrow their government by force and substitute one of our choosing?

Probably some of each, I decided. No doubt most of the country's leaders thought us capable of plotting the physical overthrow of their government. History, after all, gave precedent for paranoia. U.S. forces *had* occupied their country for more than two decades early in the century. Sophisticated Nicaraguans thought of the forty-three-year Somoza dynasty that followed as a sort of U.S. proxy. (Hadn't

Franklin Roosevelt supposedly once referred to the first Somoza as
"*our* son-of-a-bitch"?) Within the past few weeks several U.S. daily
newspapers and two weekly magazines had published leaks connecting the CIA with armed attacks in northern Nicaragua.

Yes, I realized, Nicaraguans could actually believe we were plotting their government's overthrow. But of course we were not. We
couldn't be. I had the personal assurance of Bill Casey. Like most of
my colleagues on the congressional intelligence committees, I had
taken CIA Director Casey's testimony at face value. He had told us
solemnly of "incontrovertible evidence" linking Nicaragua's Sandinista government to "Marxist" guerrilla leaders intent on overthrowing the elected government in El Salvador. Most of the weapons used
by these guerrillas, Casey informed us, were coming into that country
surreptitiously from Nicaragua. Terrorist tactics by leftist forces were
actually being directed by radio from a clandestine broadcasting station in downtown Managua, Casey claimed.

In the secret hearing of the House committee, several of us were at
pains to get one clear stipulation: The paramilitary activities being
contemplated would be designed strictly to interdict and dry up the
arms flow; this was *not* an effort to start a new war. We were not
organizing an invasion of Nicaragua.

"Please understand that this committee is not authorizing a war
against Nicaragua's government," Chairman Edward Boland of Massachusetts admonished. Ranking Republican Bill Whitehurst of Virginia agreed.

"One thing we cannot afford," I remember telling the intelligence
chief, "is another Bay of Pigs!"

Our pink-cheeked, white-haired CIA director had a minor speech
impediment that made it difficult for him to pronounce the *r* sound.
Whenever Casey spoke the subject country's name it came across as
Nicawagua. But there was no misunderstanding what he said. We
were out to shut off weapons at El Salvador's border. That was all we
were trying to do. I believed him.

Most of those who came with me to Central America in April 1982
still believed that story. Representative Mike Barnes of Maryland,
chairman of the Western Hemisphere Subcommittee, and big George
Miller of California may have been growing skeptical. But Foreign
Affairs Committee Chairman Clement Zablocki of Wisconsin and
Clay Shaw, a new Republican from Florida, entertained no doubts
whatsoever.

I must explain it clearly to these intense young Nicaraguans, I thought, before conditions deteriorate further. They must be made to see that all they have to do is shut off the flow of weapons into El Salvador.

"Look, gentlemen," I said, "if you're honestly worried about an invasion of your country, there is one clear way you can avoid it. Respect the territorial boundaries of El Salvador, and we'll respect yours. Just leave your neighbors alone and we'll leave you alone. You have my word for that."

What a terrible presumption! I realized this later, reflecting upon my naive assurance. At the time I thought I was speaking the gospel. What I said, I believed, had the sure backing of official U.S. policy.

Back at the Intercontinental Hotel, Congressman Bill Alexander and I went for a swim. I was sunning when a man named Antonio asked me if I would like a drink from the bar. I remembered this man from my trip in 1980, identifying him vaguely in my mind as a hotel employee with whom I'd once engaged in conversation about the future of his country. Antonio recalled our earlier talk.

"It is unfortunate," he said, "that things have changed."

"Tell me, Antonio," I said, "do the Nicaraguan people actually believe that my country is making war against them?"

He hesitated, clearly wondering if he should speak with candor. Then he said, "My family is from the north country, up near the Coco River. A large force invaded at Christmastime. They attacked about twenty villages. They killed some people and wounded many others. They left a lot of land mines, and these have hurt many more people. My cousin lost her foot and part of her leg when one of the mines exploded as she walked along a path."

He paused. "We brought my cousin here to Managua for medical treatment. She is at my house, not far from this place. Would you like to talk with her?"

Antonio's ancient pickup truck rumbled over pockmarked streets to the city's edge, then onto an unpaved road, coming to rest in front of a modest house of concrete blocks and a corrugated tin roof. The floor was earthen but swept clean. Cotton draperies adorned the windows. A woman whom Antonio introduced as his aunt welcomed me graciously and offered me refreshment.

Then I saw the little girl. She stood with a thin wooden crutch under her left arm. The dark, luminous eyes seemed large in her small face. Her little cotton dress was clean and neat. Her left foot was missing. She smiled at me. Suddenly my eyes filled with tears, and I couldn't speak.

I had supposed Antonio's cousin to be an adult. This girl couldn't have been more than nine, ten at the most. I didn't have the heart to interrogate her.

This, please God, was not what we had authorized—not what Bill Casey had spoken of to our Intelligence Committee. How could this little girl be involved in any flow of arms across the Salvadoran border?

It came to me with a stab of pain that U.S. taxpayers' money, with my silent acquiescence, had paid for the planting of the land mine that had crippled this child as well as for the machine guns and bullets that had killed other Nicaraguan villagers. And most of my colleagues in Congress knew nothing about it. This was a covert operation, set in motion for the sole supposed purpose of interdicting arms.

At least in El Salvador, Congress knew what we were up to. We had publicly debated and approved military and other aid to its elected government. As majority leader, I had rallied bipartisan support for President Reagan's request. We wanted to give elective processes a chance in that small, violent country where for four hundred years no freely chosen government had been allowed to complete its term.

As Antonio and I returned over dusty roads to the hotel, my mind went back to El Salvador. Two days earlier, during dinner at the official residence of U.S. Ambassador Deane Hinton, I had been deliberately seated beside Roberto D'Aubuisson, leader of the right-wing ARENA (National Republican Alliance) party that had just legally maneuvered its way into majority control of the Salvadoran Constituent Assembly. A retired army major with close ties to the military, D'Aubuisson was a celebrated firebrand, hated and feared by political opponents. Many suspected him of organizing and leading the secret death squads that had assassinated the late Archbishop Oscar Romero and were terrorizing the countryside. It was my mission that night, urged upon me by Ambassador Hinton, to convince D'Aubuisson that the U.S. Congress would terminate all aid to El Salvador if under his leadership it embarked on a reign of terror. I had pressed that message as hard as I could, and I believed it to be true.

"Look, Major," I said, "you and I ought to be able to understand one another. Like you, I'm a former military officer. Like you, I'm leader of the majority in our Congress. I know what my colleagues will accept and what they won't. Basically, they serve the American people. It's only fair to tell you that a lot of people in my country are suspicious of your intentions. Our Congress will not support any government which tolerates death squads that prey on the political opposition."

D'Aubuisson, thin and ascetic, was eating little. A tense bundle of energy, he sat at my right staring into my eyes and drumming his fingers nervously on the table. He understood the message.

"We'd surely like to see democracy work in El Salvador," I assured him. "We've been working at it in my country for about two hundred years, and we've discovered that it just can't work without some tolerance for opposing views." I could not be sure that he comprehended that.

Back at the hotel, I tried to sort out my thoughts. One thing seemed clear: My government and that of Nicaragua were on a collision course that could result in a lot of bloodshed and serve the best interests of neither.

I walked out on a balcony and looked across the pockmarked center of Managua. On a gentle rise to my right stood the monument to Franklin D. Roosevelt that had thrilled me when I first came upon it twenty-five years earlier. Above that, on a bluff overlooking downtown, rose the splendid presidential palace of the Somozas, now spurned by the Sandinista government. To the left, across a broad expanse of now-vacant land, lay the grand cathedral, the only building still functioning in the sprawling old business district, scarred by so many natural and man-made disasters.

No wonder they're paranoid, I thought. Between volcanic eruptions, earthquakes, harsh dictatorships, civil wars, and foreign military intrusions, this hard-luck country had known precious little tranquility. And none seemed likely in the offing.

Little did I suspect that for most of the next seven years I would be in the thick of efforts to resolve the twin dilemmas of Nicaragua and El Salvador. Their violence would claim the lives of 100,000 people, split the U.S. Congress into warring camps, and drive the White House to the desperate illegality of the Iran-Contra scandal.

I could know none of this at the time, of course. Nor could I have supposed that I would be drawn so forcefully into the whirling vortex of the controversy, or that my efforts to find a path to peace and democracy in the region would bring me into direct conflict with the president of the United States and subject me to scalding criticism that would contribute indirectly to the end of my legislative career.

But we are getting ahead of the story. As I look back on those events today, I really don't think I could have avoided getting involved in the ways I have just described, except perhaps by being a different person. So much of what we are, what we believe, and what we do is shaped at an early age, without our realizing it. I guess I was fated to get involved.

CHAPTER 2

A Time of Learning

The ideal condition
Would be, I admit, that men should
* be right by instinct;*
But since we are all likely to go astray,
The reasonable thing is to learn from
* those who can teach.*

—Sophocles

At some point I realized that I had a consuming interest in Latin America. I'm not sure when, or where, it began, somewhere far back in my youth. My maternal grandmother was full of true stories of the early days along the Mexican border when she ran a company store. She was one of only three gringa women in the community. "The Mexicans were very poor, Jimmy," I can hear her saying, "and some people were always warning me that they would steal. But they never stole a thing from that store. I found out that if you're honest with them they'll be honest with you."

That simple maxim, so nearly absolute to my grandmother, unfortunately encounters a few exceptions in human practice. But it became embedded in the matrix of ideas forming in my mind at the

8

age of five and six. *If you're honest with them they'll be honest with you.* Applied to the Mexican people, I was to find it a far more reliable guide than the crude stereotypes by which others in our Texas culture, nurtured on vivid accounts of Santa Anna's duplicity (see *The Eagle: The Autobiography of Santa Anna,* edited by A. F. Crawford), sometimes sought to portray Mexicans in general.

My mother was born Marie Louella Lyster, on September 11, 1894, in what then was the New Mexico Territory. Her father, Harry Hanyngton Lyster, was a native of Australia. His parents on both sides traced their lineage to County Tyrone, Ireland. Harry Lyster graduated in civil engineering from Heidelberg University in Germany and came to live with his great uncle, Charles Ligar, on a 640-acre Texas ranch that the latter had settled after retiring as Australia's surveyor general. Ligar's virgin acreage was an original land grant from the State of Texas. There it was, twenty-five miles west of Fort Worth, that Harry Lyster met and married my grandmother, Lena Crowder, the nineteen-year-old daughter of a neighbor rancher who was also the teacher at the community school. Harry was soon hired by the railroad to survey a route through the then-trackless plains and mountains along the Mexican border to California. He recruited a team and taught them the art of surveying. Somewhere on that trail he came down with undulant fever and died, eighteen months after my mother's birth.

Widowed in her early twenties and with an infant to feed and clothe, my grandmother was driven to find work nearly a thousand miles from home. Lena Lyster took a job managing the railroad commissary, the only retail store for many miles in any direction. She was one of but few women in a wide geographic radius who could read and write and "do sums." Almost all of the railroad's employees were Mexicans drawn from the local population. They were the customers.

My grandmother cherished her memories of that place and time. Some of the stories were funny, like her account of a group of men who stole away to a bend in a dry arroyo for a Sunday afternoon cockfight. Just as the diversion was getting under way, a pack of dogs owned by a local cattleman chased a stray coyote down the deep riverbed into the crowd, scattering the chickens in every direction. There were also tales of pathos—of sick babies and chronic drought and individual dignity that survived the pervasive poverty. Lena Lyster's role as proprietress of the sole mercantile establishment conferred on her, despite her youth, a certain status. While Mexican girls sometimes looked on her as a sort of mother-confessor, she was learning lessons in infant care and folk medicine from the older women. She learned something of old Mexico, its people and their culture. And, out of necessity, she learned some important things about intercultural relations.

"I found out," she said, "that if you're honest with them they'll be honest with you."

In 1914 my mother and father were married at Valentine, Texas, in the Davis Mountains. My father, James Claude Wright, was company commander of the Weatherford, Texas, National Guard unit. With other units, it was federalized by Woodrow Wilson and sent to guard the U.S. border from incursions by Pancho Villa's revolutionary forces, which had wrested control of Mexico's northern state of Chihuahua.

Many Texans in the region of El Paso sympathized with the aims of the Mexican revolution. They had applauded the statements of the visionary leader Francisco Madero and cheered when, in November of 1913, General Villa and his ragtag army captured Juárez, directly across the river from El Paso. Villa met El Paso's mayor, a man named E. C. Kelly, at the international bridge between the two cities and expressed regret over the accidental death by stray gunfire of an El Paso citizen. Villa promised full protection for all U.S. nationals within his zone of authority and vowed to meet the expected counterattack by government troops far enough south of the border to avoid the danger of bullets reaching into El Paso.

Sympathizers on our side of the border sometimes provided rations for Villa's picturesque troops with their serapes and huge sombreros. Small bands of mostly illiterate Mexican soldiers occasionally foraged into U.S. territory in search of beef or other provisions to feed their hungry, often only semidisciplined cadres. There were a few skirmishes. The mission of the National Guard, under General John J. Pershing's command, was to keep order along the skinny, twisting Rio Grande and to avoid incidents where possible.

Things grew more tense, as I would read in later years, after President Wilson ordered the U.S. Navy to intercede in April of 1914. The navy was to prevent a German merchant ship, carrying 200 machine guns and 15 million rounds of ammunition for government forces, from docking at Veracruz. U.S. Marines stormed ashore at Veracruz and three U.S. warships opened fire over their heads. Mexican casualties ran into the hundreds, mostly civilians trying to slow down the advancing troops, while the U.S. landing force suffered nineteen dead and seventy wounded. Among the Mexican dead was a group of young boys, students at a local military school, who had tried vainly to shoot it out with the marines.

The American invasion injected a new element into the boiling pot of instability that was Mexico. There was fear for a time that the intrusion of gringos would unite the Mexican people behind the hated dictator Victoriano Huerta. Even Alvaro Obregon, an enemy of Huerta's and a supporter of the constitutionalists, was advocating that Mexicans unite to expel the U.S. forces. This did not occur, as Pancho Villa argued vehemently against it. But tension grew, and our southern border throbbed with rumors as seven thousand U.S. Marines and soldiers maintained an uneasy occupation of Veracruz throughout the summer.

My father told me many years later that he had privately sympathized with the announced goals of Madero and Villa—to replace the forty years of dictatorship with a constitutional system. He thought most of the young Texas guardsmen who served with him felt the same way. So apparently did President Wilson, who in spite of his almost religious dedication to human freedom may not fully have appreciated the tremors of nationalism that coursed through Mexico in the wake of the U.S. invasion. Things were tense, and the job of the National Guard, personal feelings aside, was to keep Mexican troops on their side of the border by whatever means necessary.

One day my father, in command of a group patrolling south of Sierra Blanca, encountered a platoon of Mexican cavalry a half mile or more on our side of the Rio Grande. Dad didn't tell me this story until I was a teenager, and even then I had to coax it out of him. Each man in the Mexican patrol had a rifle and a cartridge belt of ammunition slung over his shoulder, according to my father's recollection.

"What did you do?" I asked. "Did you open fire on them?"

"Oh, no," he said. "We didn't have to do that. I just talked to them."

"What did you say?" I insisted. "Do you remember what you said?"

"Yes, I think I remember exactly what I said. I thought about it very carefully before I said it. I didn't know enough Spanish to have a long conversation. And it was important to say the right thing."

"Well, what did you say?"

"Caballeros! Momentito!"

The leader of the Mexican group reined his horse, signaled the others to rein in, and sat poised for the gringo soldiers to make their move.

My dad approached singly, stopped within earshot, and said politely, "Dispensame, pero ustedes estan en nuestro lado de la frontera." (Excuse me, but you are on our side of the border.)

At that, the commander of the Mexican troops raised his forefinger to the brim of his floppy sombrero in a salute, turned, and ordered his troops to reverse their course toward the trickle of water that formed the international boundary.

"What made them turn and go so easily?" I remember asking. "Couldn't there have been a skirmish? A fight?"

"No, no, I don't think so," my father said. "They didn't want a fight with our country, and they knew our intentions toward them were peaceful."

"How did they know that?"

My dad thought for a moment. "Maybe it was because I called them 'caballeros.' It's the Spanish word for 'gentlemen,' you know."

After another short silence, he said, "Maybe it was something else, too. Something about territory. The so-called wetbacks come across, of course, because they're hungry and they're looking for work. That's different. But a military force, that's something else. Maybe they respect our territory because they want us to respect theirs. The Latin Americans all feel very strongly about that. It's a thing called nationalism."

In years to come, I would see many examples of this thing called nationalism. I came to know it as a fact of life. It could be good or bad, but it could not be ignored.

During the summer of 1937, when I was fourteen, I spent a lot of my spare time at the Dallas Fair Grounds' Pan-American exposition. Local civic interests, seeking a second summer of tourism to capitalize on the spacious and expensive buildings erected the previous year for the Texas centennial, were sponsoring a hemispheric fair with entertainment and exhibits drawn from Latin American countries. I was fascinated by the picturesque rainbow of cultures. I met exhibitors and concessionaires from several countries and soaked up their literature like a blotter absorbing inkspots.

That summer I discovered some new heroes, men named Bolívar and San Martín, Hildago and Juárez, who had a lot in common with my old heroes—Washington, Jefferson, Sam Houston, and Andrew Jackson. In every case the names of these men were enshrined in their respective countries for deeds that involved freeing ordinary people from the yokes of foreign domination. That was a critical part of their immortality. It was foreign control against which they struggled. All of them drank from the springs of nationalism.

To me, Simón Bolívar was the most fascinating one of all. Bolívar liked the United States and wanted to duplicate its most attractive features. (More than forty years later I would visit his home in Caracas and realize just how grandly, in the Andean nations, he *still* is immortalized as "The Liberator.") In Venezuela, Bolívar modeled his independence movement on the pattern set by our founding fathers. He used Jefferson's words. He even tried to create a United States of South America. In that latter effort, Bolívar failed. Venezuela, Colombia, Ecuador, Bolivia, Peru—Bolívar led the military struggles that freed them all from their colonial bonds, but he couldn't get them to submerge their differences and unite. Trying to do so, he finally confessed, was like "plowing the sea."

It seems the people in each land cherished their minor differences, each group wanting a nation distinctly its own. That, too, was nationalism, sometimes insular and self-inhibiting, even self-destructive, but in its way understandable. Nationalism: From its common root have sprung the flowers of patriotism and the weeds of chauvinism.

For most people in our country, the discovery of Latin America begins with the discovery of Mexico. It was no different with me. During my youth I took many enjoyable trips to Mexico. Strangers welcomed me warmly. With the Mexican people I came to associate attributes of friendliness, hospitality, spontaneity, generosity. Yes, most of them were poor—by our standards, dirt poor. But there also was dignity, affable geniality. Never was I made to feel in the slightest degree unwelcome—until I was twenty years old.

In January and February of 1943, I was a newly commissioned second lieutenant in the U.S. Army Air Corps, stationed first at Davis-Monthan Field near Tucson and then briefly at Biggs Field near El Paso. In free moments I went across the border, once to Nogales and twice to Juárez. Mexicans casually met were not the same. I was not made to feel *un*welcome; I just did not feel welcome. There was a faint but unmistakable chill that left me mystified.

Unlike most of the other young American airmen who made up the 380th Bomb Group—men from New England, the Midwest, the West, the Southeast—I had been a habitué of Juárez, Nogales, Reynosa, Matamoros. Most of the fellows wanted to go at least once to Mexico. Some would return with the comment, "I don't think they like us much over there." I took issue with them. "You're mistaken," I would say. "Those are the friendliest people in the world." Still, the change I recently had experienced was troubling me.

One morning at Biggs Field two of our crewmen failed to show up for the flight-line formation. I was summoned to the operations room where a telephone call awaited me. It was one of the missing crewmen.

"Hey, Tex, we're in the hoosegow! I mean, Lieutenant! They say our commanding officer has to come over here before they'll let us out."

"That's not me," I reminded him. "That's Connery, or maybe they mean Miller."

"Cheeze! Not Miller! For God's sake, don't tell Major Miller! I thought you'd know what to do."

"Where are you?"

"Hell, I don't know," said Sergeant Welch. "We're in Juárez somewhere. We're in the stinkin' jail!"

"I'll get Connery," I promised.

Captain Gus Connery was four years older than I and maybe ten years smarter. He and I discussed the predicament on the way to the bridge. "No point in trying to throw our weight around," Connery was saying. We agreed that we could all be in trouble if we got into a fracas.

We found the jail easily enough. I tried to talk with the Mexican police officer in charge. His English was even worse than my Spanish, and I wasn't making much progress. Our two crewmen had been picked up in a street altercation about midnight. They were *muy boracho*, the police officer said.

"Very drunk," I translated. Connery looked at me and shook his head.

"Nos sientamos mucho," I stammered, trying to express our regrets. The way it came out, I was saying we regretted *ourselves*. The first hint of humor appeared in the Mexican's eye, then quickly disappeared. He began talking about the charges, a possible trial. I picked up this much.

"Podemos pagar?" (Can't we just pay a fine?) I asked, reaching in my pocket for emphasis. "Quanto tarifa?"

The police officer was pretending not to understand. Then another man walked up. He was in civilian dress, apparently a commissioner of some kind. The police officer deferred to him. To my relief the second Mexican spoke very good English. But he looked sternly at us.

"Your men were in a fight last night. They were fighting with three of our young men. We arrested them also. Your men are lucky that the officers came, because a crowd was gathering and they could have been badly hurt."

"We're very sorry," Captain Connery said. "I assure you this will not happen again—at least not with any of our squadron. We'll be shipping out in a few days, anyway. We're on our way overseas. We hope our two men have not caused you any serious trouble."

"They are not the first," the Mexican official sighed. "They did cause everyone a bit of trouble, but others have done it before. They are far away from home, and they think the uniform is their passport to anything they want to do." There was a hint of bitterness in that last comment.

I recoiled. So that's what it was—the uniform. That was what made the difference in the treatment we were receiving. I wanted to tell this man we were wearing the uniform for his country too, for anyone who didn't want to be run over by the Nazis. But I bit my lip and held my peace. It was the wrong time to get angry.

Our two crewmen had been whistling at girls on the street. Three young Mexican men thought they were insulting the girls and making inappropriate sexual propositions. "Apparently some of your people have the idea that all Mexican girls are prostitutes," said our host.

"That would be very wrong, sir. We know that isn't true," Connery was saying. "So far as we're concerned, we don't feel that way at all, and we apologize if anyone has given that impression."

There was silence while the Mexican commissioner looked at us, weighing our sincerity. Finally I asked if we could see our two crewmen.

"You may take them with you," said the commissioner. "I will discharge them to your care, Lieutenant. Yours and the captain's. There will be no fine this time. But please remember that you are guests in our country and that our young women are as precious to us as your sisters are to you."

The heroes of a nation tell something about the basic values its people exalt. All of us tend to respect those traits held up to us in our childhood as admirable. We want to emulate those examples we admire. To understand what motivates Latin Americans as a whole, it is helpful to search for the role models they hold in common.

Success was not the only, or even the primary, qualification for heroism in the southern part of our hemisphere. Mexicans think more highly of Montezuma than Cortés, for example. They reserve special scorn for a Mayan girl called Malínche who was the lover of the Castilian conqueror. In the Mexican idiom her name is a synonym for betrayal, like Benedict Arnold or Quisling. Cortés, for all his military brilliance and swashbuckling guile, is not admired; Montezuma, so naively trusting, is.

Martyrs abound in Latin America's pantheon of heroes. Peruvian history deifies an Inca named Túpac Amaru who resisted the Spanish conquest and was executed in 1569. More than two hundred years later, in 1780, an Inca descendant named José Condorcanqui led a revolt against the Spanish overlords. He abandoned his name and embraced for himself the Indian name of the early Inca. This second Túpac Amaru was tortured cruelly and slain. He is celebrated as a precursor of Latin American independence.

Or consider the aura of sanctity surrounding the memory of Augusto César Sandino, a young Nicaraguan nationalist who raised a peasant band in the mountains to wage guerrilla warfare against U.S. forces during their occupation of his country, which began in 1912 and did not end until 1933. Sandino is commonly believed to have been betrayed and shot by the first Anastasio Somoza. That may explain in part why the common people never loved the Somoza family. As in the case of Emiliano Zapata in Mexico, nobody has ever located the grave of Sandino. So many are the legends and the myths, however, and so many the verbal platitudes attributed to him posthumously, that following the successful Sandinista revolution in 1979 some Nicaraguan with a sense of humor painted the following in bold letters across a rocky Nicaraguan mountainside: "I never really said any of that stuff. —A. C. Sandino"

Many historians believe that Maximilian, Napoleon's surrogate who ruled Mexico from Chapultec palace until overthrown in 1867, truly loved the Mexican people and tried earnestly if naively to serve them well. I do not know the truth of that. But the mere suggestion that Maximilian might have been well-disposed toward them will draw a heated denial almost anywhere in Mexico. Your Mexican host will tell you that the Austrian was a cruel despot, his wife Carlotta an indulgent snob—and that he had no business being in Mexico in the first place. That's it, really. He was not *of* the Mexican people, whatever his pretensions or desires. His rule was imposed on them from outside. He was an imposter and an offense to their nationalism.

*   *   *

Over the years more than forty trips through various parts of Latin America have shown me that most people in the lands to our south hold three U.S. presidents in enormous esteem. Statues in unexpected places, faded photographs on walls in private residences, the tone of voice in conversational references all attest to popularly felt love and respect for Abraham Lincoln, Franklin D. Roosevelt, and John F. Kennedy. Not James Monroe, whose doctrine promised protection for their lands. Not Teddy Roosevelt, whose Rough Riders stormed San Juan Hill for Cuba's liberation and who built the Panama Canal. Certainly not James K. Polk or Zachary Taylor, whose invasion of their country might have freed Mexicans from a tyrant but shamed and embarrassed them in the process. Instead the people identify with Lincoln because he freed the slaves, with Franklin Roosevelt because he kept the Marines out of Nicaragua and enunciated the good-neighbor policy, with Kennedy because of the Alliance for Progress and, for some perhaps, because of his Catholic faith.

There is undeniable ambiguity in the official feeling of Latin Americans toward the United States. They covet our form of government with its elaborate protection of individual rights. They admire our economic success and would like to share in it. They would love to have an egalitarian society more like ours. But they emphatically do not want *us* telling them how to do it.

This understanding grew as I traveled to Latin America in an official capacity. When I first went to Congress in 1955, I worked on the House Public Works Committee. One project in which I took special interest was the Inter-American Highway. Stretching from Laredo, Texas, on the Mexican border to a point called Chepo, a few miles south of the Panama Canal, the Inter-American would extend for more than fifteen hundred miles, joining the United States, Mexico, Guatemala, El Salvador, Nicaragua, and Panama in a continuous ribbon of concrete. This segment of road would become the longest link in a chain of pavement known as the Pan-American Highway, destined to reach from the northern tip of Alaska to the southern extremity of Argentina in the longest paved road anywhere in the world. The vastness and boldness of the vision, given impetus during the Franklin Roosevelt administration as an important symbol of hemispheric solidarity, appealed to me, and I soon became its most active congressional advocate.

Mexican officials, with characteristic pride, declined U.S. matching funds. They vowed to complete the segment through their country with their own money. Elsewhere along the route U.S. contributions matched local expenditures financed by sometimes slender treasuries.

In 1957, along with a few other members of the Public Works Committee, I traveled long stretches of this highway by automobile. The enthusiasm of the welcoming committees moved me. Everywhere we were greeted not just by officialdom but by hospitable groups of curious citizens who showered us with the pride of their local wares. The generosity of their offerings wherever we stopped was almost embarrassing—huge platters of fresh fruit, homemade cakes and cookies, coffee and fried banana chips, an occasional locally brewed beer.

In Guatemala we were treated like celebrities. I was asked to speak to the Guatemalan congress, heady stuff for a second-term U.S. congressman. What I really wanted, though, was to get out among the people, visit a school, look at crops and local farming methods, browse through a public market, go to a bar or coffeehouse and listen to the talk, smell the air in the streets. I made time to do some of that. I was trying to appraise just what differences the highway would make in the lives of ordinary people.

Few people had automobiles, of course. Some rode horseback. More came with carts and wagons. Most walked. They moved in irregular procession along the highway's right-of-way, with their modest cargoes of bananas, citrus, coffee, cane, vegetables, and flowers. The Inter-American was a river into which many streams would flow. Its usefulness to people in the isolated mountain villages would come, I saw, only if their countries could generate revenues for a network of secondary connecting roads.

Almost everywhere was raw evidence of poverty. The gaping disparity between rich and poor that I had observed so often in Mexico was magnified in these countries to the south, except for Costa Rica. Many Central Americans, in fact, looked upon Mexico as a haven. The influx of illegals into our own country from Mexico, which reached a flood tide in the 1980s, would be matched by a similar flow into southern Mexico from Guatemala, Honduras, El Salvador, and Nicaragua.

Sometimes I carried with me a small hand-held movie camera to record picturesque vignettes. Along a river en route from Guatemala City to the ancient town of Antigua, I stopped the car to film a couple dozen women, mostly Mayan, who were enjoying what appeared to be a public outing while each did the family wash. The camera was a mistake! Their horrified expressions and verbal imprecations quickly revealed to me my insensitivity. I had invaded their privacy. This was *their* wash! I shut off the camera and, with profuse apologies, retreated to the car and resumed the journey.

As I drove away I realized the arrogance of my presumption. People were entitled to dignity. So innocent of intent can be the gesture that reveals, unthinkingly, the naked truth of our presumed superiority. These were citizens in their homeland, not animals in a zoo.

In Panama that year, 1957, I made friends with a young engineer named Tomás Guardia, Jr. Tom's grandfather had been president of Panama, and his family was involved in roadbuilding. I liked Tom very much but got the impression that the big construction contracts were passed around among a small hierarchy of wealthy patrons. Tom told me as much, acknowledging that it was not an ideal system. In Panama and Nicaragua particularly, the forms of democracy existed without its substance. Capitalism was, for practical purposes, a closed club.

The U.S. ambassador to Panama at that time was Joseph Farland. A West Virginia businessman turned diplomat, Farland had a new notion of democracy and diplomacy. He considered it his duty to represent the United States not just to the power elite of the country but to the people themselves. "People change governments more often than governments change people," he said. That made sense to me.

Too often, I had observed, our U.S. embassies were sites of lavish parties. Limousines would park in front, disgorging extravagantly dressed men and women from the paper-thin upper layer of local society. If ostentatious displays of affluence evoke scant hostility in the United States, popular reaction can be quite different in countries where a lot of people go to bed hungry every night, where most cannot afford a doctor, and where a great many don't even have shoes.

Joe Farland and I hit it off immediately. He explained his approach to what he called shirtsleeve diplomacy. "I'm not just ambassador to Panama *City*," he said. "If I'm worth anything to our country, I must be ambassador to *Panama*. I'm supposed to be ambassador to the nation, not just to a little handful of very wealthy families. I have to find ways to show the plain people of this country that the United States cares something about them. Unfortunately, a lot of them don't think we do."

Farland was compiling a list of opinion leaders throughout Panama. From the small towns and even remote villages he collected the names of teachers, labor leaders, presidents of farm cooperatives, reporters for local newspapers and radio stations—anyone who could reach and influence a considerable number of other people. "Ninety-nine percent of these people outside the capital city have never been invited to the U.S. embassy," Farland explained. "Some of them would not have the transportation to get here even if they were invited. Some would be too embarrassed to come, thinking they did not have the right clothes to wear. So I'm finding ways to take the embassy to them."

Once a month Ambassador Farland would schedule a reception in the name of the U.S. embassy in a different city or rural community outside Panama City, some place where the local people would feel comfortable. Many of these towns had never been visited by a U.S. ambassador, I was told. Farland would send personally addressed invitations two weeks in advance to active citizens and opinion makers in the communities involved. Then, he'd take down the chandeliers from our embassy and transport them, as symbols of our country's commitment, to the hall or meeting place.

He always tried to get a cross section from each community, he explained. He did not discriminate along lines of ideology or local political allegiance. Some known Marxists were among the lists of invitees, wherever they occupied positions of local leadership or influence. Often they came. Sometimes they argued with Ambassador Farland about America's purposes. He heard them out and responded with his own convictions. He felt sure he was doing some good. "The United States is not very popular here," he told me. "Some people in Washington don't like to hear this, but I have to recognize the truth if I'm going to change anything for the better. I think we're making some progress."

Joe Farland was an Eisenhower appointee. I suppose he was a Republican. Panamanians told me he was the most popular emissary the United States had ever sent. When John F. Kennedy became president three years later, there was a move in Washington to replace Farland with a Democratic appointee. At the request of people in Panama, I called Larry O'Brien, head of President Kennedy's congressional liaison team, and asked the administration to let Joe Farland continue in his work. For a time they did. I believed then—and still do—that we need more like him.

*   *   *

A short while after meeting Joe Farland I was in Costa Rica. Much there has always impressed me, including the high rate of literacy and the equality of public services. The grace and charm of Costa Rican society make it one of the most attractive countries in the world. It was at our embassy there that an important truth impressed itself on me. U.S. Ambassador Whiting Willauer had been a member of Claire Chennault's Flying Tigers in World War II. A tall, physically active man with an athletic build, Willauer had attracted the eyes of talent hunters in the Eisenhower administration. He had the reputation of being an effective ambassador.

The envoy scheduled a reception at his residence to introduce me to a group of Costa Rican officials and members of the North American business community. Before the reception began, Willauer asked if I would stick around for an hour or so after the guests had left. "There is a matter on which I would like very much to pick your brain," he said.

Throughout the reception, I kept thinking what a marvelous opportunity it must be to serve as U.S. ambassador in a small developing country like Costa Rica. After a few years in Congress, I was beginning to feel frustrated. It seemed so hard for any one member to make a major difference. What a sense of accomplishment one must feel to be the instrument of fundamental change in a country like Costa Rica, I thought. Willauer must enjoy seeing the results of his efforts firsthand. Almost envying his role, I was eager for our private conversation.

Ambassador Willauer had said he wanted to pick my brain. That was flattering. But what I really wanted was a chance to pick his brain. Finally the last of the guests departed and he motioned me to a little study where he offered me brandy and a cigar, explaining that both were products of Latin America. I lighted the cigar, savoring the moment, awaiting new revelations of the fruitful work in which he was engaged.

"What I want to talk with you about," he began, "is Congress. I'm thinking seriously of running for Congress. That's where the power is!"

The ambassador was right. Congress does wield power, sometimes unconsciously. One fundamental problem, perhaps *the* fundamental problem, in our official relations with Latin American neighbors is the low priority most U.S. policymakers assign to the region. It isn't that North Americans consciously think of Latin America as unimportant. More likely we don't think of the region at all—until there is a crisis. Then we demand an instant solution! We want the matter settled speedily so that we can get our minds back on more important things.

Foreign affairs, unless they involve war or the bugbear communism or some affront like an anti-American riot or the taking of hostages, have little sex appeal to the average voter. The day-to-day foreign-policy decisions affecting the Western Hemisphere command little attention from the average congressman, and receive low priority in the executive branch. Yet decisions made casually or even cavalierly by Congress can be extremely significant in Latin America. "How can your administration be so venal?" a Latin American friend might ask. Or "How can your Congress be so stupid?" Truth to tell, in most cases it is neither venality nor stupidity that lies at the root of the problem, but simple ignorance born of carelessness and lack of priority.

"Your government simply does not comprehend the grave injury and personal embarrassment it has brought upon us," Mexico's President José López Portillo once confided to me in a rare moment of anguished candor. He was speaking of the manner in which the United States had summarily rejected a Mexican offer to supply natural gas to help with our country's domestic shortage in the late 1970s. López Portillo had invested much of his government's money and his own political capital to build a long pipeline aimed at supplying a U.S. need. The insensitivity of our rejection brought unintended personal embarrassment.

South of the border one often hears this whimsical lament, of uncertain origin: "Poor Mexico! So far from God and so close to the United States!" An only slightly less poignant aphorism sometimes repeated by the politically conscious laments that the United States has "its mind in Washington, its heart in Britain, and its feet in Latin America."

The almost offhand way in which a great many congressmen vote on matters of considerable importance to our southern neighbors was first made clear to me in 1960. President Eisenhower officially invited the nations of the hemisphere to erect in Washington a permanent headquarters site for the Pan-American Health Organization. This is the oldest regional health institution in the world and the oldest component part of the Organization of American States (OAS). Millions throughout Latin America have looked to it for efforts aimed at eradicating malaria, pellagra, and other maladies in the region that take an appalling annual toll in human life.

One day in 1960, as presidential campaigns were getting under way, I received an urgent call from Roy R. Rubottom, then our assistant secretary of state for inter-American affairs. "President Eisenhower has a very serious problem on the House floor today," Rubottom said, "and we really do hope you can help us!" A bill to authorize construction of the health organization headquarters was scheduled for a vote that afternoon under a suspension of the rules. Not until that day, Rubottom explained, had anyone in the State Department realized the bill was in trouble. It was under attack by an unusual coalition of isolationist Republicans, partisan Democrats eager to embarrass the Republican president in that election year, and a motley bipartisan gaggle of members anxious to vote against any expenditure that smacked of "foreign aid" and didn't directly help people in their own districts.

Coming under a motion to suspend the rules, the bill would be open to only forty minutes of debate and would need a two-thirds vote to pass. If it were rejected—even though salvaged later—the defeat would set off shock waves among member states of the OAS whose representatives had voted to turn down other locations and accept Mr. Eisenhower's invitation. This could be deeply embarrassing not only to the administration but also to the United States. Clearly a rescue effort was needed, and there wasn't much time.

At Secretary Rubottom's urging, I got on the telephone and appealed to as many colleagues as I could reach individually. Then, along with several others, I joined the floor debate. The committee chairman handling the bill allotted me three minutes. What could I say to help ward off unintentional injury? I, a Democrat, and a fairly junior one at that? These words, awkward and simplistic, came to me:

> Although I did not personally vote for this President, I want everyone in this House to know that he is *my* President. If he is embarrassed in the eyes of the world, then I am embarrassed—because my country is embarrassed . . . Consider the results of so abrupt and curt a withdrawal of the president's invitation. Those nations have voted formally to accept that invitation. It remains for us to stand behind it by voting the funds to make our president's word good.

In the vote that followed the abbreviated debate that day, the bill passed by a margin of six to one. My colleagues were willing to do the right thing; most just hadn't thought about it. Speaker Sam Rayburn invited me for a bourbon and branch water in his little hideaway office upon adjournment that day to celebrate the victory. He said nobody paid enough attention to Latin America. He thought that was dangerous. He thought it would be costly in the long run. He was right.

In January of 1963, I asked Speaker John McCormack to assign me to the U.S. delegation that meets annually with Mexican lawmakers. Upon Mr. McCormack's assent, I enrolled in Spanish classes held daily at the Foreign Services Institute. I was intent on improving my Spanish so as to communicate more effectively with people in Mexico and lands to the south. At the institute classes begin at seven in the morning and are limited to four or five students in each group. Every two weeks there is a new professor from a different Spanish-speaking country. This helps the students avoid dependency on the pronunciation and idioms of any one area.

In years past, the United States sent many ambassadors and other spokesmen to Latin America who spoke no Spanish and would not try. Their principal qualification consisted of their ability to raise money for the president's political party. It rankles Latin Americans that so many North Americans expect them to speak English in inter-American communications. Latin Americans do not demand perfection in the use of Spanish, but they do appreciate effort. Unlike some French-speaking people, who will censure a foreign speaker's awkward abuse of French, Latin Americans are tolerant of errors. They work hard at encouraging people who try Spanish. They are inclined to compliment your pronunciation whether you deserve it or not. The very fact that a person makes an effort is interpreted as a compliment to their culture.

One story told to me by Mexican friends involved a beautifully conformed, sleek-coated palomino, which a Texan admired and tried to buy from its Mexican owner. The Mexican repeatedly demurred, saying, "This horse, she does not look so good."

The Texan, trusting his own sense of good horse flesh, insisted until the owner finally relented and sold him the steed. Two days later, the purchaser angrily returned the animal demanding his money back. "You cheated me!" he charged. "This horse is blind!"

Spreading his hands and shrugging his shoulders, the Mexican stammered, "But I tried to tell you, señor. I said to you three times that this horse, she does not *look* so good."

While I was still struggling with the finer points of Spanish, I learned that often a Spanish suffix attached to the end of an English adjective will communicate the intended meaning. Often, but by no means always. Once I was trying to tell some people in Mexico that I was embarrassed by a temporary shortage of funds. "Soy embarazado," I began. My friends seemed astonished.

"Otra vez!" (Say that again!) one of them exclaimed.

"Soy embarazado," I repeated with considerably less certainty. At this, my friends broke into hearty laughter.

"Usted, Señor Jim? No es possible!" one of them managed to say. He explained to me that the word *embarazada* means pregnant.

But there's something more to neighborly relations than language. It really gets down to how we *feel* about our neighbors. Speaker Rayburn said it well: "The way to have a friend is to be a friend." If we are to be understood by others, we really must make an effort to understand where they are coming from.

For the remainder of the 1960s and through the 1970s I participated actively in annual meetings with our Mexican counterparts, ultimately becoming chairman of the U.S. delegation. In alternating years we met in Mexico and invariably were received by the president of that country. I met and talked with Adolfo López Mateos and each of his five successors.

During the fifteen years or so when I was working actively with the Mexicans, two issues commanded their fervent championing. One, the Chamizal, was of little economic consequence. It was a matter of principle. It involved a few hundred acres of disputed ownership along the border between El Paso and Juárez. Since 1848 when the treaty of Guadalupe Hidalgo fixed the U.S.-Mexican international boundary at the Rio Grande, the meandering stream had shifted its course slightly southward in that vicinity.

The United States blithely occupied the few acres up to the river's new line, assuming that the border moved wherever the stream moved. Mexico contended early in the twentieth century that the natural phenomena of erosion and accretion did not change the legal boundary. In 1910 the two countries agreed to submit the dispute to binding arbitration by the International Boundary Commission. That commission, on a vote of two to one, held in favor of Mexico. But under political pressure from Texas, the United States refused to transfer the awarded land to Mexico.

The matter festered for more than fifty years while anti-U.S. interests in Mexico pointed gleefully and repeatedly to the Chamizal as proof of our contempt for Mexico and for international law. In our country, not one person in a thousand could have identified the Chamizal; in Mexico, it was a *cause célèbre*. For years it provided grist for the mill of inflammatory political rhetoric south of the border, while being totally ignored by the makers of U.S. policy.

Finally, in 1963 President Kennedy sat down with Mexico's President López Mateos and worked out an agreement. The Chamizal Treaty was signed on August 29. Under its terms, the channel was to be relocated at its original site and stabilized by lining the bottom with concrete. This cost would be split between the two countries. Mexico would pay an estimated $4.7 million to U.S. citizens for buildings transferred to its territory. Congress, belatedly awakened to the political fallout that had spewed its venom over Mexico for fifty years, passed the enabling legislation on a voice vote in the Senate and by a 348 to 5 roll call in the House. Again, Congress more often than not will do the right thing by Latin America—once it focuses on a problem and the facts.

The other issue that threatened to shatter our neighborly relations involved the question of salinity in the Colorado River. A 1944 treaty pledged to Mexico a given quantity of water each year from the Colorado, which rises in the Rocky Mountains and travels about twelve hundred miles through seven states before entering Mexican territory. On its way, the water is reused many times for irrigation, industry, and municipal purposes. Scores of communities discharge effluent from sewage plants into it. Through the years the quality of the water deteriorated badly. By 1969 it had become so brackish from increasing saline levels that it was virtually unusable when it reached the Mexicali Valley. Americans were dumping crop-destructive salt on more than a million acres of Mexico's best irrigated farmland. Ten million Mexicans depended on the river's flow for their drinking water. Clearly, we were inflicting serious injury on our neighbors. It was not unlike pouring garbage into a neighbor's well.

Fortunately, we did not allow this palpable wrong to go so long unrighted as in the case of the Chamizal. At the invitation of Mexico in 1969, I visited the Mexicali Valley along with other members of our congressional delegation and saw the damage done to the quality of life in that fertile, once-rich region. What had been a garden spot just a few years before was desolated by the brackish waters in which most cash crops simply refused to grow. Congressman Morris K. Udall of Arizona and I went to President Nixon with the problem. We appeared before the House Interior Committee, on which Udall served, to press the claim of fairness for our neighbors. Most certainly every consideration of equity would suggest that the water committed to Mexico under the 1944 treaty should be *usable* water.

On August 30, 1973, President Nixon and President Luis Echeverría adopted an agreement on water quality, limiting allowable salinity levels to not more than 115 parts per million. Congress authorized construction of corrective works, which included a desalination plant near the international border, the lining of some fifty miles of the canal route to avoid water loss and salt intrusion, and other corrective works to the tune of $280 million. It redeemed our honor. It was simple justice.

I enjoyed helping to right these wrongs. But what really aroused me was John F. Kennedy's Alliance for Progress.

CHAPTER 3

A Time of Hope

Now the trumpet summons us again—not as a call to bear arms, though arms we need; not as a call to battle, though embattled we are; but a call to bear the burden of a long twilight struggle, year in and year out, "rejoicing in hope, patient in tribulation," a struggle against the common enemies of man: tyranny, poverty, disease and war itself.

—John Fitzgerald Kennedy

The Alliance for Progress, launched by President John F. Kennedy in 1961, triggered a period of idealism and hope. It raised aspirations and set in motion a too-brief era of economic and political reform throughout the hemisphere. Finally, Latin Americans were daring to hope, someone in the United States understood the bitter legacy of problems arising from their centuries of poverty and official neglect. Moreover, someone seemed to care.

As envisioned by President Kennedy and sculpted at the Punta del Este Conference in August of 1961, the alliance would not be a quick fix but a steady, consistent ten-year undertaking to stimulate the economic and social development of Latin American nations. This would come about through a combination of financial aid from the

United States and self-help actions by the nineteen signatory countries. Latin countries promised for their part to reform unfair tax laws. They agreed to raise ten dollars of their own resources for every dollar of U.S. aid. They pledged to improve land distribution so that ordinary people could have some realistic hope of owning a parcel of land. The Latin nations also undertook to correct other longstanding societal evils that had impeded development and created recurring waves of political unrest. President Kennedy pledged $20 billion over the ten-year period, the first $2 billion by early 1962.

This was heady stuff. Along with several other young members of the legislative branch, I became an early disciple. Having seen the astounding results of the Marshall Plan in Europe, I knew that the alliance was a still bigger and more difficult undertaking. Still, I believed it could succeed. In Europe we were rehabilitating economies shattered by five years of war. In Latin America we were trying to create something that had been stifled by five centuries of cruel history.

The man John Kennedy chose to direct this effort was Teodoro Moscoso. Moscoso called one day, said he had heard of my interest in Latin American affairs, and invited me to come by his office for a visit. I was startled by the sign in his place of work: "Please be brief. We are 25 years late." To the new director, these words were not a joke but a harsh fact.

Moscoso had impressive credentials. As head of Operation Bootstrap in Puerto Rico, he had coordinated the self-help measures by which that island economy attracted investment in enough job-creating enterprises to see the average per-capita income increase sevenfold—from only $100 a year to $700—in less than twenty years. Kennedy was hoping his new director could help other Latin countries achieve similar results.

Ted Moscoso was a no-nonsense man. Liking him immediately, I invited him to bring his message to my home town and organized a reception in the autumn of 1962 under the joint sponsorship of the Fort Worth Chamber of Commerce, the Council on World Affairs, and the Export-Import Club.

"You will hear me use the word *revolution* a great deal," Moscoso said to the predominantly business audience. "It is the only appropriate word, and certainly not a word of which any American need be afraid." He explained that the revolution to which he referred did not have to be a bloody revolution. But if it were not accomplished by peaceful means, Moscoso made clear, it surely would become bloody. It was a revolution against poverty, illiteracy, social injustice, and human despair. It was not a communist-inspired revolution, he stressed, although local communist forces following Castro's lead were exerting every effort to ride the wave of discontent for their own purposes.

"The communists can only seize and pervert these revolutionary forces if we in the United States, and the real democrats in Latin America, abdicate our responsibilities and our traditions," Moscoso declared. "For the United States, there can be only one possible course—to *assist* this peaceful revolution wholeheartedly with our resources and skills, with our political and moral backing, and then to see that it is not perverted or derailed en route."

Soon encouraging signs began to appear. Most of the loan funds committed in the first year's operation were quickly put to work. Some were being used to build three thousand modest houses in Venezuela, Panama, and Costa Rica at prices poor people could afford. Chile and Peru had set up savings and loan institutions to speed their low-cost-housing programs. In May of 1962 the Dominican Republic started a land-reform program, using properties that had been commandeered for the personal pleasure of the late dictator Rafael L. Trujillo. The newly elected government was making seven-acre plots available to peasant families.

Those were measures with which people could identify. Democratically elected governments were showing that democracy could work, that plain people's dreams of a better life could indeed be realized without the sacrifice of their political liberties.

The basic idea of community-level self-help appealed to me strongly. In July of 1962, when the authorizing legislation was considered on the House floor, I offered an amendment emphasizing programs providing for "low-interest loans to individuals for farms, homes, small businesses and occupational training," and requiring that our administrators encourage participating countries to develop programs to meet these elemental needs. My amendment was adopted.

About that time, I met and formed a lasting friendship with Father Daniel McClellan, a Maryknoll missionary who had inspired what was being called an economic miracle in the high, wind-swept *altiplano* of Peru, where for centuries before Father Dan's arrival the Indian population had lived in mud hovels and tilled their farmlands with the most rudimentary implements.

Father Dan was a wiry, intensely enthusiastic Irish-American and former pugilist from Colorado. When I first met him, he was prematurely balding and wore glasses. He had gone to Peru as a missionary in 1950, I learned. Appalled at the poverty and resigned hopelessness he encountered, the priest realized that something had to be done, if for no other reason than to fulfill his role as missionary.

"People with hunger pangs won't listen to sermons," McClellan told me. The heart of the problem as he saw it was that, throughout Peru as in much of Latin America, plain people had no bootstraps with which to pull themselves up—in fact, no boots. What they needed, he concluded, was not a handout but a hand up—small loans to buy simple farm tools, seed, fertilizer, and breeding stock. This was their only hope of ever getting a foothold of any kind. For the average person such loans simply were not available. They never had been. Bankers merely scoffed, and loan sharks charged up to 120 percent interest.

Father McClellan organized a credit union among the Indians, the first of its kind in the history of Peru. Many people laughed at him. "Those Indians are beyond help," they hooted. Ignoring the critics, the priest got together twenty-three Indians who managed to scrape up among them the munificent sum of $30. This was the total capital. In just five years, under Dan McClellan's hyperactive direction, that tiny credit union grew to 275 separate credit unions, with one-third of the Peruvian citizenry as members and nearly $3 million in assets. The rate of repayment was unbelievably good. Given a chance, the simple people of the Andes were fanatically devoted to making good. Out of the first $300,000 loaned, the debt loss was less than $80.

So impressed was I by what one dedicated man had been able to set in motion that I gave a luncheon for Father McClellan in the Capitol, inviting Speaker John McCormack and other colleagues to come and meet the Maryknoller and hear his story. McCormack said he had a day full of appointments but would drop by briefly and pay his respects to the missionary. As it turned out, he was so captivated by the enthusiasm of the balding priest with horn-rimmed glasses that he stayed for three hours, asking questions and probing for ideas that would help us help John Kennedy help the 200 million people of Latin America help themselves.

Two others who contributed to the ferment of ideas in those days were former Mayor deLessups Morrison of New Orleans and James H. Boren, a Texas educator who had found his way into the Agency for International Development (AID) after organizing Senator Ralph Yarborough's Washington office.

"Shep" Morrison impressed me the first time I saw him. Nominated by President Kennedy as U.S. ambassador to the OAS, he was being grilled by the Senate committee prior to his confirmation. A dapper, smooth-skinned man of medium stature, Morrison had a quick wit to which he gave expression, at surprising moments, in his heavy, southern Louisiana accent.

When a senator asked how the mayor supposed Latin Americans might react to someone from a city so steeped in the Deep South tradition as New Orleans, Morrison raised his eyebrows in feigned astonishment and replied, "Well, that's easy. If anyone starts chanting, 'Yankee go home!' I'll just smile to myself and say, 'They sure can't be talking about *me!*'"

At Morrison's invitation, I made a couple of trips with him. In most Latin American countries, we discovered, the majority of the population was made up of tenant farmers, impoverished, deeply in debt, and without hope. Mired in the futility of a form of twentieth-century feudalism, many of them saw little promise of a brighter *mañana* through a slow and orderly process.

Part of the problem lay in their tragic history of corruptible leaders. Part of *our* problem was that too often the United States had been identified in Latin minds with unpopular and undemocratic local regimes. Military rulers had dispensed our aid as though it were their own largesse. Sometimes they had used our military assistance to shore up internal security in the manner of police states.

The vulnerabilities of Latin American societies were being exploited in those years by ambitious politicians with no particular political philosophy, as well as by aggressive local communist cadres. When Congress cut funds for the Voice of America in 1953, it was forced to abandon its wavelength to Guatemala. The Soviet Union snapped it up. China too had begun concentrating on Latin America. In 1959 it induced more than four hundred Latin American opinion makers to visit China. Students, educators, labor leaders, and writers were given expense-free trips. Peking and Moscow were beaming seventy-four hours of Spanish-language broadcasts into the region weekly. At one point Russia was credited with having a total of fifteen thousand all-expense-paid scholarships to carefully chosen Central American students to study at Moscow's Patrice Lumumba University.

Morrison and I agreed that it wasn't good enough merely to preach against communism. We had to be *for* something better. With the ambassador's support, several of us in Congress advocated trying to help freely elected governments in Latin America demonstrate that land reform could be achieved without revolution or government confiscation, through a sort of Latin American Federal Housing Administration.

We were proposing that the United States join with friendly governments to provide loan guarantees to tenant farmers so they could buy small, family-sized parcels and pay for them out of expected returns from their own crops. Nothing stabilizes a people like farm and home ownership, nor gives them a greater stake in political stability.

Jim Boren, my Texas friend, went to Peru to help set up the Alliance for Progress program. He told me he discovered a pervasive thirst among students for good reading material about the United States. "The trouble is," Jim said, "that 90 percent of those students don't have any money for books." He recommended that we set up mobile lending libraries with inexpensively bound copies of the best American literature in Spanish. Soon I was advocating such a program to the alliance officials.

Jim Boren is a heavyset man with a round, bland face and large opaque eyes through which he would stare, as if uncomprehending, at anyone who tried to tell him that one of his ideas was too much trouble to try. He has a sense of humor and a penchant for cutting through layers of verbal dross to the core of a matter. It was this habit that led him to create the Partners of the Alliance. Soon after he had gone to Peru to administer our government's AID program, the former professor saw that grandiose projects and high-sounding phrases just were not getting through to ordinary farmers and workers.

"The people in the villages," Boren told me on his first trip back from Peru, "aren't interested in economic philosophy. They talk of very simple things. They want *agua, desagüe, y luz* (potable water, waste disposal, and lighting).

"The most civic-minded among them will express hope for *escuelas y caminos* (schools and roads)," he went on, "but beyond that, they'd just like to be left alone by the politicians in the capitol and the military in the barracks."

Most government programs, he saw, were skimming over the people's heads. Their needs were local and immediate. As a former educator, Boren also got excited about the need to awaken North

Americans to the world south of the Rio Grande. He conceived the idea of a people-to-people component as a means of making the alliance come alive and of buying time until its larger reforms could take effect. In 1963, after months of importuning, Boren got the green light from Ted Moscoso and President Kennedy to organize local groups in the United States and link them with companion groups in cities and villages throughout Latin America. The function of the North American chapters was to provide immediate, usually inexpensive items that would make a direct difference in the lives of ordinary people.

I traveled with Boren to several cities where we organized local chapters of his nonprofit Partners of the Alliance. One village had a night literacy program in which adults, after work, were learning to read and write by candlelight. In another village, a similar group was studying by kerosene lamp. One way Boren's organization could help was by sending small U.S.-made generators; they could be bought and transported by air freight for $135 each. One would operate for five hours on a gallon of gasoline, providing energy for six 50-watt bulbs. People in another rural village had erected a community center and dug a water well. We found a group of American Partners who wanted to buy those people a pump for $285 so that they could enjoy uncontaminated water.

Volunteers in another Latin American locality had built a school, but the villagers needed material for the doors and windows. A Partners chapter in our country put up the money, which came to about $250. Another chapter raised $1,200 and sent a jackhammer unit to help another group of villagers dig their own irrigation system, which they had been attempting to do with only picks and shovels. Simple things like a cement mixer and wheelbarrows made work easier for other self-help projects where community residents were building their own medical outposts and day-care centers.

But the North American chapters were not to think of themselves as "adopting" a Latin American community. The program should not be paternalistic, Boren insisted. It had to be a genuine *partnership*. "This is not an old-clothes charity program," he would say. "We are not patronizing our partners. They have some things to share with us, too."

Not surprisingly, Jim enjoyed teaming Peruvian and Texan communities. To head the statewide organization in Texas, he recruited Ed Marcus of Dallas. Soon Neiman Marcus, then managed by Ed's brother Stanley Marcus, was sponsoring art exhibits from Peru.

In several Latin American countries, Boren organized business and cultural groups not just to receive but also to send local products to U.S. communities. "The United States needs your help," he would say to the Latins. "We need access to your best products, and to your cultural riches—your art works and literature and music." Neither side was to be considered exclusively as a recipient. Both were to be participants.

By 1970, when Jim Boren left the State Department, the Alliance for Progress had been phased out. Its premature demise was a major disappointment to me. Policymakers in the Johnson administration considered it too costly and too cumbersome a project to carry on at the same time we were putting so much energy and effort into the Vietnam war. But Boren's people-to-people Partners of the Alliance survived. Twenty-five years after its inception, it is the only still-functioning facet of the grand experiment. It operates now as a private nonprofit association under the name National Association of the Partners of the Americas. Boren has taken up a new career as a humorist, poking good-natured fun in books and speeches at the follies of the bureaucracy. But his brainchild endures. Today it involves volunteer efforts of more than twenty-two thousand people working in thirty-one countries. That, by any measure, is a success!

When President Lyndon Johnson sent U.S. troops into the Dominican Republic in 1965 to ensure the safe evacuation of U.S. citizens during a bloody military coup, he immediately sought the approval of the OAS. Within three days its council adopted a resolution calling for an immediate cease-fire and an international security zone as a haven for foreign citizens. Acting under the provisions of the OAS resolution, the U.S. Marines provided security for the international security zone. In those rampant cold war days, when Castro and Che Guevara were riding high, there was widespread fear that any revolution ousting a military junta might be taken over by communists.

The OAS forwarded an eight-point program calling for elections under inter-American supervision. In the elections, Joaquin Balaguer outpolled former President Juan Bosch. Most liberals in the United States favored Bosch. Dominicans I questioned following that election told me they had voted for Balaguer because he campaigned more vigorously. They thought Bosch was intimidated by threats on his life into limiting his public exposure.

At President Johnson's request, I made several trips to the Dominican Republic, trying to evaluate ways to stabilize the political ferment and help the economy. One idea I brought back involved the creation of corporations to build local plants to convert Dominican raw materials into finished products. Oranges and tomatoes grew abundantly in Dominican soil. But bottled orange juice and canned tomato paste, a staple of the local diet, had to be imported. Why not promote home industries that could not only provide jobs and keep local dollars at home but also—and here was the novelty—spread the base of ownership? A long-time friend, Bernard Rapoport of Waco, Texas, had introduced the basic idea to me. This was before the days of federally encouraged employee-stock-ownership plans, but that is exactly what we were trying to pioneer.

More specifically, we wanted U.S. investors to establish plants to bottle orange and tomato juice and to can and freeze tomato paste and sectioned fruit for consumption in the local market, replacing imports. The investors would set aside 50 percent of the stock for distribution among workers at the plant and family farmers who sold produce to it. To qualify for stock, a farmer would commit a certain number of his acres to improved agricultural methods for better yield and quality and consign a major percentage of his crop to the indigenous industry.

Over and above their wages and the prices they got for their crops, workers and farmers would share in company profits, giving many more people a stake in the economic and political future of their country. It would be harder for propagandists to drive a wedge between owners and workers. Our hope was gradually to replace peonage with a sort of people's capitalism.

President Balaguer was enthusiastic about the idea. So was his secretary of agriculture. Our U.S. AID administrator, a smart, bushy-haired career man named Alex Firfer, after a period of initial skepticism, warmed to the idea and brought in some agronomists from an American land grant college. Their mission was to give advice about the best locations for plants and the most modern methods for improving crop yields.

Rapoport and I, after a lot of trial and error, recruited five potential U.S. investors who were ready to put money into the projects if our government would provide them an extended-risk guarantee against confiscation or physical destruction of their property in case of another violent political upheaval. For months we sought State and Treasury Department approval for the extended-risk protection. It became the victim of repeated bureaucratic delays. President

Johnson, to whom I explained the proposal, liked the concept. He was willing to support it, he said, if his technical people agreed.

But now, in 1966, the administration was deeply immersed in the problems of Vietnam. Things had stabilized in the Dominican Republic. It was no longer a crisis. The investors Rapoport and I had attracted to the experiment began losing interest, one by one. The demands of their own businesses would not wait indefinitely for the government to make up its mind. There was no one person who had an immediate financial interest in persevering to make the dream come to fruition, and both Rapoport and I had other things to do. Neither of us would have profited financially from the venture. We could spend only so much of our own time and money trying to promote an idea. I was becoming more involved in the domestic aspects of Johnson's Great Society legislation. In the end, our idea died aborning. But it was, I am still convinced, a good one.

A decade of hemispheric idealism began to fade in the late 1960s. It would be replaced by an era of gradual financial retrenchment on the part of the United States and reliance on the CIA and other intelligence agencies to do furtively what other U.S. interests were unwilling to undertake, or unable to achieve, openly.

In 1971 and 1972, U.S. intelligence agents were active in efforts to destabilize the government of President Salvador Allende in Chile. U.S. involvement in the attempt to overthrow the left-leaning president was first denied by officials in the Nixon administration and later admitted by President Gerald Ford in one of his first televised news conferences. Former Secretary of State Henry Kissinger has personally assured me that the CIA had nothing to do with Allende's death, apparently by suicide, during the coup that took over that government. It did work, nevertheless, to destabilize that country's economy.

From the viewpoint of our national credibility in Latin America, however, the entire episode seems to have been both a grave miscalculation and an avoidable tragedy. We can but imagine the outrage with which we would react if some other nation were caught deliberately plotting to destabilize and undermine our government and our economy. Allende's coalition had won the congressional elections a few months before the coup, and his regime was riding a crest of popularity. Some Chileans with whom I have spoken believe, nevertheless, that Allende and his forces would have lost the upcoming presidential election. Nobody accused him of doing anything to subvert or circumvent the electoral process. The people themselves could have changed the leadership by democratic means if that is what they had wished.

By helping in the destabilization, the United States managed to become identified with the unpopular, undemocratic regime of General Augusto Pinochet. His dictatorship interrupted one of the longest periods of electoral democracy in Latin American history. Pinochet suspended the constitution and ruled with an iron hand, refusing for seventeen years to permit elections.

In the wake of this violent change, I began to note in my trips to Latin America a growing paranoia toward the CIA and a tendency to excuse failures of one kind or another by blaming the U.S. agency. For instance, when Mexican President Luis Echeverría broke tradition to speak at the University of Mexico City in 1973, he encountered an embarrassingly hostile student demonstration. Echeverría, who thought of himself as leader of the underdeveloped nations, was stung. Unwilling to acknowledge his own error in judgment, he blamed the incident on the CIA. He claimed that U.S. agents had organized the outbreak. There apparently was no truth whatsoever to the charge. Interestingly, Echeverría had worked with the CIA while minister of the interior before his ascension to the presidency. But he knew our CIA would be a popular whipping boy.

Even before the coup in Chile, I began to encounter wild rumors about our intelligence activities. On February 7, 1971, the *Miami Herald* picked up a story from an antigovernment newspaper in Costa Rica alleging that the U.S. agency was plotting the overthrow of President José Figueres and his administration. The next day, the story got headline play in papers throughout Central America. Suspicion was rife.

By coincidence, I arrived in Costa Rica on the evening of February 7 along with a congressional subcommittee inspecting the Inter-American Highway. After reading the *Herald* story and sensing the vibrations it had set in motion, I asked for a personal conference with our ambassador, Walter C. Ploeser. Ploeser assured me the rumor was false. He believed it had been planted by a political group with a strong anti-U.S. bias.

On the following day, the Costa Rican government was hosting a luncheon for our committee. Figueres, the grand old man of Central American democracy, was present. When called upon for comments, I publicly attacked the rumor, formally denied it on behalf of our government and made a strong and heartfelt statement in praise of President Figueres personally and all that he stood for throughout the Americas. Figueres, obviously moved, spoke for nearly an hour. He thoroughly disavowed the rumors, denied ever having named any American persona non grata in his country, and stated in a ringing declaration that those who circulated the falsehoods were friends of neither the United States nor Costa Rica.

But fact, as usual, was slow in catching up with rumor. Two days later, on February 10 at a press conference in Mexico City, I discovered that President Figueres's emphatic disavowal in Costa Rica had not even been covered in the press. A reporter for United Press International, oblivious to the Figueres denial, asked me to comment on the CIA "plot" against the president of Costa Rica.

The secret agency, because of the mystery that shrouds its activities, is a convenient whipping boy for nationalistic demagoguery. Since nobody knows exactly what clandestine activity may be afoot, it is easy to blame almost any economic calamity or failed policy on the CIA. The indubitable facts that U.S. agents had been deeply involved in the violent overthrow of Guatemalan President Jacobo Arbenz in 1954 and had sponsored an undertaking in the 1970s to destabilize the elected government of Chile make many Latin Americans deeply resentful of the CIA and anxious to believe almost any rumor involving the agency.

Shortly after Jimmy Carter became president, he expressed the frustration of defense, state, and other agency officials who dealt with classified information in having to testify before a proliferating number of congressional subcommittees that claimed some sliver of jurisdiction over their activities. Some leaks had occurred. Moreover, the task of preparing and giving testimony to so many diverse panels was consuming time and energy that Carter felt could better be spent in carrying out the government's missions.

Speaker Tip O'Neill and Senate Majority Leader Robert Byrd responded to the president's concerns. They asked a group of us to draft legislation creating intelligence committees in the House and Senate to be the official congressional repositories of the government's official secrets. The president and his subordinate administrators were required by law to report any clandestine activity to these two committees. As the newly elected House majority leader I served, along with Minority Leader Robert Michel, as an ex officio member of the House committee. In this capacity, for the next ten years, I listened to reports from CIA directors Stansfield Turner and William Casey, as well as from our military intelligence operatives.

There is an absolutely legitimate, even necessary role for the CIA. That role, however, is gathering intelligence, not overthrowing governments. In a complex world where agents of other governments practice deception and terrorism has become a way of life, our country needs every available source of reliable information. Gathering and sorting that information and presenting it to our nation's policymakers is the necessary work of intelligence agents. Sometimes they risk their lives in desperately hostile environments. More often, if the identity of an undercover agent is publicly disclosed, his or her confidential sources in faraway lands are in mortal jeopardy.

In the late 1970s, a handful of rogue former CIA agents began publishing the names and descriptions of erstwhile teammates. At least one CIA operative lost his life as a result when a car bomb shattered the automobile in which he was riding. Other agents reported that their sources, fearful of retaliation from anti-U.S. elements, were abruptly breaking off relations. The impairment of U.S. intelligence-gathering capacity was intolerable. As majority leader, I introduced a bill that now makes it a federally punishable offense to publicize the identity of an on-duty secret intelligence agent of the United States. Surely we owe this much protection to those who risk their lives to serve our country.

There can be no question, however, that misuse of the agency to carry out secret, deliberately disruptive operations in other countries has cost us good will in important parts of Latin America. When Stansfield Turner became director in 1977, he vowed to get the agency out of self-generated adventures and back into the business of gathering information.

I have spoken of the sensitivity of Latin Americans to any foreign intrusion into their internal affairs. That is well known. The two phrases most often heard from Latin statesmen are "nonintervention" and "self-determination." These ideals are enshrined in the Mexican constitution of 1917 and in almost every subsequent Latin American–related policy document, including the Rio Treaty and the charter of the OAS. Many Central American officials can recite, with undisguised disapproval, the surprising number and exact details of armed intrusions by U.S. military forces into their countries during the twentieth century.

If there is any one universal principle that unites Latin Americans, it is their common insistence on self-determination. They abhor military intrusion, or any attempt by any outside force, overt or covert, to violate any nation's political independence. They believe in the equality of states, big and small, and in the right of each to set its own course. Benito Juárez of Mexico put it in these words: "Respect for the rights of others is peace."

This most fundamental fact was brushed aside by a group of zealous Reagan administration officials in the 1980s. Their actions led to the most internally divisive clash of philosophy and of will since the Vietnam war. That, in turn, led to Irangate.

CHAPTER 4

The Road to Irangate

Our reflections on the United States and its present predicament lead to the question: Will it be able to resolve the contradiction between empire and democracy? At stake are its life and its identity.

—Octavio Paz

No foreign policy issue since the Vietnam war has been so politically polarizing as the Reagan administration's efforts to overthrow the Sandinista government using the Contras as a proxy force. The American people split, and Congress fractured into two near-irreconcilable camps, each side claiming moral superiority. One was determined to avoid another Cuba, the other to avoid another Vietnam. Taunts such as "Communist!" and "Warmonger!" shattered the calm of reasoned debate. There was little room in the middle for creative solutions or constructive maneuvering.

During the last year of the Carter administration, Congress had established itself as an active participant in formulating this country's policies toward Nicaragua. On a broader scale, the Intelligence Oversight Act of 1980 required the executive branch to keep Congress "fully and currently informed" not only of ongoing activities but also of "significant *anticipated* intelligence activities" (italics added).

Throughout the latter half of the 1970s domestic political opposition to the Somoza regime in Nicaragua both spread and deepened. It grew to include not only the influential Chamorro family, publishers of that nation's largest newspaper, which spearheaded the movement, but also a broad group of businessmen and industrialists, a cadre of university students, and a substantial segment of the Roman Catholic priesthood, which was preaching "liberation theology."

Upon the fall of Somoza in July 1979, the newly installed government inherited an economy devastated by civil war and a decade of corruption. A massive earthquake seven years earlier had killed ten thousand people and damaged 80 percent of Managua's buildings. Hundreds of millions of dollars for relief and reconstruction poured in from the United States and elsewhere, but Somoza kept tight control of the money, doling out construction contracts to his own family and a few political cronies. Relatively little of the money had served its intended purpose, and the city was still a shambles.

Fleeing into exile, the Somoza regime took with it much of the nation's remaining wealth. It left a national debt of $1.64 billion and only $3.5 million in the national treasury—slightly more than a dollar per person for the entire population of that war-ravaged land. Five years of intensive civil war had destroyed a billion dollars' worth of industrial facilities. The country was in desperate need of foreign assistance if it was to rebuild its shattered economy.

President Carter moved swiftly to transfer small amounts of emergency aid, including food and medicine. Secretary of State Cyrus Vance said, "We cannot guarantee that democracy will take hold there. But if we turn our backs on Nicaragua, we can almost surely guarantee that democracy will fail." In November 1979 Carter requested swift passage of a $75-million economic-aid bill. Many conservative congressmen, however, bridled at the revolutionary rhetoric of the new regime. They came to view the victors in the civil war as communists and wanted no part in helping the devastated country. The hostage crisis in Iran and Soviet intervention in Afghanistan hardened feelings and heightened wariness. Fears of Cuban or Soviet intervention in Central America began to emerge in the public dialogue. These doubts intensified during March of 1980 when four high-ranking Sandinista leaders traveled to the Soviet Union, where they publicly decried the U.S. "imperialist policy of interference" in Latin America.

As a result, final passage of the $75-million aid package requested by Carter would not be attained until July of 1980. Meanwhile,

Cuban cadres of teachers and health workers, armed with medicine and vaccines, began to flock into the smitten country. It was almost as though, fearing the intrusion of leftist influence, we were paralyzed into a failure to compete against it.

My first personal contact with the Sandinistas came in June of 1980. At the personal request of President Carter, I took a small delegation to Nicaragua to see what was going on, to ask questions, to appraise our chance of influencing the rapidly moving events, and to report our findings back to the president.

On the eve of our delegation's departure, the House faced a vote on an amendment by Representative Robert Bauman of Maryland to strip away all the money earmarked in the supplemental appropriation bill for emergency Nicaraguan aid. Feeling that we must salvage at least the option to compete for the stricken country's friendship, I offered a substitute. My amendment would allow the aid, but provide that the president report to Congress every ninety days on the internal situation in Nicaragua, including that government's observance of human rights. Addressing the House, I revealed that President Carter had asked me to lead a small delegation to Nicaragua that weekend. I appealed to my colleagues to approve our participation in the devastated country's reconstruction:

> Let me have the tools by which I can say to the people in Nicaragua: "The people of the United States have not deserted you. We haven't given you up for lost. We do want to work with you. We do expect you to establish free political institutions. We expect you to have regular, free elections. We want you to respect private property and human rights. . . ."
> I would have no credibility at all going to Nicaragua . . . if I were speaking for a Congress . . . which had . . . publicly asserted its disdain for the government and people of Nicaragua. . . . Let us, I appeal to you, have the tools by which we can help salvage their friendship.

By a ninety-nine-vote margin, the House adopted my substitute, retaining $25 million in emergency aid. This would be the widest margin of any vote on aid to a Central American country during the entire decade of the 1980s.

The little delegation had to be assembled in a hurry. Mr. Carter had assigned us the use of a military aircraft. We had arranged for the respected Nicaraguan banker, Arturo Cruz, to fly to Managua with us. I asked three Democrats to accompany me. Bill Alexander of Arkansas and Stephen Neal of North Carolina were regarded as moderates. Kent Hance of Texas was considered a conservative. Republican leader Bob Michel tried but was unable on short notice to round up a couple of Republicans to join us. I asked John Paul Hammerschmidt of Arkansas and Don Clausen of California, but neither could arrange his schedule to accompany us.

In Nicaragua that June, we met with people from all sides—Enrique Dreyfus, spokesman for local business interests; Frank Bandana, head of the coffee growers; Pedro Joaquín Chamorro of *La Prensa,* the major privately owned newspaper; and his younger brother Carlos Chamorro, who edited *Barricada,* the official Sandinista newspaper. The brothers were sons of *La Prensa*'s crusading publisher, Pedro Joaquín Chamorro Cardenal, whose murder in 1978 had galvanized the Somoza opposition, precipitating a general strike and hastening the end of Somoza's regime. The victim's widow, Violeta Chamorro, had been part of the original governing junta that took power upon the fall of Somoza. She had resigned from that political post shortly before we arrived. Our delegation talked with her, and with Alfonso Robelo, a moderate and businessman who had also left the regime and spoke now of running for president as soon as elections could be held.

Everyone with whom we talked believed the United States should work with the new regime. They all felt that a show of friendship by the United States would influence political developments for the better. None of the scores of people we consulted wanted Cuba to be the principal purveyor of assistance to the needy country.

Meeting with Daniel Ortega and five members of the governing junta, we pressed hard for assurances. "Will your government respect private property?" asked Kent Hance.

"Everyone's rights will be respected," replied Ortega. "No property will be taken from anyone except by legal means, and with just compensation." The thirty-six-year-old *comandante* said an enormous amount of land "already belongs to the nation," having been held apart by Somoza and never used for anything except his "personal profit and enjoyment." Ortega hoped that this could be distributed in family plots to landless peasants and "legal titles" awarded.

"Can we assure our president and our colleagues in Congress that Nicaragua will protect civil liberties?" Bill Alexander persisted. Upon Ortega's affirmative response, Bill demanded specifics. Free speech?

Free press? Freedom of assembly? Even for the political opposition?

"All of these things are being guaranteed in our new constitution," insisted Ortega. "None of them existed under Somoza, and that is why our people revolted!"

Steve Neal wanted some elaboration on the "mixed economy" and "pluralistic society" about which the new leaders had spoken. Were these code words for a form of socialism?

Things were just now evolving, said Ortega. "We are looking at many models." The banks and public utilities could be "owned by the people" and run by public officials. "The same as in many other democracies," he declared. "Beyond this, we want private business in private hands. We want them to be successful. We want them to make money. We want private citizens to own land. We want *more* of them to own land, and more of them to own businesses. We want *more* of our people to be capitalists."

"When will you have elections?" I asked.

"Just as soon as possible. Just as soon as we can get enough tranquility to have *real* elections. The people of our country have never had a real election. One time Somoza pretended to have an election, but it didn't mean anything. Nobody paid any attention and nobody voted. We want *real* elections. We want everybody to participate."

Afterward, U.S. Ambassador Lawrence Pezzullo seemed pleased by the meeting and the answers we had received. "Extremely positive," he said. "The most positive responses we've had to date."

Our group reported to President Carter that the economic aid had taken on symbolic importance. Everyone with whom we talked considered it potentially decisive in shaping the future of U.S.-Nicaraguan relations. I told our colleagues in the House that, from all we had learned, the direction of the new government in Nicaragua was still to be determined.

A month later, Mickey Leland of Texas and Esteban Torres of California were in Nicaragua as guests of that government. Others in Congress were invited to help celebrate the revolution's first anniversary, but most lawmakers had other commitments. Many, wary of the Sandinistas' intentions, played it safe by declining. The irrepressible Leland, a free spirit with effervescent curiosity, saw Fidel Castro sauntering through the festive crowd in Managua, escorted by three members of Nicaragua's governing junta. Mickey engaged the Cuban strongman in conversation. After a few minutes of banter, the loquacious Castro turned to his Nicaraguan hosts. Pointing to Torres and

Leland, he declaimed, "You are fortunate to have these men here. You should appreciate the help of the United States. If that country had been willing to work with us after we overthrew Battista, Cuba would not have the problems it has today."

Both Leland and Torres talked with me later about these remarks of the enigmatic Cuban. None of us could be sure exactly what they meant—and whether they were directed at the Nicaraguans or at us. I encouraged my colleagues to discuss the conversation with President Carter.

In early September of 1980, I had a surprise visit in Washington from Ambassador Pezzullo. He was disturbed that Daniel Ortega's brother, Humberto, who served the fledgling junta as minister of defense, had made a public statement that Nicaraguan elections would not be held until 1985. In view of the junta's assurances to our group in June, the ambassador thought it would be useful for the four of us who had heard them directly to lodge a strongly worded complaint. I dictated a letter. Alexander, Neal, and Hance all joined in signing (the complete original letter can be found in the appendix).

Humberto's public statement, we wrote, came as "a major disappointment to those of us in Congress who have held out hope that Nicaragua, with our understanding and help, could move swiftly toward a truly Democratic society."

To be confronted now, after the verbal assurances we thought we had received during our personal visit to Nicaragua in June, with the dismaying announcement that elections will not be held until 1985 is appalling in the extreme. Our people recall with bitter irony the grand promises made by Fidel Castro in Cuba in 1959 that there would be free elections in due course. Twenty-one years have passed from that date. No free electoral system has been established. Cuba remains a dictatorship, its leader having crassly betrayed that solemn promise. In our country, people vote today who were not even born when that promise was made in 1959. . . .

We had hoped and believed that the Nicaraguan people can find their own destiny, free from outside domination, while fully respecting private property, judicial procedures, free speech and press, and the other necessary habiliments of a free society which cannot exist without an orderly electoral system in which the people themselves are given frequent and

regular opportunity to choose those by whom they will be
governed. . . .

Those of us in the United States who want so strongly to be
friends of the Nicaraguan people and your beautiful country
earnestly hope you will share these thoughts with others in
the governing junta and that you will reconsider and give to
civilized humanity the reassurance that an orderly system of
political democracy will be established through free elections
in the near future, much nearer than five years hence.

The campaign of 1980 raised the decibel level of the debate over
Central America, making a bipartisan consensus more difficult.
Throughout that election year, Ronald Reagan's campaign rhetoric
scathingly attacked President Carter's policies. Reagan inveighed
against our "Marxist" neighbors in the Caribbean. He repeatedly
charged that the Nicaraguan leaders were "Cuban-trained, Cuban-
armed and dedicated to creating another Communist country in the
Hemisphere." The Republican platform deplored the "Marxist Sandinista takeover of Nicaragua" and opposed Carter's aid program.
Some Sandinista leaders, reading the Republican candidate's harshly
critical descriptions of themselves, came to believe that a Reagan
administration would try to undermine their government no matter
how they conducted its affairs.

Reagan's victory and the election of a Republican-controlled Senate intensified differences between Democrats and Republicans over
Central America. As floor leader for the House Democrats, I sought
to find common ground. On February 17, 1981, after new Secretary
of State Alexander M. Haig, Jr., told House and Senate leaders he
had "evidence" that leftist insurgents in El Salvador were receiving
weapons from "Soviet-bloc nations," I moved to close ranks in the
face of what was perceived and represented to us as a threat to the
independence of El Salvador. "Central America is probably more
vitally important to us than any other part of the world," I told the
press following that briefing at the White House. "Our response to
what is happening there requires a bipartisan, unified approach, and
I fully expect that is what the president and the secretary of state will
receive."

The Reagan camp was not content, however, with protecting the
territorial integrity of El Salvador. Emboldened by the president's
electoral victory, Reaganites construed this as proof of public support

for the use of U.S. power and influence to control the shape of other governments in the hemisphere. Reagan's new ambassador to the United Nations, Jeane Kirkpatrick, had made a public distinction between "authoritarian" and "totalitarian" governments. Some now wanted to make a further foreign policy distinction between "rightist" and "leftist" leadership. Military dictator Augusto Pinochet of Chile was acceptable; the new group in Managua was not.

Reagan quickly suspended the sale of American wheat to Nicaragua and terminated economic aid. He attributed these actions to Nicaragua's alleged encouragement of rebel forces in El Salvador. The suspension distressed U.S. Ambassador Pezzullo, who felt it left him no bargaining room. Nicaraguan leaders viewed the embargo on wheat sales as an act of economic "aggression." Several members of the Sandinistas' internal opposition expressed similar sentiments. They were "dismayed," one said.

Ambassador Pezzullo met with CIA Director Casey, arguing that the Sandinista revolution was still popular inside Nicaragua. Any open attack on it by the United States would only strengthen its hold on the population, Pezzullo warned. He expressed deep concern that the United States was destroying its own position, forfeiting its chance to influence events for the better. The Sandinistas wanted a friendly relationship with the United States, he insisted. Making an open break, as the administration was doing, undermined his efforts to improve relations.

Casey and others in the administration were not moved by our emissary's warnings. They disagreed, and ultimately Pezzullo was replaced as ambassador.

The administration's rhetoric grew harsher. In November of 1981, the CIA met in the White House with the National Security Council to propose a $19-million covert-action program. On December 1, the president signed a "finding," as required by law, stating that a covert action was in the "national interest." William Casey came to Capitol Hill to inform the House and Senate intelligence committees of plans for political and paramilitary operations against Nicaragua. These activities would be limited at first, however, to thwarting Nicaragua's "support of subversion" in neighboring El Salvador.

On November 14, 1981, Arturo Cruz, who had been appointed Nicaraguan ambassador to the United States in the spring of that year, resigned his post. It was Cruz who had accompanied me to his country the previous year, introducing my group to people on all sides of the political spectrum. His resignation was partially in protest of the Sandinista arrest of private-sector leaders, and partially in protest of Reagan-administration policy.

"What the United States does not realize," Cruz wrote in his resignation statement, "is that its continuing mistrust of the revolution might be pushing the Sandinista government to the left and forcing it, in spite of itself, to use just the kind of measures that the United States finds so troubling. . . . Washington's hard line continues to encourage the armed aggression of the counter-revolution."

Cruz's resignation came at the end of three months of private talks between Assistant Secretary of State Thomas Enders and the Sandinistas. The talks attempted to establish a foundation for U.S. tolerance of the Sandinista government. Enders negotiated for an end to Nicaraguan support of insurgent movements in Central America and for a lessening of security ties between the Sandinistas and the Eastern bloc. In reciprocation the United States would agree to tolerate the Sandinista government. By the end of October, however, the talks seemed inconclusive and Enders was ordered by higher-ups to terminate them. In an op-ed article in the December 9, 1981, issue of the *New York Times,* Arturo Cruz pleaded for another effort at rapprochement and warned

> the United States' continued suspension of bilateral economic assistance and the threat of even more severe economic sanctions oblige the Nicaraguan Government to move closer to the Socialist bloc. The possibility of military measures pushes my Government to seek security in ways that the United States find threatening.

Early 1982 signaled the beginning of a concerted campaign to rally public support against the Nicaraguan government. Skeptics in the press and in Congress had been pressing for proof of the anti-Sandinista charges. Administration officials now arranged closed-door briefings where they presented secret aerial photographs to bolster their claim of a dramatic Nicaraguan arms buildup. Later, the House Intelligence Subcommittee on Oversight and Evaluation would write that the briefing was "flawed by several instances of overstatement and overinterpretation."

On March 12 the State Department presented to the news media an account of a nineteen-year-old Nicaraguan supposedly trained in Cuba and captured in El Salvador and sent by his government to fight with the Salvadoran rebels. The publicity stunt backfired badly when the youngster, whose name was Orlando José Tardencillas Espinosa, confronted the press and repudiated the entire account. He reported that he had been tortured by military captors in El Salvador and threatened into conspiring with Salvadoran and U.S. officials to fabricate the story. He now said he had never been trained in Cuba, and was not sent by his government. He had traveled to El Salvador to fight on his own initiative. The story of the hoax made page one of the *New York Times* on March 14, 1982.

During that month details of the secret war in Nicaragua that originated in 1981 began to appear on the front pages of major newspapers. Anti-Sandinista guerrillas badly damaged two major bridges along the Nicaraguan-Honduran border, spurring the Sandinistas to declare a state of emergency.

In April of 1982, there was a crisis of sorts in El Salvador. It was partly in response to this crisis that the House delegation went to Central America. The first Constituent Assembly elections held under El Salvador's new constitution resulted in a three-way split. President José Napoleón Duarte's Christian Democrats won a plurality, but not a majority, of the seats in the Constituent Assembly. The more conservative ARENA party, headed by charismatic firebrand Major Roberto D'Aubuisson, was a close second. Now D'Aubuisson was maneuvering behind the scenes, meeting with the leaders of other right-wing parties to form a coalition to freeze out the moderate-to-liberal Christian Democrats. According to reports, the Christian Democrats under D'Aubuisson's plan would have no chairmanships, no seats in the cabinet, no representation in government agencies.

This development threatened to destroy hopes of internal political stability. The fledgling democracy, so patiently nursed through its first real elections by Duarte, seemed doomed to the politics of dissolution. Many in the United States feared D'Aubuisson's close ties to the military and his outspoken extremism. Death squads had terrorized the Salvadoran countryside for years. The ganglike assassination of Archbishop Romero and the brutal slaying of three North American nuns and a lay missionary were only the most flagrant examples in a chain of violence that many observers believed to be directed secretly by Salvadoran military officers.

The United States had invested heavily in the Salvadoran experiment in democracy. Two years earlier I had visited Duarte in his country and had been impressed by his decency. For the first time in the little nation's whole violent history, someone was making an effort to subdue the military and make its officers amenable to civil law. Now, U.S. observers feared, all of this could be in jeopardy. U.S. Ambassador Deane Hinton shared this concern. He briefed our delegation on the internal dangers inherent in a right-wing/military cabal. Knowing the deep dependence of the military establishment on U.S. aid, he asked me to talk informally with D'Aubuisson. Hinton wanted me as House majority leader to stress the apprehensions in Congress over death-squad activity, and the likelihood that aid could be terminated entirely if it appeared that extremists were silencing voices of moderation and reason in the government.

Seated beside the vigorous young militarist at dinner in the ambassador's residence, I sensed the tension. D'Aubuisson's body was like a tightly coiled spring. He drummed his fingers on the tablecloth and tapped his feet beneath the table in an almost incessant venting of nervous energy. When he spoke it was in staccato bursts that reminded me of machine-gun fire. He talked too rapidly for my poor Spanish to follow, and I had to call upon a State Department translator to sit between us and help.

D'Aubuisson had the kind of political magnetism that can both attract and frighten. But he did have the ability to listen. By the time dinner was over, I was sure Roberto D'Aubuisson had received the message. He knew that the U.S. Congress would not support a reign of terror.

Throughout the entire decade, our desire to promote democracy in El Salvador was inseparably linked to our snarled relations with Nicaragua. Our delegation left the violent little country and traveled to Managua, where we confronted the Sandinistas with the demand that they respect their neighbor's border. After that visit to Nicaragua, the one in which I encountered the little crippled girl, my uncritical acceptance of the CIA's description of events between the two countries, and of our purpose in financing the paramilitary intrusion, began to be shaken increasingly by events. Try as I would to justify the administration's official story, it just wouldn't wash. Others in Congress, including several other members of the House and Senate Intelligence committees, were having the same problem.

Skeptics worried increasingly that the real purpose of the covert operation was to overthrow the Sandinista government. One House Democrat, who requested anonymity at the time, summed up the growing concern in Congress, saying the overthrow of foreign governments was simply "none of our goddamn business." Even Nicaraguans openly opposed to the Sandinistas disputed Reagan administration tactics. "When the moderates are all hanging in the streets of Managua," said disaffected former junta member Alfonso Robelo, "the United States says 'Look what the Sandinistas did to the moderates' and uses it as a pretext for an invasion!'"

During the months ahead the Nicaraguan insurgent force continued to grow. Contra leaders began openly expressing their central goal—the overthrow of the Sandinista government. In the late summer and early fall of 1982, a torrent of press reports highlighted comments to this effect. *Newsweek*'s November 8 issue included the following account:

> When the time is right, the Somocistas say, they will draw their loose circle of camps together in toward Managua and force the Sandinistas out. And then? "Come the counterrevolution, there will be a massacre in Nicaragua," promises one contra officer. "We have a lot of scores to settle."

Speaker Thomas P. O'Neill became adamantly opposed to Contra aid in any form. The speaker's ninety-one-year-old aunt who died in 1981 had been a Maryknoll nun, one of the founders of the order. Hers was a strong and penetrating influence, and "Tip" felt a close kinship to Maryknollers. A Maryknoll missionary named Peggy Healy, based in Nicaragua, often corresponded with O'Neill. Sister Healy felt keenly that the CIA's support of the Contras was wicked. I met with her at the Speaker's request. She was outspoken in her denunciation of the terror, bullying, and needless violence perpetrated by the growing bands of armed resistance. "I believe every word," Tip O'Neill told an aide following a meeting with Sister Healy. Opposition to the Contra war mounted. Meanwhile, increasing numbers of CIA-trained Contra forces, based in Honduras, were making hit-and-run attacks on northern Nicaraguan villages, then fleeing to sanctuary across the Honduran border.

Finally, on December 8, 1982, Intelligence Committee Chairman Edward Boland moved on the House floor to prohibit the use of any U.S. funds to overthrow the Nicaraguan government or to provoke a military exchange between Nicaragua and Honduras. Some, including Boland, had begun to fear that CIA operatives were plotting to draw Nicaraguan troops into conflict with Honduran forces as a prelude to and excuse for upping the ante on U.S. military aid to the Contras. Boland did not speak often. When he did, his words carried weight. A slender, bespectacled New Englander with a deep voice,

Eddie Boland had a reputation for fairness and assiduous attention to detail. His amendment carried by a big vote.

The very next day, CIA Director Casey met with the Senate Intelligence Committee. He argued that arms interdiction remained the principal goal of the Reagan administration's efforts. But he acknowledged that the CIA was hoping also to "harass" and pressure the Nicaraguan government into becoming more "democratic." During that meeting, Senator Patrick Moynihan raised a question: Just how and where did the United States draw the line between deliberate harassment and the effort to overthrow? He asked if the U.S.-financed Contras, regardless of *our* intentions, were fighting to overthrow the government and gain power for themselves. Bill Casey did not directly answer that question. Moynihan later wrote to Casey stating that the Senate committee supported the Boland Amendment and that he expected the CIA to conform to both its letter and spirit. Moynihan subsequently introduced the Boland Amendment in the Senate, where it passed. Reagan signed it into law on December 21, 1982, prohibiting the use of any U.S. funds to attempt an overthrow of the Nicaraguan government.

Immediately following passage of the Boland prohibition, Casey's CIA counsel, Stan Sporkin, assembled a task force composed of the agency's best lawyers. As noted in Bob Woodward's book, *Veil—The Secret Wars of the CIA, 1981 to 1987,* Sporkin told the task force, "This thing [the Boland Amendment] is going to come back and bite us in the ass like nothing you've ever seen." Other lawyers disagreed, feeling the agency only needed to ensure that nothing was done for the ostensible "purpose" of overthrowing the Sandinistas. The group came up with a list of guidelines and cabled it to the Honduras CIA station that was monitoring the Contra operation. The cable took the Boland Amendment literally, stating that nothing should be done for the "purpose" of overthrowing the government of Nicaragua—there would be no equipment, training, support, or even conversations.

Senator Patrick Leahy of Vermont, a member of the Senate Intelligence Committee, visited Central America for a firsthand look. Leahy took with him Rob Simmons of Senator Goldwater's staff, three other Senate staffers, and a CIA legislative liaison officer. In Honduras, Leahy's party was briefed on Contra training and projected combat-unit movements. Although he saw Casey's cable on the Boland prohibition tacked to a bulletin board, Leahy concluded that the information he was receiving confirmed an actual effort to overthrow the Sandinista government.

Worse, Honduran armed forces chief General Gustavo Álvarez told Leahy, "We'll have our soldiers in Managua by Christmas." Per Woodward's account in *Veil*, when the senator pointed out that U.S. policy specifically forbade activities to overthrow the Sandinistas, General Álvarez replied, "Oh, yeah, but wouldn't it be great to do anyway?"

On the group's next stop, in Panama, Leahy asked for specific information on the Nicaraguan program. The CIA station chief said he had orders from his division chief, Dewey Clarridge, not to respond. Eventually Clarridge came to Leahy's hotel where he informed the senator of a top-secret undertaking to train Contra rebels in Panama. Clarridge reported that the strongman leader of Panama, General Manuel Noriega, had been a key undercover provider of information and assistance for the CIA. General Noriega was helping the CIA build a secret Contra training center in Panama. Leahy was irate. This clearly had nothing to do with arms interdiction. He and the Senate staffers put together a top-secret report concluding that the CIA operation in sponsorship of the Contras was bigger in nearly every respect than it had been officially described as being.

During 1983 the administration launched a massive campaign to win Congress over to its agenda on Central America. Increasingly the issue was stated in anticommunist terms. President Reagan emphasized the perils of falling dominoes and the Marxist threat in the Western Hemisphere. His style became more confrontational. UN Ambassador Jeane Kirkpatrick, returning from Central America in February, spoke of growing Soviet influence in the region and called for more funding to fight that menace.

A few urged caution. Assistant Secretary of State Thomas Enders viewed the late-1982 Boland Amendment and other congressional actions as warning signals. Insistence on a militant policy was putting the White House and Congress on a collision course. But most senior appointees did not see that as a problem. Members of this inner circle advised the administration to take its case aggressively before the American people.

By the spring of 1983, armed Contra groups had grown from five hundred to fifty-five hundred men. John McMahon, executive director of the CIA, began to worry that so large a military operation strained the capacity of the CIA. He suggested that the Contra operation belonged in the hands of the Defense Department. Defense Secretary Weinberger reportedly nixed this idea. Since a force so numerous defied the stated purpose of arms interdiction, Congress became increasingly concerned that the law was being evaded. An effort to bar all funding for the Contras gained momentum in the House.

"There is no question that the numbers increased far beyond what the committee anticipated," said Republican House Intelligence Committee member William Goodling. "I think as the force increases and diversifies, controlling it would be an impossibility."

During April of 1983, thirty-seven members of the House wrote to President Reagan stating that continued financial support for so large an anti-Sandinista force bivouacked in Honduras was a "violation of the Boland Amendment." Administration response to the charge exacerbated the conflict. CIA attorneys argued that U.S. aid to the Contras was technically legal because, regardless of the intentions of the Contras, the *goal* of the U.S. agencies that supplied the money was innocent of intent to overthrow the Nicaraguan government.

By mid-1983 Contra rebels were engaging Sandinista military units in large clashes. Contras were blowing up bridges. A granary and ranch had been hit. Then a power plant was attacked. The CIA explained that the power plant was a "military" target, although approximately 90 percent of the power was reserved for civilians. Soon Eddie Boland began to speak out, denouncing the administration's noncompliance with the Boland Amendment. On April 27, 1983, he and House Foreign Affairs Committee Chairman Clement Zablocki introduced H.R. 2760, a bill "to prohibit United States' support for military or paramilitary operation in Nicaragua."

On the same day President Reagan addressed a joint session of Congress. He raised the stakes, insisting that

> the national security of all the Americas is at stake in Central America. If we cannot defend ourselves there, we cannot expect to prevail elsewhere. Our credibility would collapse, our alliances would crumble, and the safety of our homeland would be put in jeopardy. . . . Who among us would wish to bear responsibility for failing to meet our shared obligation?

By stressing to Congress and the American people the "national security" aspects of Central America and hinting that he would blame Congress for failure, Reagan hoped to line up congressional support for his Nicaraguan agenda.

Six days later, the House Intelligence Committee voted nine to five along straight party lines to support the Boland-Zablocki bill and halt all U.S. support for the military operation.

Just prior to this vote, Assistant Secretary of State Enders devised a last-minute proposal that would limit the number of Contra troops and reform the Contra leadership. Enders thought the right policy would be to remove the Soviets and Cubans from Nicaragua by renewing a dialogue with the Sandinistas. But Reagan and Casey questioned the personal loyalty of anyone wanting to carry on a dialogue. The Nicaraguan government, they had decided, was the enemy. On May 27, Enders was transferred away from the Latin American desk and given a new assignment as ambassador to Spain. He chose to resign in July, replaced by an administration hard-liner contemptuous of the congressional role in foreign policy.

This drove another wedge between the branches of government. By early May objections to the president's Nicaragua policy spread to the Senate. There, the Intelligence Committee voted thirteen to two not to authorize funds for covert operations in Nicaragua until the president submitted a new finding delineating the purposes of such operations. A compromise by Senator Barry Goldwater continued funding for an additional five months but made any further sums contingent upon the credibility of a new presidential finding.

In the House, Speaker Tip O'Neill strongly censured the president's efforts to sell his Central America war on national security grounds. O'Neill put the issue plainly and harshly: "The President of the United States broke the law and then laughed to the American people that he broke the law."

On June 6 U.S.-Nicaraguan relations deteriorated further when Nicaragua expelled three American diplomats. The Reagan administration retaliated by expelling twenty-one Nicaraguan diplomats the next day. Each side accused diplomats from the other side of spying.

As the domestic debate escalated, it became more partisan. Most Democrats did not support any Contra aid. Some, however, were deeply disturbed by growing insinuations that opposition to arming the "freedom fighters," as President Reagan began referring to the rebel forces, would be interpreted as "helping the communists." Almost unanimously, the Republicans supported Reagan's program of military aid to the Contras.

The floor debate on the Boland-Zablocki Amendment was bitter and personal. House Intelligence Committee member William Whitehurst, Virginia Republican, cautioned of a "Marxist triumph throughout all of Central America" if the measure passed. "I do not want my name sullied with the irrefutable charge that I lost Central America," he said. Opponents of the president's policy declared that we were literally playing with dynamite and endangering the lives of another generation of young Americans. Some began charging the president with leading the country into another Vietnam. Boland asserted his apprehension with a reference to that unpopular conflict:

> When we adopted the Gulf of Tonkin resolution we did not have all the facts. We could not—many of us could not—see where it would take us. Today the House does not suffer from that disadvantage. You have heard in secret session the numbers of fighters armed, the cost of the program, the plans for expansion.

I felt the polarized debate and hardening positions needed a new focus. It really wasn't a question of whether we approved of the Sandinistas. It was a question of whether we had a right to dictate their violent overthrow. Beyond that, it was a question of how to resolve the conflict. I offered an amendment calling for a regional approach:

> The question is this. Do we go it alone? Do we postulate ourselves as a sort of Lone Ranger riding throughout the hemisphere shooting silver bullets at people who misbehave from our point of view? Or do we call on that organization [the OAS] which has been created for that express purpose? . . . I believe we should do the latter.

My amendment directed the president to seek intervention by the OAS to resolve the conflicts in Central America. It also prohibited direct or indirect support by U.S. intelligence agencies for military or paramilitary operations in Nicaragua. A majority liked my approach. The Boland-Zablocki bill, with my amendment attached, passed the House on July 28. The vote was 228 to 195.

While this measure was pending in the Senate, a series of disastrous leaks about administration policy surfaced. One story reported that the CIA was seeking presidential authorization for twelve to fifteen thousand Contra rebels, roughly twice the current number. By far the most damaging revelation, however, laid bare administration plans for two large military exercises off the Honduran coast. The plans called for a U.S. Navy battle group housing sixteen thousand sailors and five thousand U.S. ground troops. The maneuvers, according to administration officials, were designed to intimidate Nicaragua. The revelation sent chills of apprehension through Congress. Secretary of State Shultz, according to reports, had not been informed of the decision of the National Security Council (NSC) to launch these maneuvers. Nonetheless, he had to defend the action to members of Congress who were outraged by news of the escapade. Not one congressional leader had been informed of the maneuvers ahead of time.

In a letter to President Reagan on July 28, House Speaker O'Neill and Senate Minority Leader Robert Byrd expressed dismay "that officials of your administration did not foresee the need to consult with the Congress prior to initiating such serious action."

The military maneuvers in Honduras marked the rise of the NSC, which would later orchestrate the Iran-Contra affair. But at this stage in 1983, the CIA still directed anti-Nicaraguan activity. William Casey was determined to do everything possible to protect his Nicaraguan operation. With congressional support eroding, things were getting out of hand. The administration needed to regain the initiative. Casey told Clarridge, his CIA division chief in Latin America, to "get something." He needed "news" to establish credibility for the Contras within Nicaragua. Two U.S. senators would soon experience that news firsthand.

Senator William S. Cohen, a Republican from Maine, served on the Senate Intelligence Committee. He wanted to support the administration on Nicaragua and had told the president he would. But Cohen had apprehensions. Casey suggested that Cohen visit Nicaragua. Thus, in September he and Democratic Senator Gary Hart of Colorado departed Washington on a C-140 bound for Managua. One hour outside Managua, the pilots received word that the Augusto César Sandino Airport was closed due to an air attack. A twin-engine Cessna with a 500-pound bomb strapped under each wing had been shot down over the airport.

Eventually arriving in Managua, Hart and Cohen found vast destruction. The crash had wiped out part of the terminal, hurling oil and glass over the surrounding area. Both the pilot and copilot were killed. The Nicaraguan news media arrived, and one reporter attributed the bombing attack to a CIA-sponsored Contra raid.

"The CIA is not that dumb," Cohen retorted.

Nicaraguan officials, however, produced a briefcase retrieved from the plane. Cohen and Hart, looking through its contents, found a manifest instructing the pilot to meet a person in Costa Rica at a particular restaurant. In the briefcase were the pilot's Florida driver's license and American credit cards, along with code identifications for the operation—authentic CIA paperwork.

In a meeting with the CIA station chief, Cohen and Hart unloaded. How could the CIA think it would achieve anything by bombing a civilian airport? Civilians could have been killed, turning the Nicaraguan population even more firmly against the Contras. The station chief retorted that the operation was intended to show that the Contras were serious and could strike the capital. Moreover, he dissembled, the Contras were free agents, and the CIA could not control their targets. Hart railed at how stupid the operation had been. Who would carry his CIA paperwork in a briefcase on a covert bombing raid? An utter idiot? Returning to Washington, Cohen and Hart made clear to Casey their disdain for the bombing. But it had been done. Adventurism. Two men dead. Sandinistas riled. Nothing gained.

During the fall of 1983, a national intelligence estimate produced by the CIA concluded that the Contra forces, in spite of the buildup in their numbers, did not have the military capability and political support to overthrow the Sandinistas. The Nicaraguan government would not fall in a military confrontation with the U.S.-backed Contras, the study declared. This evaluation, however, did not deter the administration from enlarging its covert war.

During September, Congress demanded, and the administration attempted to define, a logical political rationale for U.S. actions. On September 19, President Reagan signed a new finding. Now the officially stated reason for equipping and training paramilitary forces was "to bring the Sandinistas into meaningful negotiations and constructive, verifiable agreement with their neighbors on peace in the region." As worked out with the Senate Intelligence Committee, the finding also encouraged the United States to "seek support of and work with other foreign governments and organizations as appropriate to carry out this program." The committee voted thirteen to two to accept the amended finding.

Undeterred, the House voted twice more before the end of 1983 to stop all covert operations against Nicaragua. The White House pulled out all stops in an intense lobbying effort to keep the program alive in the Senate. President Reagan put his prestige on the line with personal telephone calls to individual senators. The effort paid off. The Senate continued to support the administration. Senate spokesmen, pointing to the new presidential finding, argued that the 1982 Boland Amendment was no longer necessary. While the two houses debated, that provision expired with the end of the fiscal year on September 30, 1983.

House and Senate conferees on the defense bill finally agreed on November 18 to provide $24 million for the Contras for fiscal year 1984. Some senators had wanted as much as $50 million. In exchange for permitting even the smaller funding level, the House insisted on banning the use of CIA "contingency" funds or "reprogrammings" to supplement the money for the rebels. Any additional funds would have to pass both houses.

During the process of this agonizing legislative battle the NSC, acting on its own and without informing the congressional oversight committees, approved an increase in the authorized strength of the Contra rebels, up to a force of eighteen thousand. With the new presidential finding, planners in the administration felt the time was ripe for economic warfare. "Let's make the bastards sweat," Bill Casey reportedly said, per Woodward in *Veil*. With this, the war entered a new and much more aggressive phase.

On October 11, 1983, CIA-trained speedboat teams conducted a predawn raid against Nicaraguan fuel storages at the port of Corinto. Five storage tanks, supposedly housing most of Nicaragua's oil reserves, were blown up. Some twenty thousand residents of the city were forced to evacuate because of fires. Three days later the CIA-sponsored teams hit Puerto Sandino, another major Nicaraguan port. Next came the sabotage of a Nicaraguan pipeline. Evidence began to surface that CIA employees not only helped plan these attacks but actually executed them. This was something new. If true, it violated assurances given to Congress that no U.S. personnel would take part in covert attacks against Nicaragua.

There also was a new team directing the war. Anthony Motley had replaced Tom Enders as assistant secretary of state for inter-American affairs. Motley had convened a working group on the Contra operation called the RIG (Restricted Interagency Group). Motley, Clarridge of the CIA, and Lieutenant Colonel Oliver North of the NSC formed the core. It was at a private meeting of this group, Congress later would learn, that Clarridge had proposed mining the Nicaraguan harbors. Casey presented the reckless and illegal plan to the president, who approved.

Now the wraps were off. No more Marquis of Queensberry. No more kowtowing to fastidious congressional rules. No more squeamishness about legalities. A determined cabal had the bit in its teeth. It was out to do whatever it took to bring Nicaragua to its knees.

CHAPTER 5

The Secret Government

*They decided that the policy embodied in the Boland
Amendment was wrong, and they went about to violate it over a
long period of time and then to lie about their activities to
prevent the Congress and the public from finding out. . . . If the
court were not to impose such a penalty [imprisonment] here . . .
its action would be tantamount to a statement that a scheme to
lie and to obstruct Congress was of no great moment.*

—Federal District Judge Harold H. Greene
upon sentencing John M. Poindexter,
June 11, 1990

*When the cause obliterates the distinction between falsehood and
truth, between ends and means, the cause has destroyed
everything good, including itself. When expediency is
transformed into principle, chaos is unleashed.*

—Gary Hardaway, free-lance writer

From early 1984 through late 1986, a secret government conducted a secret war against Nicaragua. This government
made decisions behind closed doors and carried them out in stealth.
Congress was not informed, as the law required—it was, in fact,
deliberately lied to—about the activities of this clandestine government. As Representative Norman Mineta of California would com-

plain to me upon discovering the deception, "They treat us like mushrooms. They keep us in the dark and cover us with manure." Zealots in the secret coterie no doubt thought they were acting with President Reagan's blessings. They believed their fervency in the cause of anticommunism justified making their own rules while violating national and international laws.

Ironically, this closed cabal was plotting its first fateful ventures at the very time a high-level bipartisan group was publicly seeking a basis for national consensus. The National Bipartisan Commission on Central America was the brainchild of Democratic Senator Henry M. Jackson of Washington. Appointed by President Reagan, it consisted of twelve members of both political parties, and twelve senior counselors. I was one of the latter. Choosing former Secretary of State Henry A. Kissinger as its chairman, our group became known as the Kissinger Commission.

We heard testimony from literally hundreds of people and spent nine days in Central America listening to heads of state and opposition leaders, as well as many others. The commission submitted a 132-page report to President Reagan on January 10, 1984. This report evaluated the crisis in Central America, calling it urgent. That crisis "must be addressed at once and simultaneously in all its aspects," the commission warned. "Ultimate resolutions depend on economic progress, social and political reform. But insurgencies must be checked if lasting progress is to be made on those fronts."

The objective of U.S. policy, according to this nonpartisan study, must be to "reduce Central American conflicts to Central American dimension." Indigenous reform, even indigenous revolution, posed "no threat to the U.S.," the commission concluded. "But the intrusion of outside powers exploiting local grievances for political and strategic advantage is a serious threat." The United States, it said, "must make a long-term commitment and stick to a coherent policy."

Pointing to the distressing economic decline throughout the region, the bipartisan commission recommended a $400-million supplemental appropriation "to stabilize economies now going downhill very fast." It proposed a five-year economic-assistance plan in the range of $8 billion. Immediately, we should provide an emergency loan to the Central American common market, encourage commercial banks to renegotiate loans "at the lowest possible interest rates," and otherwise "take an active role in efforts to resolve the external debt" of the region.

The commission agreed that "consolidation of a Marxist-Leninist regime" in Central America would create a serious threat. A majority of the members felt that the United States should support continued assistance to El Salvador, "conditioned on terminating death squads" and establishing "the rule of law," as well as continued "incentives and pressures for the regime in Managua to negotiate seriously."

Both Democrats and Republicans on the panel urged the U.S. government to support a "comprehensive regional settlement" and to "commit itself to respect results of elections within countries" that observe "pluralism at home and restraint abroad."

The report ended with a ringing call for consensus: "The people of Central America are neither Republicans nor Democrats. The crisis is nonpartisan, and it calls for a nonpartisan response."

When news of the mining of Nicaraguan harbors reached Congress, however, it effectively torpedoed any chance of consensus. Positions hardened, almost calcified. The first dispute, a harbinger of battles to come, arose with a renewed request by the administration for more Contra funding. Assistant Secretary of State Tony Motley agreed with William Casey that the Contras needed much more than the $24 million Congress had appropriated for 1984. The way he went after it betrayed contempt for congressional rules. Instead of dealing with the Senate Intelligence Committee, which had legal jurisdiction over authorizing new funds, Motley tried an end run. He carried a request for an additional $21 million directly to Alaska Senator Ted Stevens, who headed the Senate Appropriations Subcommittee, asking him to sneak it through without legislative authorization.

Barry Goldwater learned of the ploy and was enraged. The White House was bypassing Senate rules. Goldwater and Moynihan, the ranking Democrat on the Intelligence Committee, wrote to President Reagan denouncing the violation of normal procedure. That letter brought an apology from Secretary of State George Shultz. The Senate intelligence panel would ultimately vote approval for the extra $21 million, but a bad taste lingered. It was only the first, and perhaps the least consequential, in what was to be a series of procedural and legal transgressions by members of the new secret government.

As if responding to the Kissinger Commission's call for the United States to respect democratic elections, the Managua government announced that national elections would be held that November

(1984). Ortega ordered the lifting of press censorship imposed under the emergency law. He also proclaimed freedom for political parties to organize and hold rallies.

Alfonso Robelo, the U.S.-educated business leader whom I had met first in 1980 on the mission for President Carter, told a group of congressional leaders in March that he believed there was a chance for an upset in the elections. Robelo had left Nicaragua and was working in Costa Rica with Edén Pastora, a popular hero of the 1979 anti-Somoza revolution. Pastora, remembered by the people as "Commander Zero," had grown disillusioned with the Sandinistas and gone into exile. Robelo felt that Pastora was a natural to oppose Ortega for the presidency in the November balloting and was trying to persuade his associate to make himself available. As a progressive moderate, the revolutionary hero would be an attractive alternative and more likely to garner support than the more right-wing dissidents, some tainted by old Somoza connections, whom the United States was supporting financially.

But his principle goal, Robelo told us, was to remove what he saw as the root cause of hostility between our two countries. He would do this by bringing enough pressure to ensure open and free elections. Robelo thought the Sandinista government could be prevailed upon to show its good faith by opening the ballot box to exiles—letting estranged Nicaraguans return and have their say with votes in the national election rather than with rifles in the mountain passes.

Alfonso Robelo asked if several of us would write to Ortega commending him on the decision to hold elections and appealing to him to make a reality of his promise that all parties would be allowed to participate equally. Ten of us signed such a letter on March 20 and mailed it to Daniel Ortega. We wrote, "with the hope that the initial steps you have taken will be followed by others designed to guarantee a fully open and democratic electoral process." The letter continued:

> We note that some who have become exiles from Nicaragua
> have expressed a willingness to return to participate in the
> elections, if assurances are provided that their security will be
> protected, and their political rights recognized. Among these
> exiles are some who have taken up arms against your gov-
> ernment, and who have stated their willingness to lay down
> those arms to participate in a truly democratic process. If this

were to occur, the prospects for peace and stability throughout Central America would be dramatically enhanced. . . . A decision on your part to provide these reasonable assurances and conduct truly free and open elections would significantly improve the prospect of better relations between our two countries.

Signatories joining me in this appeal were Chairman Edward Boland of the House Intelligence Committee; three subcommittee chairmen of the House Foreign Affairs Committee—Mike Barnes of Maryland, Stephen Solarz of New York, and Lee Hamilton of Indiana; three members of the House Appropriations Committee—David Obey of Wisconsin, Matt McHugh of New York, and Bill Alexander of Arkansas; as well as Bob Torricelli of New Jersey and Robert Garcia of New York, both members of the House Foreign Affairs Committee (the complete original letter can be found in the appendix).

Scarcely did we dream, even in the emotionally charged atmosphere of the day, that our letter with what we considered its reasonable appeal would subject us to personal attack. We supposed almost everyone wanted the very result for which we pleaded—truly free elections. Our disillusionment came swiftly.

A small band of dedicated enthusiasts of the armed resistance in early April began a series of long, hostile speeches on the House floor. The principal spokesman for the group, Newt Gingrich of Georgia, told me that he had mailed copies of the speeches to newspapers in the home districts of signatories to the Ortega letter, asking for editorial condemnation of our efforts. In a case of classic overstatement, Gingrich wrote, "There is no modern example of so blatant an effort by one faction of American politicians. . . . This letter is almost certainly illegal and unconstitutional . . . a clear violation by legislators of the executive's right to deal with foreign governments. . . . These ten congressmen clearly undercut the efforts of their own government to apply pressure to the Nicaraguan regime."

His hyperbole rendered the attacks ineffectual. Letters from members of Congress to foreign heads of state were not uncommon. Only recently some of those objecting now had petitioned the head of the Soviet Union on behalf of a more permissive Jewish emigration policy. The harsh fervor of the small group of Republicans who mounted the denunciation, however, and the frantic intensity with which they pursued it, awakened the ten of us to the growing shrillness of debate over Central American issues. On April 12 I responded briefly in the House:

> The Nicaraguan government has announced at last that it will have elections. We are trying to gain assurances that those elections be truly open, free, and fair. That is what we were asking in the letter, and I do not apologize for that. That is what I think most of us in Congress are for.
>
> I will forever try, if I can, to stand ready to assist in opening the door to a reconciliation with any nation on Earth that has bad relations with us. Even when it does not work, we must be willing to try again. I think that is what is expected of us. I would rather be a peacemaker than a warmaker. I do not think we have to apologize for that.

President Reagan's instinct was to discount the Nicaraguan elections as unworthy of notice. In an interview with the *New York Times,* he had told a reporter that covert attacks would stop when the Sandinista leaders "keep their promises and restore the democratic rule and have elections" (March 29). Reminded that elections had been scheduled for November, Reagan dismissed them peremptorily: "There isn't anything yet to indicate that the elections will be anything but the kind of rubber-stamp that we see in any totalitarian government."

That afternoon, Senator Moynihan, vice chairman of the Intelligence Committee, took stern issue with the president. The statement revealed, he argued, Reagan's real preference for a military solution. "If the president is so sure that the government there cannot be changed by elections," he asked in a speech on the Senate floor, "how *is* it to be changed save by violent overthrow? That is a necessary if unintended conclusion to be drawn from the president's statement" (italics added).

By autumn it would be apparent that those now calling the shots in administration policy had no interest in pursuing either elections or a policy consensus as set forth in the Kissinger report. Their singleminded goal was to bring so much misery on Nicaragua's three and a half million people that its government would just collapse.

If Congress passed laws forbidding U.S. participation in efforts to overthrow that government, the secret interagency group would find ways to achieve that goal and make it appear that someone else had done it. So the CIA study said the Contras lacked popular support and could not defeat the Sandinista army? The secret group would supplement the Contras' efforts and tighten the screws on Nicaragua in other ways.

The United States was applying an economic stranglehold. Not only did the president cut off Nicaragua's sugar quota and declare a boycott on trade. U.S. representatives in international lending institutions (the World Bank and the Inter-American Development Bank), began pressuring those agencies against making any loans to Nicaragua. Now private U.S. banks, which had dealt with Nicaraguan borrowers, were importuned against extending those notes. With these measures, Nicaragua's already impoverished economy was gasping for breath. Now, reasoned the secret planners, it was time to close the fingers on Nicaragua's economic windpipe. Mining harbors would reduce the little nation's shipping capacity. It would also intimidate shippers from other nations that still traded with the hard-bitten regime.

One night in late February of 1984, the deadly business began. Trained frogmen started stringing underwater mines in Nicaragua's three busiest harbors. It would be almost six weeks before the fingerprints of the U.S. government would surface.

On Thursday night, April 5, Barry Goldwater stood on the Senate floor attempting to salvage the extra $21 million requested by the administration for Contra aid. He castigated his colleagues for "congressional meddling with the efforts by the President to defend the national security." As Goldwater spoke, Senator Joseph Biden sat at his desk reviewing a classified memo stating that the CIA had played a direct role in mining three Nicaraguan harbors. This was the first Biden had heard of the mining.

He delivered the memo to a fellow Intelligence Committee member, Republican Bill Cohen. After reading the startling revelation, Cohen carried it over to Goldwater, now through with his speech, and demanded an explanation. Goldwater was stunned. He gained permission to speak again and began reading the classified memo to his Senate colleagues. His staff director, Rob Simmons, rushed over abruptly, interrupting Goldwater's delivery. This was highly classified material! Simmons and Goldwater stared at one another in dismay. This was the first either had heard of the minings. Simmons later had Goldwater's reading of the secret memo excised from the *Congressional Record*. Few senators had been on the floor when he was reading it. Some may not have grasped its full import. However,

Dave Rogers, a reporter for the *Wall Street Journal*, heard it. He wrote a story about the episode that was published in the next morning's edition. The headline read: "U.S. Role in Mining Nicaraguan Harbors Reportedly Is Larger Than First Thought." Now the lid was off.

Senator Edward Kennedy branded administration policy in Nicaragua "illegal" and "indefensible." On the previous day, Kennedy had sponsored an amendment to slash all of the $21 million from the bill. Despite official assertions that the aim of the Contra aid program was to pressure the Sandinista regime into change, Kennedy had argued that the real purpose was to help the guerrillas seize power by force.

Just prior to the vote on the Kennedy amendment, Majority Leader Howard Baker had read a letter from Reagan to Senate members. Reagan pledged in the letter, "The United States does not seek to destabilize or overthrow the government of Nicaragua; nor to impose or compel any particular form of government there." The Senate, thus formally reassured, passed the bill, including the $21 million, by a vote of seventy-six to nineteen. Now, one day later, doubt cast an ominous shadow over the president's solemn assurance. Did Reagan not know of the illegal mining, or had he deliberately deceived the Senate?

News of the real scope and dimension of the minings trickled in slowly to members of congressional committees. Approximately seventy-five mines had been laid on the bottom of three Nicaraguan harbors. Some of the mines had up to 300 pounds of C-4 explosive, enough for a gigantic explosion. On February 25 two fishing boats had hit mines and sunk at the Caribbean port of El Bluff. Two more vessels suffered damage. Two crew members were killed and seven were wounded. On March 1 a Dutch dredging ship hit a mine at the Pacific port of Corinto. Five people were injured and damages were assessed at $1 million. On March 7 a mine explosion at Corinto cracked up a Panamanian freighter. On March 20 a Soviet oil tanker was seriously crippled when it ran over a mine at the Pacific port of Sandino. Five crewmen suffered injuries.

Goldwater was incensed. He fired off a scathing letter to CIA Director Casey condemning the minings.

On April 6, press reports began to appear revealing direct CIA participation in the mining of Nicaraguan harbors. These stories prompted a rash of recriminations on Capitol Hill. Members demanded to know why nobody in Congress had been notified in advance. This was outlawry, indeed a flagrant violation of international law. The United States had once gone to war when its own harbors were mined! Who could have put the country in so untenable a position?

Both houses were up in arms, shaken by the audacity and bald deception of the scheme. On April 10 the Senate voted 84 to 12 to pass a forcefully worded "sense of the Congress" resolution condemning the mining. On April 12 the House followed in a 281 to 111 vote. Some of the president's strongest Senate supporters backed the statement. Senator Barry Goldwater said, "I am forced to apologize to the members of my committee because I did not know the facts of this case. . . . I apologize to all members of the Senate for the same reason."

During a state dinner for the president of the Dominican Republic, President Reagan said of the resolution and overwhelming votes by which it passed, "If it is not binding, I can live with it. I think there is a great hysteria raised about this whole thing."

Nicaragua formally protested the mining before the World Court at The Hague, Netherlands. The U.S. administration refused to appear, declaring disdainfully it would not respect the tribunal's authority over U.S. actions in Central America. On May 10, 1984, the court issued a preliminary ruling condemning the CIA's involvement in the mining of Nicaraguan harbors as a violation of well-established principles of international law. The ruling called on the United States to "immediately cease and refrain" from all such mining operations in Nicaraguan territory. As a matter of fact, the United States already had ceased. The dangerous adventure had been counterproductive in very important ways. It had cost our country respect in the world community, and it was costing the administration support in Congress.

Goldwater left for a trip to the Far East on April 13, leaving Moynihan as acting chairman of the Senate Intelligence Committee. Later that day Moynihan saw an article in the *Washington Times* quoting statements made by NSC Adviser McFarlane about the mining. "Every important detail," McFarlane claimed, had been "shared in full . . . as provided by law" with the oversight committees. Moynihan, who had drafted the 1980 Intelligence Oversight Act requiring the committees to be *"fully and currently* informed on *all* intelligence activities" (italics added), knew that McFarlane's claim was untrue. In all the oversight committee hearings, there had been only fleeting reference to any possibility of minings. That reference constituted twenty-seven words in a presentation that lasted well over two hours—one sentence in a transcript of eighty-four pages. Moynihan considered McFarlane's statement a complete dismissal of a serious evasion of law and a brash rejection of Goldwater's letter of complaint to Casey.

That afternoon, in an interview with David Brinkley, Moynihan said, "Senator Goldwater made his judgment as clear as words could do, and four or five days after that they still reject his judgment. So they now have *my* judgment in the only way I can make it, which is to say, *I resign!*" Later that day Pat Moynihan formally resigned his position as vice chairman of the Senate Intelligence Committee.

That weekend President Reagan joked about the controversy. At the White House Correspondents Association annual black-tie dinner, the president quipped, "What's all that talk about a breakdown of White House communications? How come nobody told me? Well, I know this: I've laid down the law, though, to everyone there from now on about anything that happens, that no matter what time it is, wake me, even if it's in the middle of a Cabinet meeting."

But the displeasure in Congress was not to be laughed off so easily. Sensing that angry lawmakers, particularly in the House, were unlikely to approve more arms aid for the Contras in the absence of a big change in public opinion, Reagan on May 9 went on the offensive in a nationally televised address. He tried to portray Nicaragua as a threat to the entire Western Hemisphere. The United States had a "moral obligation" to support the Nicaraguan "freedom fighters," Reagan insisted. "The Sandinista rule is a communist reign of terror." Despite his forensic efforts, House and Senate conferees could not reach a consensus on the $21 million in Contra aid. On May 24 the House, on a 241 to 177 vote, again rejected further aid.

During June of that year, 1984, Senate support for the administration's effort began to decline. Several Senate Democrats who had previously supported the president changed positions. Senator Daniel Inouye of Hawaii gave the following reasons: The program was no longer secret; the United States did not have control over the Contras; the program had "gone beyond" its initial purpose of halting the flow of arms from Nicaragua to El Salvador; and the high visibility of the CIA operation was "slowly but surely eroding whatever credibility" the agency had left. From that point, Senate Republicans and the president were forced—temporarily, at least—to give up the fight for the $21 million.

Following a series of White House discussions, Casey obtained a decision from the president that until the November election the CIA would conduct a "holding action" in the covert funding program. When Reagan was reelected as he expected to be, the administration would somehow renew the fight and win more funding from Congress for the Contra war.

But the secret government had not given up. Back in March, Casey had written a highly classified letter to Robert McFarlane asking him to explore funding alternatives with the Saudis, Israelis, and others. Later that spring, McFarlane met with the Saudi ambassador to the United States, Prince Bandar, a man with access to great wealth. The two men agreed that the Saudis would contribute $8 to $10 million to the Contras at the rate of $1 million per month. The contributions, both men agreed, would have to be handled with the greatest secrecy.

According to Woodward's *Veil* and Cynthia Arnson's book, *Crossroads: Congress, the Reagan Administration and Central America,* here is how they worked it: Bandar obtained a Saudi government check for $8 million. McFarlane acquired a secret bank account number from the BAC International Bank in the Cayman islands. Bandar, given the account number, traveled to Geneva, Switzerland, on June 27 to transfer the funds through a Swiss bank. Handing the $8 million to an official from the Swiss Bank Corporation, Bandar instructed that it be deposited in the corporation's general account. He directed that $1 million a month be transferred to the Cayman island account. This way the money's origin could not be traced. The initial $1 million was transferred on July 6.

Thus, in mid-1984, Arabs were persuaded to do clandestinely what our government was forbidden to do legally. The Saudis were funding the Contras. McFarlane informed the president, who expressed his appreciation. Congress and the public would not learn of this until a year and a half later.

On July 24, in a nationally televised news conference, Reagan renewed his public offensive. He said the United States had a "responsibility" to prevent Nicaragua from becoming a Soviet "base in the Western Hemisphere." He embellished the appeal with revived statements about Sandinista arms shipments to the Salvadoran guerrillas and the totalitarian nature of Sandinista rule.

On August 2, the House, by a 294 to 118 vote, at first rejected Contra aid entirely for fiscal year 1985. The Senate, in the year-end omnibus spending bill, provided $28 million the president had requested for the Contras in the coming year, fiscal 1985. House conferees agreed to a compromise, allowing the president to spend $14 million, but only after February 28, 1985. To do so he would have to submit a report to Congress after February 28 certifying that the money was needed to fight Sandinista *expansionism*.

Boland, ecstatic over the compromise, spoke of the measure on the House floor:

> No funds available to the Central Intelligence Agency, the Department of Defense, *or any other agency or entity of the United States involved in intelligence activities* may be obligated or expended for the purpose of . . . supporting, directly or indirectly, military or paramilitary operations in Nicaragua by any nation, group, organization, movement, or individual [italics added].

The measure passed the House 294 to 118. It became known as the Second Boland Amendment. The funding bill cleared Congress on October 10.

There would be one more major flap growing out of the secret war in 1984. The Associated Press reported in October that the CIA had approved distribution of a printed manual by Contra troops among Nicaraguan villagers. Titled "Psychological Operations in Guerrilla Warfare," it was classic revolutionary indoctrination on how to disrupt and upset civil order. One section of the manual advocated "neutralizing" Sandinista government officials. Most American readers interpreted the word *neutralize* to mean *assassinate*. Subsequent investigations revealed that the manual had been produced by low-level CIA officials. Chairman Boland said the manual glorified "the doctrine of Lenin, not Jefferson." President Reagan disavowed any connection with political assassinations in Nicaragua. Still, the issue became a steamy one in the final quarter of that year.

Elections were coming, both in the United States and in Nicaragua. Arturo Cruz, the international banker who had accompanied me on my 1980 trip and who had served briefly as Nicaragua's ambassador, told me that he wanted to run for the presidency of his country. He took one well-publicized trip to Nicaragua, making several speeches and testing the waters. Arturo told me upon his return to the States that he had drawn large crowds. No impediments had been put in his path. He thought he could win. Two weeks later he told me that the U.S. State Department and the White House had dissuaded him from running. That puzzled me, because Cruz thought he could have won.

Bob Woodward reports in his book, *Veil*, that just prior to Reagan's landslide victory in 1984 Secretary of State George Schultz devised a Nicaraguan peace plan that he wanted to deliver directly to the president. Defense Secretary Weinberger and UN Ambassador Jeane Kirkpatrick strongly objected. Bill Casey made clear to Shultz, according to Woodward's account, that if he went forward with the recommendation, a score of high-level resignations would follow. Shultz did not proceed. I was not aware of any of this at the time. But it soon became clear that there would be no serious peace moves in the immediate offing.

Daniel Ortega won the 1984 election in Nicaragua, leading the Sandinista Party to victory with slightly over 60 percent of the popular vote. Arturo Cruz might have been a formidable opponent. After he pulled out of the race at White House urging, there was little suspense. There was, however, a heavy voter turnout. Whether it was a real contest and a fair count, I cannot say. International observers from several Latin American and Western European nations thought that it had been.

Our government officially ignored the Nicaraguan election and declined to send observers. *Newsday* reporter Roy Gutman maintained that certain people in the Nicaraguan opposition and the Reagan administration collaborated to keep Cruz from participating in the election so that it would attract less international attention and could be more easily discredited.

Reagan was reelected in November, winning a large electoral plurality—every state but Minnesota—over Democratic nominee Walter Mondale. The House remained in Democratic hands while Republicans held a slim majority in the Senate. Domestic issues dominated the campaigns, and no serious analyst claimed that a mandate had emerged, one way or the other, concerning Central America. But the size of Reagan's victory seemed to inspire his followers.

On January 15, 1985, Lieutenant Colonel Oliver North of the NSC proposed a plan to seek congressional approval for Contra funds "adequate to achieve victory." North wrote later that month that "with adequate support the resistance could be in Managua by the end of 1985." Lifting the Boland restrictions of October 1984 was the "primary goal."

During his February 1985 State of the Union Address, Reagan told Congress, "We must not break faith with those who are risking their lives on every continent, from Afghanistan to Nicaragua, to defy

Soviet-supported aggression and secure rights which have been ours from birth. . . . Support for freedom fighters is self-defense . . . the struggle is tied to our own security."

The 1984 law prohibiting Contra aid allowed the president to make a new request on or after February 28, 1985. But it would have to be based on a showing of a Nicaraguan expansionist threat to other countries. Many in Congress did not believe such a showing could be made. However, events in Nicaragua took a critical turn that solidified congressional opinion, for the time being, against the Sandinistas. Daniel Ortega and his followers had an almost uncanny knack for alienating members of Congress, and at the most inappropriate times from the Sandinista point of view. As he had done before and would do again, Ortega proceeded to snatch legislative defeat from the jaws of victory. The Sandinista leadership, perhaps emboldened by its own electoral success or embittered by the continuing bloodshed, increased its harassment of political opponents and imposed new restrictions on the press. Those who had opposed funding efforts to overthrow the Sandinista government were livid. It was beginning to seem like a bizarre contest between the Sandinista leaders and the secret plotters in the White House to see which could outperform the other in some outrageous deed calculated to offend the U.S. public and inflame the Congress.

About the time attitudes against the Sandinistas hardened, opinions of the Contras improved slightly. In early January of 1985, Arturo Cruz said that it would be a "terrible political mistake" for the United States to halt support for the Contras before the Soviet Union ended its support for the Sandinistas. Within two months Cruz had signed a joint statement with Contra political leaders, formally joining the rebels.

Democratic Representative John Spratt of South Carolina said the presence of former Sandinistas like Cruz in the Contra directorate "represented to me a genuine opportunity for social democracy in Nicaragua." Other Contra leaders, however, continued to express their goal of overthrowing the Sandinistas. "We will defeat the Sandinistas militarily," said Contra leader Indalecio Rodriguez. Many in Congress still remained skeptical of administration objectives.

During February of 1985, pro-Contra rhetoric escalated. President Reagan referred to the Contras as "our brothers," equating them with "freedom fighters" like Lafayette and Simón Bolívar. In one press conference Reagan said that the goal in Nicaragua was to have the Sandinista government removed "in the sense of their present structure," not overthrown but made to "say 'Uncle.' "

The Reagan administration targeted members of Congress and the general public with an intensive propaganda blitz. One objective was to popularize the Contras. Administration consultants prepared newspaper editorials appearing under the signatures of Contra leaders and arranged appointments for the leaders with the major media. Then from February 21 to April 21, the administration coordinated a week-by-week blitz, launching over seventy publications briefings, conferences, and meetings with editorial boards to advance the Contra effort. Opponents of the covert war, unable to counter this coordinated campaign, grew apprehensive.

Funds from third countries for Contra military aid continued to grow in 1985. The Saudis doubled their contribution from the 1984 pledge of $1 million per month. During February Lieutenant Colonel Oliver North (under the name "Steelhammer") wrote to Contra leader Adolfo Calero ("Friend") asking him to keep the expanded Saudi donation quiet.

On April 4, Reagan unveiled a request for $14 million in military aid for the Contras, attaching to it a peace proposal that would withhold arms money and provide only humanitarian aid for sixty days while the Catholic Church attempted a peace dialogue between the Contras and Sandinistas. At the end of this sixty-day period, the president could revert to military funding if he determined that the peace dialogue had not been satisfactory. Senator David Durenberger dubbed this plan an "apple with a razor blade."

The *New York Times,* on April 17, published sections of a leaked document in which the president asserted that "direct application of U.S. military force . . . must realistically be recognized as an eventual option, given our stakes in the region, if other policy alternatives fail." In the wake of this article some members of the House became convinced that the president was committed to sending U.S. troops into Nicaragua. This made his "peace" proposal more suspect, less attractive. The pendulum had swung again. Reagan's double-barreled formulation would probably not pass.

In a letter to Senate Majority Leader Robert Dole just before the Senate vote on April 23, President Reagan dropped his request for military aid and agreed to provide assistance to the Contras only for food, medicine, clothing, and general survival. He knew, of course, that Saudi arms money could keep the war going; lawmakers at that point did not know. The Senate, thus mollified, voted 53 to 46 to approve the president's altered request. The House, dubious about the last-minute maneuver, on the next day defeated Reagan's Contra aid proposal by a 248 to 180 vote.

The men who formed the secret government were not deterred. If Congress would not fund the war in Nicaragua as an expression of U.S. policy, they would find other ways to keep that war going. Lieutenant Colonel Oliver North proposed in a memo to Robert McFarlane that the president solicit private donations to the Contras from the public. McFarlane approved the creation of the Nicaraguan Freedom Fund, Inc. This fund would act as a tax-exempt conduit through which wealthy donors could funnel tax-deductible contributions to the Contra army. Then North and his collaborators began developing a secret plan to get two of America's friendliest client states in Asia, South Korea and Taiwan, to make contributions to the Contras.

As the seekers of funding went further underground, the first faint outlines of what was to be the Iran-Contra connection began to emerge. During May of 1985, William Casey reviewed a memo from Graham Fuller, his national intelligence officer for the Near East and south Asia. Fuller argued in the memo that denying arms to Iran as a response to Iranian-sponsored terrorism had become counterproductive. He advocated a more daring policy: Work *with* Iran.

Several days later, Casey found that a draft national security decision directive, drawn up for the president's signature, would include U.S. authority to sell weapons to Iran. Shultz disagreed with the plan. Weinberger wrote the word *absurd* on his copy and returned it. The objections of these two senior department heads would ultimately be overruled.

After another American, David P. Jacobsen, was kidnapped in Beirut on May 28, North devised a plan. He reported word from someone he considered a reliable informant that $200,000 would secure the return of two American hostages. McFarlane gained the president's approval for a plan to raise the $200,000 privately. A promise of that amount was elicited from Texas billionaire H. Ross Perot. Later North informed McFarlane that the $200,000 would only constitute a downpayment. His source now said the price had gone up. The hostages would be set free for $1 million each. Perot's $200,000 was sent to the source. Nothing happened.

In June, Casey received information that the Iranian Foreign Ministry wanted to trade hostages for TOW (tube-launched, optically tracked, wire-guided) antitank missiles for use against Iraq.

Meanwhile, the fickle balance in Congress shifted again. Reagan had nobody to thank for this unexpected boon but his old nemesis, Daniel Ortega. On April 24, 1985, Ortega, now duly installed as Nicaragua's elected president, departed for the Soviet Union on a working visit. Everyone presumed the Nicaraguan leader was petitioning the only outside source available to him for money and weapons to defend against the Contra military forces. Congress saw red. The prospect of renewed Soviet influence in the hemisphere sent chills through the sensitive political body.

Senator James Sasser of Tennessee, who recently had responded on nationwide television with a brief speech against arming the Contras following one of President Reagan's appeals, now felt obliged to hedge his position: "For him [Ortega] to be going to the Soviet Union at this time," said Sasser, "indicates that the Sandinista leader is either naive, incompetent or not as committed to negotiations as recent statements would indicate."

Some Democrats became convinced that a show of toughness toward Nicaragua's government was important now for Democrats in general. Certainly nobody wanted to be called soft on communism. Representative Dan Daniel of Virginia voiced this warning in a letter to his Democratic colleagues:

> Last fall, we were trampled at the polls in the presidential election. The score for the states was 1 to 49. Post-election polls indicate that one of the reasons for that political loss was the perception that the Democrats were soft on defense. If we now fail to oppose the spread of communism in this hemisphere, and we are once more perceived to be soft on defense, and communism, then we could be shut out completely in the next election.

President Reagan's crusade approach to Contra aid kindled an accusatory debate on Capitol Hill. Republican Representative Dan Burton said during the House debate in June, "My friends, don't be soft on communism!" Representative Newt Gingrich called a vote restricting military aid to the Contras a "vote for the unilateral disarmament of the side that favors freedom in Central America." On the House floor, I described these assaults as "to some degree" reminiscent of McCarthyism.

On the eve of the House vote Reagan sent a letter promising to "pursue political, not military solutions in Central America." This letter assured the president at least a down payment on the long-denied victory he was looking for. On June 12, 1985, the House reversed itself and voted, 248 to 184, for $27 million in *humanitarian*—not military—aid for the Contra forces.

With increased Contra funds in pocket, William Casey concentrated on the plan to exchange arms with Iran for American hostages. On August 8, the president attended a meeting with Vice President George Bush, George Shultz, Caspar Weinberger, Don Regan, Casey, John Poindexter, and Robert McFarlane. A plan evolved for Israel to ship TOW antitank missiles to Iran, the United States to replenish Israeli stocks, and Iran to obtain the release of American hostages held in Lebanon. The CIA would not conduct this operation, it was decided. Lieutenant Colonel Oliver North would be the operational commander.

During August and into the fall of 1985, a continuous stream of rumors and press reports suggested that the NSC was circumventing congressional restrictions on Contra aid. House Intelligence Committee Chairman Lee Hamilton and Western Hemisphere Subcommittee Chairman Michael Barnes finally wrote to National Security Adviser McFarlane, requesting information and documents relating to Colonel North's contacts with the Contras. But the president's Intelligence Oversight Board sought to evade a complete response. Board Counsel Bretton G. Sciaroni wrote a legal opinion concluding that the Boland Amendment did not apply to the NSC. Sciaroni apparently reached that conclusion without reviewing key documents portraying North's role in Contra fund-raising activities and in the procurement of weapons.

In written correspondence with House committee chairmen (September 5, 1985) and in private meetings with Senate Intelligence Committee members, McFarlane denied NSC involvement. Per Arnson's *Crossroads*, McFarlane said, "At no time did I or any member of the National Security Council staff . . . solicit funds or other support for military or paramilitary activities either from Americans or third parties." Committee members, of course, had no knowledge at the time that third countries were funding the Contras; nor did they know that the United States was illegally selling arms to Iran.

Arms sales between Israel and Iran were complex because of the legacy of distrust between the two countries. North selected Manucher Ghorbanifar as the key intermediary. Ghorbanifar secured a loan from a Saudi Arabian businessman, Adnan Khashoggi, who contributed $5 million for the purchase of 508 TOW missiles. Then, on September 15, came the release of Reverend Benjamin Weir, an American hostage.

Two months later, North arranged for a CIA-supplied aircraft to fly eighteen Hawk missiles, claimed by U.S. officials to be oil-drilling parts, from Israel to Iran. That plane had been scheduled the same day as the flight to Iran to carry a planeload of ammunition to the Contras. John McMahon, CIA deputy director, learned that the CIA aircraft had flown arms to Iran without his approval. He instructed that no additional CIA activity supporting the NSC operation be undertaken in absence of a presidential finding to authorize covert action.

The next day, November 26, 1985, CIA General Counsel Stanley Sporkin drafted the finding, which provided *retroactive* approval of all preceding covert missions involving the Iran undertaking.

Robert C. McFarlane announced his resignation as national security adviser on December 4, to be effective December 11. Following his resignation from that official post, McFarlane would continue his activities in the arms for hostages operation. President Reagan appointed Vice Admiral John M. Poindexter, McFarlane's deputy, to replace his old boss as NSC presidential adviser.

Reagan met with Shultz, Weinberger, McFarlane, Poindexter, and McMahon on December 7 to discuss the Iran program. The finding authorizing the CIA's role in that operation was signed by the president. Poindexter put the only copy in his safe, sending word to the CIA that the finding had been signed. Congress was not advised. It would not be told for almost a year.

This was an absolute breach of law. The National Security Act, in unequivocal and unambiguous language, set forth a definite requirement. The heads of "*all* departments, agencies, and *other entities*" of the United States are commanded by that law to report "fully and currently" to House and Senate intelligence committees on "*all* intelligence activities" and any significant "anticipated" activities (italics added). In the event of circumstances so "extraordinary" that prior notice could not be given to those committees, then the *president himself* was required to give prior notice to a bipartisan group of eight specified people, including the elected leaders of both parties in each House. This requirement was also flouted. No such notice went forth.

On January 6, 1986, the president, the vice president, Shultz, Weinberger, Casey, Don Regan, Poindexter, and Attorney General Edwin Meese met again to discuss the situation. Poindexter unveiled a plan to continue to pursue further arms sales to Iran. The sale would occur in a thirty- to-sixty day period; in exchange, Iran would produce the remaining five American hostages. The congressional intelligence committees would not be informed, the group agreed privately, until after the hostages were released. Apparently nothing was said about the president's legal responsibility to notify the leadership *in advance* of any such action. (Shultz and Weinberger were reportedly opposed to the plan, but Reagan appeared amenable.)

Between February 15 and 18, another 1,000 TOW missiles were shipped to Israel. Half of them went on to Iran. However, no hostages were released. Ghorbanifar, the international arms merchant chosen by North as the go-between, explained the dismaying discrepancy by claiming that Iran no longer wanted the TOWs, so they did not count. Doubts already had begun to arise about Ghorbanifar's veracity. At this point Poindexter, according to some reports, wanted to halt the whole operation, but North persisted.

As the secret arms for hostages effort moved forward, President Reagan initiated a new request for increased Contra arms aid. In February 1986, he asked for $100 million in military assistance, pulling out all the rhetorical stops.

Though aware of the secret Contra-resupply financing from other countries and the private fund-raising activities of Oliver North, President Reagan, per Arnson's *Crossroads*, left the impression that Contra forces were bereft of equipment. "You can't fight attack helicopters piloted by Cubans with Band-Aids and mosquito nets," he said. Speaking to a group of Jewish professionals, Reagan declared that overlooking the strategic danger posed by Nicaragua would result in a "map of Central America covered in a sea of red, eventually lapping at our own borders." Presidential speeches and public comments also spawned images of terrorists and revolutionaries "just two days' driving time from Harlingen, Texas."

Other administration officials joined in. White House Communications Director Patrick Buchanan wrote in the March 5 *Washington Post* that, by obstructing Contra aid, "the National Democratic Party has now become, with Moscow, co-guarantor of the Brezhnev doctrine in Central America. . . . With the vote on Contra aid, the Democratic Party will reveal whether it stands with Ronald Reagan and the resistance—or Daniel Ortega and the communists."

In spite of, or perhaps because of, such verbal overkill, Reagan's request for $100 million to buy weapons for the Contras was rejected by the House on March 20, 1986. The vote was close, 210 to 222. In his closing statement just before the vote, Speaker Tip O'Neill said that

> there is a difference between debating the effects of policy and questioning the motives of those who advocate those policies. . . . My conscience dictates that I vote nay, not only for the Administration policy but to its tactics as well.

Shortly after the House vote, Reagan branded the action "a dark day for freedom" and declared his "solemn determination to come back again and again until this battle is won."

The Senate on March 27 approved the $100 million to arm the Contras but withheld the bipartisan victory Reagan wanted. The Senate tally was also close, 53 to 47.

Within a few days of these votes, the Nicaraguan army made a hit-and-run incursion into Contra base camps on the Honduran side of the border. The administration responded in fury, citing this occurrence as justification to increase Honduran military aid, to airlift troops into the border zone—and to blame the incident on Congress for not having approved more Contra military aid. A year later, Congress would learn that the White House and the CIA had disregarded State Department estimates that discounted the military or diplomatic significance of the incursion. As Arnson noted in *Crossroads*, when the Honduran government balked at requesting "emergency" aid as a result of the incident, U.S. Ambassador John Ferch told Honduran officials, "You don't have a choice!"

During April, Reagan's Central American envoy, Philip Habib, wrote to Democratic Representative Jim Slattery responding to questions about the Contadora group, the elected presidents of several Latin American nations who were meeting intermittently in search of an avenue to peaceful settlement of the bloody Central American war. Habib said he understood a Contadora peace proposal then under consideration would involve among other things the end of financial support from the United States to the Contra army. Habib indicated the Contadora group's proposals might be worth exploring. Conservative Republicans, livid, demanded Habib's recall. The new assistant secretary of state for Latin America, Elliott Abrams, assured conservatives that Reagan would not abandon the Contra war to any diplomatic settlement.

The president's promise to strive toward a peaceful settlement in Nicaragua had influenced Congress to renew Contra funding during 1985. Now the administration, by Abrams's account, seemed unwilling to consider negotiation in any form.

By April of 1986, North had begun integrating the Iran and Contra operations. In an internal memo, he wrote that a major portion of the $15 million expected to be paid by Iran for the arms could be diverted to the Contras. Poindexter apparently approved the diversion. From this point until November, the two operations moved closer and closer until they fused.

In a May 16, 1986, meeting of the National Security Planning Group, administration officials agreed to step up the solicitation of third-country funding sources. In late May, McFarlane, North, and other officials traveled to Iran. Their talks, unfortunately, did not secure the release of hostages. In mid-July sources passed word to the Iranians that the United States would make no further moves until a hostage was released.

By June the peace process initiated by the Contadora presidents had reached a stalemate. The Nicaraguan government refused to sign any peace treaty requiring reduction in its own military forces and expulsion of foreign advisers unless the United States ended support for the Contras and also called off U.S. military maneuvers in the region.

Prior to the third Contra-aid vote in June, the administration made an extraordinary effort to maximize party discipline among House and Senate Republicans. GOP House members told Democratic friends of stepped-up pressure within the party caucus to close ranks behind the White House on Central America. During April conservative groups wrote GOP presidential candidates and Republican National Committee Chairman Frank Fahrenkopf, Jr., asking them to deny support to any House members who voted against rebel funding. Ronald Reagan, calling on his personal charm and the prestige of his office, met with potential vote switchers at the White House. Republican Representative Larry Hopkins, when interviewed by Daniel Schorr on National Public Radio, June 28, 1986, offered the following assessment of that meeting:

I'm from Wingo, Kentucky. I never thought I was ever going
to be in the Oval Office, much less even see a president.
You're overwhelmed by that but this president, I think, puts
you at ease. . . . He's the kind of guy you just want to help.
One of the better things that's happened in my life is the
opportunity to visit with him just for a brief time. I'm proud
to stand in his shadow.

On June 25 the House vote shifted, a majority approving Reagan's
Contra aid program 221 to 209. The House agreed to a Republican-
sponsored plan allowing Reagan to provide $100 million to the Con-
tras, including up to $70 million for guns, ammunition, and additional
military supplies. The House's acceptance of the modified package
sent the matter back to the Senate, which had approved Reagan's original proposal on March 27. The Senate ultimately came around to the
House formula and passed the bill on August 13 by a 59 to 41 margin.

On July 29, 1986, the Reverend Lawrence Jenco was released from
Lebanon following almost seventeen months of captivity. On the
same day Vice President George Bush received information from the
Israeli antiterrorism adviser, Amiram Nir: the United States and Israel were dealing with Iranian radicals who were trying to extract as
much as they could from Americans in exchange for the hostages.

In August, Assistant Secretary of State Elliott Abrams obtained an
additional $10 million in nonlethal assistance to the Contras from
the government of Brunei. Oliver North's private network was directing regular airdrops of military equipment and supplies to the
Contras.

On October 5, the Sandinistas shot down an airplane loaded with
ammunition and supplies for the Contra forces in northern Nicaragua. Three crew members were killed. Another, a U.S. citizen named
Eugene Hasenfus, parachuted to safety and was captured. Hasenfus
carried Salvadoran air force identification indicating that he was an
"adviser." One of the dead passengers bore an ID card issued by
Southern Air Transport, formerly operated by the CIA. President
Reagan denied any U.S. connection with the flight. (Later, Oliver
North would testify, "I was the U.S. Government connection.") Following the Hasenfus incident, North undertook a major housecleaning,
ing, trying in vain to shred all written memos that referred to the
Contra diversion.

On October 7, a New York businessman named Roy M. Furmark informed Casey that two Canadians who helped finance the arms sales had not been repaid and were threatening to reveal the affair.

On November 2, David P. Jacobsen was released from Lebanon following seventeen months in captivity. The next day, a Lebanese magazine, *Al-Shiraa,* reported that the United States had secretly been supplying arms to Iran, and that McFarlane had secretly visited Tehran. When Reagan met with Jacobson at the White House on November 7, he told reporters that this story had no foundation.

But now no amount of dissembling could cover the trail. Discovery was inevitable.

My wife Betty and I were enjoying a rare afternoon of leisure together at our home in suburban Virginia when the call came from the White House. Would I come right away to the southwest gate and enter on the lower level across from the Executive Office Building?

Senator Robert Byrd was just arriving as I disembarked in the narrow alleyway between the White House and the ornate old executive mansion that once served as home for the State Department. Byrd and I congratulated one another. In the elections just a few days earlier, Democrats had reclaimed the Senate and improved our position in the House. I would be Speaker of the House, and Bob would resume his interrupted role as Senate majority leader.

"Know what this is all about?" I asked as we walked toward the door.

"No," Bob said. "I was just going to ask you."

We soon discovered, to our initial disbelief and then our growing dismay. Poindexter conducted the solemn briefing. Present were Vice President Bush, Senator Dole, House Minority Leader Michel, Byrd, and I. The president was not there; neither was Tip O'Neill. The meeting had been hastily put together. We listened as the story unfolded. TOW missiles had been delivered to Iran. The presidential finding authorizing the adventure almost a year earlier had not been reported to Congress as the law required.

We would not be told until a day later, in a second briefing by Attorney General Meese, that funds from the missile sales had been diverted to buy weapons for the Contras. But already we could tell that several provisions of law had been violated. The National Security Act required prior notification of the congressional leadership before launching any such venture. The Anti-Terrorism Act and the Arms Export Control Act both prohibited the sale of weapons to

Iran. The Defense Department Appropriations Act prohibited the shifting or covert transfer of funds to "any intelligence or special activity different from that previously justified to the Congress" without first giving formal notice to the appropriations committees.

In a nationally televised speech on November 13, 1986, President Reagan described the arms shipments to Iran as good-faith gestures to establish contact with Iranian "moderates." He strongly denied that he ever had engaged in an arms-for-hostages trade. Then during a November 19 press conference he defended the Iran operation: "I don't think a mistake was made. . . . I don't see that it has been a fiasco or a great failure of any kind." He denied four times that he had "condoned" the Israeli shipments. Immediately following the press conference, however, Reagan issued a correction, stating that he *had* condoned a shipment by another country.

On November 21, Congress began investigations into the Iran arms program with closed hearings by the House and Senate intelligence committees. In testimony about meetings with the Iranians, CIA Director Casey referred to "an NSC official." When asked who that person was, Casey replied that he was not sure. Lieutenant Colonel North's name was never mentioned.

That same day, Attorney General Meese contacted NSC head Poindexter asking that he gather all relevant documents. When Poindexter came upon the December 5, 1985, finding (now almost a year old) that portrayed the Iran operation as a straight arms-for-hostage deal, he tore it up and put it in a bag to be burned. Later that evening North entered his office and directed his secretary, Fawn Hall, to assist him in shredding documents, memos, and messages from his safe and files.

Reagan announced the resignation of Poindexter and the dismissal of North on November 25. He cited evidence discovered by Meese that funds from the Iran arms sales had been diverted to the Contras as the reason for North's firing. In the announcement, Reagan denied knowledge of the Contra diversion, saying he had not been "fully informed" about the Iran arms project.

By mid-December the president had appointed a three-member commission headed by former Senator John Tower to investigate the NSC, the Senate Intelligence Committee launched a full-scale investigation, and Lawrence E. Walsh was named as independent counsel in the Iran-Contra affair. Several committees in each house of Congress were eager to get into the act. This was the juiciest thing since

Watergate. So many interests were involved that it would be hard to deny a right to hearings by the Senate Foreign Affairs and House Foreign Relations committees, the armed services committees, and the judiciary committees, which had purview over constitutional relations between the two branches of government.

Bob Byrd and I met with Dole and Michel. They were as concerned as I. Headline-hungry members on several of these committees might be tempted to make "Irangate" into a year-long feeding frenzy. Hearings could degenerate to partisan name calling and sensational exhibitionism. The matter was too grave, I thought, to be handled as a three-ring circus, each committee vying with the others for sensation and attention. I told the other leaders of my desire to appoint a special blue-ribbon committee for developing the facts in a dignified public way. They agreed, so I designated Majority Leader Tom Foley, judicious and calm; sage, laconic country lawyer Ed Jenkins of Georgia; three senior committee chairmen—Jack Brooks (judiciary), Dante Fascell (foreign affairs), Louis Stokes (intelligence); and Lee Hamilton of Indiana, a top member of both the Intelligence and the Foreign Affairs committees with a reputation for reason and fair play.

Dole, Michel, and Byrd each appointed a similar number. For the first several months of 1987, the hearings of this committee commanded prime time on national television as its members delved and probed and persisted until they got the truth out where the public could see it all in some perspective and draw informed conclusions.

My hope was to lay it all out with dignity and decorum, to avoid rancor wherever possible, and to discourage any future escapades in secret government. But, then, I was new at being Speaker. I had high hopes.

CHAPTER 6

A Chance for Peace

I returned, and saw under the sun, that the race is not to the swift, nor the battle to the strong, neither yet bread to the wise, nor yet riches to men of understanding, nor yet favor to men of skill; but time and chance happeneth to them all.

—Ecclesiastes

One day in mid-July 1987, Tom Loeffler came by my office with a startling proposition. I liked Tom and had missed seeing him since he left Congress the year before to run for governor of Texas. Cowboy boots jutting out beneath the neat pinstripe and a big grin told me Tom hadn't changed.

There have always been two distinct sides to this husky Texas Republican. For an accomplished horseman and former football star, Tom could be fastidious. Other players who scrimmaged with him at the University of Texas say he never wanted to wear a soiled jersey. During his campaign for the Republican gubernatorial nomination in Texas in 1986, someone claimed to have seen Tom step out of the shower wearing shower caps on his feet to protect against athlete's foot.

Whatever the truth of such tales, I liked and trusted Tom Loeffler in spite of our rival party affiliations. During his years in Congress he had rounded up votes on the House floor for the GOP, and the two of us sometimes compared notes. I had always found him absolutely trustworthy.

"I thought I should come by and tell you, Mr. Speaker, that President Reagan has asked me to help him organize the effort to get more military aid for the Nicaraguan Contras," he began.

"He couldn't have picked a better person," I said. "He chose a man for a man's job. That won't be an easy task."

More like nearly impossible, I was thinking. That's what I had told Howard Baker one day in early spring when he came by to tell me he was taking the job as White House chief of staff. Baker and I were discussing the climate of incredulity created by the Iran-Contra revelations, and I offered him a word of gratuitous advice: In my opinion, any further military aid to the Contras was doomed. "The people are disillusioned and Congress won't vote for it." I suggested that President Reagan would be wise to initiate talks aimed at a peaceful settlement while the Contras still had some money in the pipeline rather than waiting for it to run out and expecting Congress to renew it. "If he waits for that and insists on that, he's likely to be rejected, Howard, and then he won't have any leverage at all," I had said. "But if Reagan took the initiative now and called for talks aimed at ending the war, he could seize the high ground—like Eisenhower in 1952. Remember the electricity when Ike said, 'I will go to Korea?' " Baker said it sounded like good advice. I was thinking of that conversation as Tom Loeffler continued.

"I know it won't be easy to renew military aid, Mr. Speaker," Loeffler was saying. "Some of our people think we got a real shot in the arm from Oliver North's testimony. They think it gives us a chance at getting more money for the Contras. Either way, it'll be a bloodletting. My personal instinct is that we can do something much better than that."

"Like what?" I asked.

"If the president and the Speaker could make a joint call for a peace settlement, that would make a huge impact in Central America. I'd like to know if you would be willing to join Ronald Reagan in a bipartisan initiative aimed at settling the whole thing once and for all?" I wondered if Tom has been talking with Howard Baker. I listened as he made his case.

"The reason we haven't had any clout in Central America," Loeffler argued, "is because the president and the Congress have been fighting like strange bulldogs. I'm convinced that Mr. Reagan is tired of this war and he'd like to end it on decent terms, but he doesn't have a lot of credibility down there right now. If you and he were to join a peace offensive, that would carry a hell of a lot of weight. The people know you down there. They trust you. And everybody in Central America would pay heed to a position on which the president and Congress were united."

The idea was intriguing. Still, I was skeptical. I didn't think Tom Loeffler was laying a trap, but I could see some serious pitfalls. Would the president's pro-Contra advisers be cynical enough to float a phony peace initiative with the expectation of its failing, and then use the preordained failure as an excuse for renewing the war? I mentioned this thought to Tom, told him some Democrats were sure to be suspicious.

"Mr. Speaker, I know there's a lot of suspicion on both sides," Loeffler said. "There's a lot of mistrust. The reason I came to you is because you and I can talk straight to each other, and because you're the only one who can make this happen. I'm convinced that the president is sincere in wanting a peaceful settlement. I think you know me well enough to know that I wouldn't have come to you unless I felt that. There is always a chance that you could be left out on a limb, but I don't believe that will happen in this case."

We talked for about thirty minutes. I mentioned the new initiative by President Oscar Arias of Costa Rica. We talked of the necessary ingredients for a workable peace plan—get the Russian and Cuban military out of Nicaragua, an agreement between Nicaragua and its neighbors to respect one another's boundaries, cessation of hostilities, restoration of constitutional rights in Nicaragua, and free and honest elections.

I remembered the conversation I'd had at the Carter Center in Atlanta the previous November. Jimmy Carter had called and asked me to speak at a conference of elected Latin American leaders on November 17. At dinner the evening before, the former president summoned me from a table where I was sitting to join in a spirited conversation he was having with Nicaraguan Vice President Sergio Ramírez. I put the question straight to the Sandinista leader: "What would it take for you to expel the Cuban and Russian military, live in peace with your neighbors, stop giving aid to those who want to subvert the government in El Salvador, and restore the constitutional rights of free speech and press and assembly that you suspended in your emergency law?" Ramírez replied, "We are not interfering in El

Salvador. For the rest, it would take one thing only—for your government to stop financing the invasion of our country. When that is done, there will be no need for an emergency law, and we will be glad to do everything you have mentioned."

Thinking back on this as I sat there talking with Tom Loeffler, I wondered. The Ramírez statement could not necessarily be taken at face value. But maybe it had to be tested, and maybe this was the time.

Finally, I said to Tom, "Go back and check your sources again, Tom. Tell them that I don't want any part in setting up a halfhearted effort doomed to failure as a prelude to a greater military push. But tell them that if they are absolutely sincere in wanting to negotiate a peaceful settlement, I'll do everything within my power to help."

After Tom left, I walked to the window and looked out. A midsummer haze shimmered over the lush green of the east Capitol lawn and softened the outlines of the Library of Congress beyond. My mind flicked back over the long panorama of my involvement with Latin America—my pleasant days on the Public Works Committee promoting the Inter-American Highway, the years of parliamentary exchanges with Mexican lawmakers, and my great early enthusiasm for President Kennedy's Alliance for Progress and my disappointment when it was abandoned.

Since childhood I had been a frequent visitor to the region. I had met and talked with Mexico's last five presidents and with most of the recent Central American heads of state. I understood at least something of their problems. I didn't consider myself an authority on the region, but I was an informal student of it. For thirty years I had traveled throughout Central America, knew some of its history and many of its legends. I liked its people. Could I help end the agony and bloodshed that afflicted those nations and kept splitting the U.S. government into hostile camps? If the president was really interested in conciliation, I surely could not refuse to try.

As floor leader for the House Democrats, I had often clashed with President Reagan over domestic issues and spending priorities. He had resented it, I felt, when Congress asserted its own initiatives, as we were doing on the economic front. In the first years of his presidency, I repeatedly had faced defeat when trying to rally votes against Reagan's budgets. But in the first six months of 1987, Congress had overridden presidential vetoes on clean water and highway bills while the House had passed its own budget, the first major initiative for the homeless, and a far-reaching trade bill—all opposed by Reagan. Would this inhibit his and my ability to unite in an appeal for peace? If things were handled correctly, I decided, this history might even add credibility to such a joint appeal.

Over the years, I had been a sort of occasional troubleshooter for presidents in Latin America and had enjoyed that role. I'd gone to Costa Rica and to the Dominican Republic for Johnson, to Nicaragua for Carter, and to El Salvador for Reagan. In three separate trips to observe elections in El Salvador I had grown to admire and be good friends with its tough, craggy-faced president José Napoleón Duarte. In May of 1984, I had risked ostracism by fellow Democrats to make an impassioned and successful appeal for continued aid to the embattled democratic government there. There was no doubt that I had pulled the administration's chestnuts out of the fire that day: We won by 212 to 208.

In foreign affairs, bipartisanship had been my forte for most of my career. I had enjoyed helping the Reagan administration gain passage for the Caribbean Basin Initiative, and I could think of nothing more satisfying than to help the old cold warrior make peace in Central America if that's what he wanted. Too much blood had been spilled in its jungles and its poverty-stricken barrios.

But I wondered if President Reagan was prepared for the shift that would have to be made in our policy toward Nicaragua. I thought of the long, sad history of our involvement in the affairs of that bedraggled country—of the Tennessean William Walker, who invaded with a private army and declared himself Nicaragua's emperor in the nineteenth century, after which we kept U.S. Marines there as a virtual army of occupation for twenty-one years on the thin pretext of protecting Americans; of the forty-three years of the U.S.-backed Somoza dynasty; of the Sandinista revolution in 1979 and our ill-concealed efforts to overthrow it—six years of U.S.-financed war, mining their harbors, boycotting their goods, pressuring commercial banks and international lending institutions to extend their government no credit, rhetorical bombasts by our president vowing to make their leaders "cry uncle."

My visits to Nicaragua had convinced me that, much as their economy was hurting, the left wing would retain control just so long as it could credibly blame its failures and the people's miseries on a U.S. "imperialist" effort to break and dominate them. Nationalism was a more powerful force in Latin America than Marxism—of this I was certain. Nicaraguans, even more than most Latin Americans, had a love-hate relationship with the United States. They secretly wanted to be like us, but they'd be damned if we were going to tell them how to do it.

The time might be ripe for a package of major concessions from the Sandinistas. We would not wring this from them at the end of a rifle barrel, however. We might get it from them at a conference table. And this would require an alteration in our approach. We would have to treat them like equals and embrace the hallowed Latin principle of self-determination.

During the next few days I made a series of contacts. I wanted to know two things: whether Tom Loeffler was reading President Reagan correctly, and whether a joint appeal from Reagan and me would make any decisive difference to Latin Americans. I tried to probe the climate at the White House and in Central America. Chief of Staff Howard Baker told me President Reagan was aware of Tom Loeffler's overture and would be supportive.

I asked Richard Peña, who had recently left the professional staff of the House Foreign Affairs Committee, to feel out some of our contacts in Costa Rica, Guatemala, and El Salvador, including the ambassadors and foreign ministers. Richard had accompanied me on two recent trips, spoke excellent Spanish, and was known by most of the leaders. I called my old friend and friend of the president Bob Strauss to see if he had any indication of a changing sentiment in the administration.

Bob had managed to maintain good relations with cabinet and White House officials in four successive administrations. Once at a dinner party at my home I had been asked to prophesy who the next president would be. "I haven't the faintest idea who the next president will be," I replied, "but I'm absolutely certain who the next president's best friend will be. Bob Strauss!" Bob, present at the time, gruffly pretended to take offense but enjoyed the quip.

In less than two days Bob called me back to say that he believed there probably had been a change in Reagan's view toward Central America: "I think he really would like to make peace, and principally because Nancy would like for him to go out of office as a peacemaker. I had this from several very good sources, including the best source of all—Mrs. Reagan."

Wherever I turned for insight into Central American thinking, and for light on whether a bipartisan call from the president and the Speaker would bear fruit, I got encouragement. The Arias plan, announced a few weeks earlier by the Costa Rican president, seemed broadly acceptable in substance. But nobody was willing to predict that it would produce results in the absence of a nod and a nudge from the United States. If official U.S. pronouncements either ignored the Arias plan or damned it with faint praise—as Reagan had done to appeals by the Contadora group—the Arias plan would probably meet the same fate. It could just die on the vine. That was the consensus among Salvadorans, Hondurans, and Costa Ricans whom I consulted.

Richard Peña's contacts suggested a sense of urgency. The presidents of the five Central American countries were to meet on August 6 and 7 in Guatemala at a place called Esquipulas. If they failed to make real progress toward an accord—or worse yet, broke up in vocal disagreement—the best opportunity would be wasted. Another chance would not come soon. Resulting bitterness might even poison the well of future dialogue. If a bipartisan U.S. pronouncement was to have any significant effect, then, it should precede the summit. But there wasn't much time. It was just two weeks away.

And a major effort would be necessary in Congress. Detente between congressional partisans might be a peacemaker's most daunting challenge. The Contra issue had polarized the House. Outraged by the secret plotting in the White House basement, anti-Contra lawmakers were aggressively insisting on an immediate end to all U.S.-sponsored military involvement in Nicaragua. Militant conservatives, emboldened by Lieutenant Colonel Oliver North's six days of televised testimony in the recent hearings, were mobilizing for a legislative counteroffensive.

On July 23 the conservative wing lined up fifty-seven Republican members for pro-Contra speeches under the one-minute rule that each day precedes House business. Some came equipped with slides and displays from Colonel North's briefings for private contributors. This spurred anti-Contra Democrats to taunt the Ollie North enthusiasts with references to their "dog and pony show." The issue was emotional, the atmosphere combustible.

By House tradition, the Speaker alternates one-minute speeches between the parties, recognizing a Republican, then a Democrat, then a Republican, until all who wish to speak have had the opportunity. Some of the early speeches contained strong rhetoric. The temptation of opponents to utter audible remarks of disparagement was almost irresistible. That could not be allowed. This issue was incendiary, and as presiding officer I had to act as fire extinguisher.

For almost an hour I remained in the chair to make certain that decorum prevailed. I was determined to tolerate no slight to any Republican member. At the first sign of verbal discourtesy, I rapped the gavel sternly and insisted on order. I repeated this twice until the message soaked in. This was to be a day of assiduous civility. It was important that nobody be given an excuse to develop hurt feelings. We were going to need all the good will we could nurture.

On Friday, July 24, I flew to Puerto Rico with the Puerto Rican delegate to the House, Jaime Fuster, and his wife Mary Jo. I had promised to speak at the annual Commonwealth Day festivities on Saturday, July 25. My grandson Erik accompanied us for a day of swimming and jet skiing. We had dinner at the magnificent old governor's palace, La Forteleza, and I picked the brain of Governor Rafael Hernández Colón, a sincere and helpful man who knew and had frequent contacts with other Caribbean leaders.

At the colorful public ceremony, attended by more than 100,000 festive people on Saturday night, I had a chance to visit briefly with Rodrigo Arias, brother of the Costa Rican president. I learned that Oscar would begin a tour of the Central American countries on Monday, talking with each of the presidents preparatory to the Guatemala gathering. On Sunday I called President Arias and told him the gist of what Loeffler had suggested to me. We made an agreement to talk again on Wednesday after his tour.

On Monday I called José Napoleón Duarte in San Salvador. He was not sure what might emerge from the Esquipulas meeting but thought it well worth a major effort. "A lot depends on Daniel [Ortega] and whether he thinks the rest of us are serious. The pressure of our collective opinion must get from him what the Contras have been unable to get. We may not do any good, but we are going to try. If the United States is solidly behind us, and the president and Congress are speaking as one, that would be a big help." Duarte also stressed the importance of what he called symmetry—a *simultaneous* effort to stop the insurgencies in Nicaragua and El Salvador.

Tom Foley and Tony Coelho, House majority leader and whip, expressed skepticism as to the administration's motives. They believed Loeffler was sincere but doubted that right-wing elements and diehard Contra supporters would let the president go through with a real peace effort. "Their goal is to overthrow the Nicaraguan government," Tony insisted, "and I don't think they want to settle for anything short of that." Both agreed, however, that we had a responsibility to pursue the peace opening if it was for real. We asked Republican Leader Bob Michel, House Foreign Affairs Committee Chairman Dante Fascell, and ranking Republican Bill Broomfield to meet us Tuesday to discuss what was being proposed.

That meeting produced an agreement that Bob Michel and I would call the Nicaraguan ambassador, Carlos Tünnermann, and ask him to come for a private visit in H-201, the "hideaway" office just off the Capitol rotunda at the end of a second-floor corridor. I did not feel optimistic about any peace initiative unless it could be truly bipartisan. Previous debates had left too much bitterness. We needed the help of congressional Republicans from the very beginning if we were to expect their cooperation later. Both Bob Michel and I thought it was necessary to find out, if we could, what attitude the Nicaraguans would have toward a peace offensive.

Tünnermann came on July 28 accompanied by an associate named William Vigil and a young woman, Sophia Clark, the English-speaking niece of Sandinista Foreign Minister Miguel D'Escoto. She served as translator for some of the exchanges.

Tünnermann's opening comment came as a surprise: "I've been in Washington as Nicaragua's ambassador for three years, and this is the very first time anyone in the U.S. government has asked to see me or talk with me about anything whatever."

Bob Michel and I both pressed for a definitive commitment that Nicaragua would get rid of any weapons that threatened the United States, patch up its relations with its neighbors, and restore constitutional rights to its own citizens if U.S. military aid to the Contras were terminated. The ambassador agreed and gave essentially the answer I had received in November from Sergio Ramírez. He even handed us copies of proposed treaties that he said his government had offered to each of its neighbors guaranteeing the sanctity of their borders.

At the end of the meeting, Michel and I agreed that there was at least a chance the man might be faithfully stating a new Sandinista policy. An initiative seemed timely and worth pursuing. Bob agreed to bring the rest of his leadership into the effort.

That afternoon President Arias called from Costa Rica. He had just completed a tour of the region. Arias believed the time was ripe for a serious effort. He told me of his meeting with Daniel Ortega and of the wretched economic conditions he had seen in Managua.

"Daniel is in trouble, and he knows it. The whole economy is in shambles. There are no goods on the shelves in the stores. Inflation is rampant. As Ortega and I drove down the street in a jeep, I saw some men on the sidewalk making visible signs of disapproval. I have never seen this before in Managua."

I asked if he thought that mattered greatly to Ortega. "Yes, it must matter. I believe that the junta which governs the country is divided. Tomás Borge and Bayardo Arce are ideologues. They follow the Marxist line. But the others are wavering. They are discouraged by the failure of their experiment. Ortega is probably not a Marxist. I think he is a pragmatist. He sees that it hasn't worked. He knows the society must have a breathing spell. Your country's trade embargo has hurt perhaps more than the Contras have. They need investment, new life. I believe he would be willing to make major concessions to bring the war to an end and open up trade."

"What chance is there to get democratizing reforms in case we can get a cease-fire?"

"If all the other presidents will stick together, I believe there is a decent chance that we can get Ortega to disband the most oppressive restrictions on the people immediately and allow a truly democratic society to develop," Arias replied. "This is what we must insist upon. But he must not be seen as bowing to pressure from the United States. That would kill him in Nicaragua. The pressure must come from the rest of us. It would help for the United States to show an interest in the peace process and some flexibility, but the terms of the settlement should not seem to be dictated by your country. You and the president could help at just this time by expressing an interest in our success at Esquipulas and an intention to support a reasonable initiative by the Central American presidents."

Arias suggested the first step should be a sixty-day cease-fire, during which time the United States should suspend military aid to the Contras, and Nicaragua should deny any use of its territory to the FSLN (National Sandinista Liberation Front) guerrillas making war against the government in El Salvador, as well as take concrete steps to restore civil rights to all Nicaraguans. On that last point, he said "there must be verification committees established to make certain that everyone keeps his promise."

When I asked Arias if the other presidents agreed on that basic outline, he said that Duarte of El Salvador really preferred a cease-fire to occur after the sixty-day performance, not before, but that most of the other presidents did not think that would be workable.

Later that afternoon, I got a small bipartisan group of House leaders together with Howard Baker, Tom Loeffler, and Will Ball from the State Department. George Shultz was out of town but would be back within a day. I discussed my conversations with Arias and Duarte, and Bob Michel gave a report on our meeting with the Nicaraguan ambassador. Everyone in our core group (Foley, Michel, Fascell, and Broomfield) agreed it was a window of opportunity and that we should try to pursue the opening. Howard Baker reaffirmed Loeffler's pledge that the president really would like to see the effort work. Tom Foley stressed to Baker that I would be endangering my credibility with the Democratic members unless there were unqualified support from the president. Baker said he understood that.

Foley was absolutely right about the reaction of our Democratic colleagues. The suggestion of a joint statement with the president made some of them very nervous. A few of the staunchest liberals still smarted over my saving aid for the Duarte government in El Salvador a few years earlier, although most of them had come to appreciate the genuineness and integrity of the durable Salvadoran president's efforts. There was greater distrust of the administration than ever in the wake of the Iran-Contra disclosures, however, and great uneasiness at the suggestion of any bipartisan effort in Central America. Many Democrats would have preferred to kill all Contra aid and let nature take its course.

The next day was a Thursday, July 30. I was anxious to get a cadre of key supporters organized in both the House and Senate before the weekend. Only a week remained before Central American leaders would be gathering at Esquipulas.

Tom Foley and Tony Coelho and I carefully assembled a cross section of Democrats who had been active on various sides of the Contra issue. We gathered around a long table in H-201 of the Capitol with a group of about fifteen activists. The group included Dave Bonior of Michigan, who was to undertake a major role in coordinating the peace activities. Also present were Lee Hamilton, Matt McHugh, Dave McCurdy, Wayne Owens, Mel Levine, and George Miller. That first discussion was a free-for-all. I told them of all the meetings we'd had, expressed my belief that there was at least a chance for peace, said that I wanted to explore every possibility of a carefully crafted bipartisan appeal, and asked for their support.

George Miller, the big Californian who had consistently opposed aid to the Contras and earlier had been against working with Duarte in El Salvador, came right to the point. "This is very dangerous, Mr.

Speaker; it could be a trap. The administration would love to get us divided among ourselves."

David Bonior was cautiously supportive. "I'm with you, Mr. Speaker. So long as there is any chance this might work we ought not to foreclose the opportunity. Still, I can't help being suspicious of the administration coming to us just before a vote with some concession that is more apparent than real, simply to throw us off stride. They have done that several times before, as we all know. The past record contains nothing to convince me that Ronald Reagan is serious, and he surely knows he doesn't have the votes in this climate to keep Contra aid alive."

Someone asked, "Why does the administration need Congress to join with it? If Reagan has a real peace plan, why doesn't he just offer it?" Somebody else suggested that the president would not have the support of his own right wing if he made a genuine offer, and that he needed a show of bipartisanship to cover his left flank. "Otherwise, he could become isolated with both sides shooting at him," said Matt McHugh. "Still, Jim, I think most of our Democratic colleagues would like to see some concrete good faith on the president's part before you stick your neck out publicly. If you go out front without the president's outspoken support, *you* could end up being the one mistrusted by both sides."

Mel Levine spoke up: "As I see it, Mr. Speaker, we're being asked to bring credibility to an administration that has lost all credibility in the Iran scandal and can't get anybody to take them seriously if they did have a peace plan."

"He's the only president we have right now, Mel," I said. "He's the only one who can speak for the country. If he is truly serious about wanting a peace effort, and if the Iran-Contra revelations have embarrassed some on the far right into temporary quiescence, maybe we ought to do what we can to *give* him the credibility he needs to negotiate on the country's behalf."

Wayne Owens said, "The stakes are important enough to take a chance, in my opinion. You recognize the personal risk you're taking, Mr. Speaker, but I admire you for being willing to take it. The prize is worth the risk. More than seventy thousand people have died in those two countries in the last six years. Do we realize that, considering comparative populations, this is the equivalent of perhaps as many as three million deaths in the United States—more than we've lost in all the wars in our history combined? If you can do anything to stop the bloodshed, Mr. Speaker, I think it's worth doing."

That seemed to sum it up. I sensed a turning point. I was watching George Miller and saw him nod assent. The thrust of the conversation changed perceptibly. Now we weren't discussing whether to do it; we were discussing *how* to do it. Tom Foley was becoming fully supportive but cautioned against any expectation of a quick fix. "Whatever plan might be set in motion will take at least six to eight months to have a real effect," he observed. "We can't expect everything that needs doing to be done within a sixty-day cease-fire period, but I agree we ought to form a plan within the next week if possible to give maximum encouragement to the peace-seekers at the Guatemala meeting. That assumes, of course, that the White House is on board!"

Someone noted that the National Conservative Union was running a pro-Contra ad on the ABC network in prime time. "If the president is for peace, he ought to ask his friends to call off the emotional public agitation. That's damn counterproductive!"

It was agreed that I would dictate a draft of the proposed joint statement, see if George Shultz and the president would approve it, touch base with the Senate leadership, and bring them up to speed on everything that had been happening. We had set up a meeting with George Shultz, new National Security Adviser Frank Carlucci, and Tom Loeffler for later that afternoon. Bob Michel and Will Ball would also be there. I called Senate Majority Leader Bob Byrd and made an appointment to go by his house that evening.

In the Thursday afternoon meeting, Secretary Shultz seemed puzzled. He had just returned from a trip abroad, there had been scant opportunity for his White House colleagues to fill him in. He came accompanied by Frank Carlucci, Will Ball, and Tom Loeffler. Loeffler made the opening comment. "We're all on the team," he pronounced.

I said this was the very best opportunity we'd had to work together. A successful peace effort with a real cease-fire could *null prosse* the whole question of Contra military aid. We could avoid that partisan bloodletting in the future if things really worked. I said that House Democrats in the end would be supportive if the aim was to make peace, but that if the goal was to float an initiative and be turned down, we wanted no part in it.

Shultz said, "It isn't a question of diplomacy *or* military pressure. The two have always gone together. It's what we call the two-track approach."

I said we had to be very clear that we were serious about negotiations. "Otherwise it won't work."

Shultz wondered if we had considered making the Contra leaders part of the process at this stage, but everyone else thought that would be premature.

At the end of our meeting, I agreed to dictate a draft for a proposed statement to be made jointly by the president and the Speaker. I told Shultz I would have a copy for him within twenty-four hours so he could review it and suggest any changes.

We talked about the upcoming Central American summit and the best ways to encourage the leaders to act. Shultz expressed doubt that Ortega would agree to anything effective. I told him of a suggestion by President Arias that Phil Habib should contact President Cerezo of Guatemala. When Bob Michel and I told the secretary of our talk with Nicaragua's Ambassador Tünnermann, Shultz showed more interest. Finally he said, "The world is starved for leadership and the only place it can come from is the United States. We need something that Ronald Reagan, Jim Wright, Bob Michel, and all the rest of us can agree on. You can count on me to help. We need a solution."

At that point, I stressed that the administration should cool its rhetoric about Contra military aid. In the coming days, we didn't want anything to split us apart again. Shultz agreed to take that message back to the White House. He said he would talk to the president and suggest he postpone any media blitz aimed at promoting such aid. We insisted that Reagan should not ask Congress for more military funds while the peace process was ongoing.

The lingering sun cast patches of shadow over George Washington Parkway as I drove toward Senator Robert Byrd's house that night. He lived in a fashionable section of McLean called Evermay, about a mile from my house in nearby Langley Oaks. Bob was alone when I arrived at his door. He had shed his coat and dapper trademark vest for a comfortable, loose-fitting jacket. I told him of all that had been happening in the past, beginning with Loeffler's first visit. As we talked, the white-maned West Virginian showed increasing interest. He agreed that we should give the effort every chance to succeed and asked if I could meet with the Senate leaders the next day in his office off the Senate floor. He would call Bob Dole, Sam Nunn, Claiborne Pell. I left with the feeling that I had an enthusiastic ally.

A minor setback stalled us briefly on Friday morning. It was July 31, 1987, and time was running out. I had asked Foley, Coelho, and Bonior to join me for an early breakfast in my hideaway room in the

Capitol. When I arrived they were reading the *Washington Times*. Above Frank Carlucci's picture a headline proclaimed, "Carlucci Cites Contra Gains, Claims Media Ignore Them." It quoted Reagan's new security adviser as saying, "The freedom fighter effort is on target. . . . There will be results that will influence Congress when the time comes." The story, not confirmed in any other news report, went on to say that "President Reagan is expected to make an address to the nation to press his case for assistance to the resistance before he leaves Washington on August 13 for a 25-day vacation in California." It quoted an unnamed "senior U.S. official" as saying that the president's speech would be made "after Congress adjourns" for its August recess. To Carlucci it attributed a statement that Mr. Reagan "intends to push the issue" of military aid to the Contras "in a series of speeches."

This was disquieting. It ran absolutely counter to the signals we had been getting from the White House. I did not believe the story, but saw its potential for disruption. It could panic Democrats, already suspicious of the president's motives, and build resistance to any joint peace effort. If the scenario it projected were actually intended to be carried out, it would render our work futile.

I called Frank Carlucci, whom I had known and regarded highly when he served as ambassador to Portugal. He assured me the *Times* story was without foundation. He had been both misquoted and quoted out of context, he said. He had heard from President Arias, and the peace process was on track. Carlucci believed my conversation with Arias had paved the way for a useful compromise with Duarte over which would come first, democratization or cease-fire. Under the new scenario, they would occur simultaneously. President Reagan appreciated my efforts and wanted them to succeed, Carlucci insisted.

Reassured, I went back to my office, called Janice Joyner of my staff, and dictated the first formal draft of what was to be the Reagan-Wright plan, or as the White House was to suggest, the Wright-Reagan plan. It came to a page and a half double-spaced on legal-sized paper. I had copies hand-delivered to Shultz, Baker, Carlucci, and Democratic and Republican leaders in the House and Senate.

The peace plan I committed to paper recognized the forthcoming summit in its first paragraph, made a three-point declaration of the U.S. interest regarding Nicaragua, and proposed an immediate end to hostilities and a process of reconciliation based on six points.

Concerning Nicaragua, I stressed our three legitimate concerns: (1) that there be no Soviet, Cuban, or communist-bloc military base in Nicaragua, (2) that there be no staging ground for any military threat or subversion of duly elected governments in the hemisphere, and (3) that the Nicaraguan government redeem its pledges made to the OAS in 1979 for free speech, free press, religious liberty, and a regularly established system of free, orderly elections. Beyond this, the statement declared, the United States has "no right to influence or determine the identity of the political leaders . . . nor the social and economic system" of that country.

The six points generally involved an immediate cease-fire, U.S. suspension of military aid to the Contras, a simultaneous Nicaraguan halt to aid from Cuba and the Soviet Union, immediate suspension of the emergency law, restoration of "all civil rights and liberties," and establishment of an "independent, multi-party electoral commission" to revise the laws for elections "to be supervised and guaranteed by an international body such as the OAS." The draft further suggested withdrawal of foreign military personnel and suspension of combat maneuvers by the United States in Honduras "as a demonstration of good faith when the cease-fire is in place."

As part of a process of negotiation among the countries involved, my draft pledged U.S. participation in "bilateral discussions with the governments of the region—including the government of Nicaragua—concerning security issues." This was later to become a sticking point of misunderstanding.

The plan contemplated "national reconciliation and dialogue among citizens of Nicaragua, including amnesty for former combatants and equal rights to participation in the political process." It pledged that both Nicaragua and the United States should "encourage and support the reintegration of demobilized forces into Nicaraguan civil and political society on terms guaranteeing their safety."

To complete the circle and bring our country into a welcome participatory role, the plan called for "expanded trade and long-range economic assistance for the democratic governments of Central America, for which Nicaragua might qualify through strict compliance with the terms of the agreement.

Later that morning, Costa Rican Ambassador Guido Fernández came by. He was leaving that day to meet over the weekend with President Arias. He would go with Arias to Esquipulas. The five

Central American foreign ministers would meet there on Tuesday, August 4, and the five presidents would meet on August 6.

Fernandez is a man of pleasant countenance, cordial manner, and excellent English. I had seen him many times and knew him to be very close to President Arias. He carefully read my first draft of the proposed joint statement and asked if he could take a copy with him to Costa Rica. I cautioned him that the White House had not yet studied it and it might be altered substantially before formal approval. He liked its contents, he said, and wanted to know if I could come to Guatemala in the next week for the Esquipulas summit. I told him I didn't think that would be appropriate, nor even possible given the number of things we had to accomplish in Congress prior to the August recess. As he left, he said, "I feel better about the prospects for peace than I have felt in a long, long time."

That afternoon, true to his word, Bob Byrd had assembled five senators in the smaller of the two meeting rooms that adjoined his office just west of the Senate floor. I looked up and saw on the fireplace mantel a big, oversized workshoe that had belonged to his grandson, killed a few years earlier in an auto accident. Once, with a dreamy faraway look in his eye, Bob had told me the sad story of his grandson's death. He kept the shoe in his office as a reminder. I saw him look toward it as the meeting began and wondered if it had any relevance to the fact that we were talking about saving the lives of a lot of other young men in our hemisphere.

After I walked the group through the conversations with administration officials, someone asked if I had seen the *Washington Times* article touting a new dose of Contra aid. I told them of my talk with Frank Carlucci and his disavowal. Claiborne Pell, in his aristocratic, understated way, said he thought Nicaragua might be ready to accept the terms of a peace offer but doubted that Ronald Reagan was prepared to do so. At this, Byrd asked if Howard Baker had told me the president would go along with the plan. I replied that he had. Secretary Shultz, I explained, had not been a party to the earlier discussions but had pledged cooperation and was probably bringing himself up to speed at that very time.

Somebody wondered aloud if the White House would have deliberately kept George Shultz out of the first preliminary discussions. I said I could not imagine any reason for doing so, the secretary had simply been out of the country. The question reminded me again of the degree of suspicion and the sense of intrigue that surrounded this issue.

Sam Nunn and Byrd said they would like to get Howard Baker, Frank Carlucci, and George Shultz into a broader meeting with a cross section of legislators and asked if I could have our House people available for such a meeting Monday morning. I promised to do so, invited Byrd and Dole to bring whomever they wished, and suggested we meet in the Speaker's private dining room at 10:30 on Monday morning, August 3.

Things began to fall rapidly into place on Monday. A large group convened in the Speaker's dining room that morning, George Shultz and Howard Baker joining a bipartisan collection from both houses of Congress. I referred to the Friday story in the *Washington Times* and said that if we expected a cease-fire in Central America, there really had to be a cease-fire in the fight between Congress and the administration over Contra aid. Secretary Shultz agreed.

"The only way we'll have an impact is if we are not quarreling among ourselves," I stressed. "Secretary Shultz has referred to a two-track system. We have been emphasizing the military track. Now we must emphasize the negotiating track. If we expect Central Americans to trust one another and work together, then certainly Democrats and Republicans are going to have to trust one another and work together. We Democrats are going to have to accept at face value President Reagan's sincerity in wanting this effort to work. Republicans are going to have to accept the genuineness of our desire to bring about a real change in Nicaragua.

"Mr. Secretary," I said, turning to Shultz, "we're proposing a moratorium on military activity in Central America. We'd like to propose also a moratorium on inflammatory rhetoric between the president and the congressional leadership over this issue. If we really believe there's a chance this can work, we all need to be playing on the same team. We need to wage peace with the single-minded determination of a successful war. If the Sandinistas show any willingness to do the things we're asking them to do, we need to avoid saying or doing foolish things to throw the train off track."

George Shultz and Howard Baker agreed that there would be a moratorium on further request for military aid if our joint appeal produced any results in Central America, and if serious peace talks were proceeding or serious progress was being made. Now I felt much better about our overall prospects.

David Bonior contacted Sophia Clark of the Nicaraguan embassy and gave her a copy of the proposed peace plan. Baker and Shultz had indicated that it was generally acceptable, although they might want cosmetic alterations. I had a call that afternoon from Miguel D'Escoto, the former Roman Catholic priest who served as foreign minister for the Sandinista government. I had known him since 1979 and never quite been able to peg him ideologically. He called to say that my paper was being "studied" in Managua. That was noncommittal, but I considered the fact of his call a positive development.

Later that afternoon, Secretary Schultz returned with a few longhand notations penned onto the script of our proposed joint statement. They didn't change the meaning. They were semantic improvements, I thought. Shultz said the president was "very enthusiastic." He said Reagan would give it "the long shot." He would let it have "the main track," would launch no pro-Contra effort during the August recess of Congress, and none into September if the process should seem to be working.

The next day I shuttled between meetings of senators in Byrd's large conference room and Democratic House members assembled by David Bonior in the "squirrel's nest" room on the third floor of the Capitol, where the Steering and Policy Committee meets each Thursday morning. In the Senate meetings, Secretary Shultz assumed the principal burden of defending the document. I learned later that at one point during my absence Senator Chris Dodd of Connecticut and Secretary Shultz had agreed to delete references to our engaging in "bilateral" talks. Rather, we would agree to participate in "multilateral" talks. We would face the question of bilateral discussions on an ad hoc basis as the situation unfolded.

This was to change the nature of our proposal in a way that I had not anticipated. For the next several days I supposed, wrongly as it turns out, that we were offering to sit down directly with the Sandinistas and hammer out an agreement for them to banish all Cuban and Russian military presence and any long-range weapons we considered threatening in exchange for our renewing trade and normalizing relations, assuming they did the other things required by their Central American neighbors. This was the only misunderstanding that arose between us, but it might have been an important one.

On Wednesday, August 5, I met with President Reagan at the White House. Along with Shultz, Howard Baker, and Will Ball, we sat in the Oval Office and talked of how to launch the joint statement for maximum effect. It was agreed that the president and I would walk together into the White House press room, hand out copies of our joint declaration, each make a brief statement, and then answer questions. I would hold a second press conference on Capitol Hill (the complete statement can be found in the appendix).

As we left the Oval Office, President Reagan handed me a second piece of paper and said, "This memorandum outlines my under-standing of what we're proposing." I didn't have time to read it then, as we were just walking out the door to talk with the press. I put it in my pocket and promised the president I would study it later.

The White House press corps disappointed me with the paucity of its questions. We might have entered the room without sufficient advance notice, or else a lot of the reporters were at lunch. Clearly they were not expecting an announcement of this significance.

That afternoon, the joint leadership of Congress and a large num-ber of my House Democratic colleagues stood with me in the statu-esque old Cannon Caucus Room across the street from the Capitol and answered a barrage of questions from the Capitol Hill press corps. At least there was a lively interest.

Later that day, I remembered the piece of paper in my pocket, the one handed me by President Reagan. Scanning it, I was taken aback. As I recall now the typed manuscript covered twenty-one points. Most of them seemed written with the anticipation that our effort would fail. They addressed how to recoup the military initiative following a breakdown in talks. One point asserted the assumed right to resume full-scale military action if the Sandinista government failed to accept all of the conditions of our proposal within two weeks, or if the Nicaraguan leaders failed to carry them out in their entirety by September 30.

Obviously, this would not do. Public circulation of such a docu-ment would pull the plug on the negotiators at Esquipulas. It would replace the friendly entreaty with a threat, the olive branch with a clumsy club. Even if the Sandinistas wanted to accept our terms, their nationalistic machismo would force them to reject an ultimatum of that type. By either accident or design, the twenty-one points amounted to a shotgun blast at the nervous dove of peace.

I picked up the phone and called Chief of Staff Howard Baker. When I described the paper, he knew exactly what it was. He had not been aware that the president had handed it to me. "Mr. Speaker, I hope you'll just forget that piece of paper," he said. "That was writ-ten by Cap Weinberger on his own, and it doesn't represent anybody else in the White House. I don't think the president even had a chance to read it all the way through. It does not represent our position, and I think you'd do us all a favor if you just got rid of it." That's what I did.

Later that afternoon, I had a call from Costa Rican Ambassador Guido Fernández. He was at the meeting of foreign ministers in Guatemala. Things had begun well, he said, but he believed it terribly important that I have a "personal representative" present for the Thursday meeting of the five presidents. I said I'd send Richard Peña. A commercial plane was leaving National Airport in approximately fifty minutes for a Miami connection to Guatemala City. Peña, contacted by my office, had time only to pick up his passport, no change of clothes. Eastern Airlines actually held up departure by eight or nine minutes, and Peña got aboard out of breath from sprinting and dodging cars and passengers at Washington's crowded terminal on the Potomac River.

The telephone awakened me at 4:30 on Friday morning, August 7, 1987. It was Costa Rica's amiable ambassador. Fernández was ebullient. "President Arias wanted you to be the first to know," he announced. "The five presidents have just signed off on an agreement in principle. It is being drafted now. They will review it in written form within a few hours, and I am confident that they all will sign it."

I couldn't go back to sleep. I didn't want to. It was going to be a magnificent day, and I could think only to thank God for my early notice of the day's arrival. Betty, now awake, sensed my excitement. "It's wonderful, isn't it?" she said.

"Yes, Betty, it's wonderful. Really wonderful."

"I'm happy for you," she said. Then, after a pause, "Of course, I'm happy for everyone. But especially for you."

"I'm happy, too," I told her. I thought a minute. For whom was I really happiest? "I guess I'm happiest for people Ginger's age," I said, referring to my eldest daughter. Her sons were thirteen and fifteen. "Do you know that in Central America kids the age of Chris and Erik are dying in battle?"

Later that morning, Richard Peña called me at the office from the Guatemala airport. He spelled out the details of the agreement. The presidents had concurred that none of them would supply aid or permit use of their territories to any rebellious group aimed at undermining the government of any neighbor. A process of reconciliation and amnesty would be declared in both El Salvador and

Nicaragua. Under the direction of a reconciliation commission, de-mocratization would take place, with certain specific standards of individual liberty to be guaranteed to all. The five foreign ministers would meet in fifteen days, and within ninety days there would be a simultaneous cease-fire.

The Esquipulas agreement embraced fully three-fourths of all the points included in the Wright-Reagan plan. President Arias had in-sisted to Peña that I understand our initiative had been the stimulus that was needed to bring all five of the presidents together. "President Arias asked me to tell you specifically, Mr. Speaker," said Richard, "that it was your insistence on the separation of the peace initiative, clinically and surgically, from any threats of military action which made it possible for the Central Americans to accept it and to pre-serve their dignity at the same time."

At my daily press conference in the Capitol that day, I announced the outlines of the historic agreement that had just been signed. I expressed satisfaction and support. Someone asked if this meant the U.S. government was officially supportive. "You'll want to get a statement from the president, of course," I replied, "but it is abso-lutely inconceivable to me that our government could be anything but fully and enthusiastically supportive."

It was a great day, one of the finest in my life. That night I slept on a cloud of euphoria.

CHAPTER 7

Esquipulas and Arias

If you have built castles in the air,
Your work need not be lost;
that is where they should be.
Now put foundations under
them.

—Henry David Thoreau

On Saturday, August 8, I asserted my prerogative to use the five-minute Democratic response that followed the president's weekly radio broadcast. I spoke of the peace initiative launched in Guatemala and stressed the bipartisan approach that led to it. The theme of my message was "give peace a chance." Then I went home and collapsed in a lawn chair on our deck, intent on enjoying an idyllic Saturday afternoon.

My reverie was soon interrupted by a call from the White House. Someone wanted to know if I would be willing to talk with Adolfo Calero, acting chairman of the Nicaraguan resistance forces, if he were to call me. "Of course!" I said. I knew Calero, had visited with him on several occasions. A big balding robust man with a moon-shaped face, Adolfo Calero had been a Coca-Cola executive in Nicaragua in the Somoza days. He left the country to join the Contra movement after the Sandinistas firmed up their hold on the government. He was considered a hard-liner with friends in the United States but was probably not as popular among the people inside Nicaragua as Edén Pastora or Alfonso Robelo.

Soon the phone rang again. It was our ambassador, Everett Briggs, in Tegucigalpa, Honduras. Calero was with him in the chancery office. They both expressed pleasure that Ortega had signed the Esquipulas accord, agreeing to abolish military law and restore the democratic process in Nicaragua. Calero admitted to a lingering disbelief that Ortega could be trusted to carry out the promise. "I know Daniel," he declared, "and even if he wants to keep his word, there are others in the junta who will make it hard for him." But Calero pledged that he and the Contras would abide by the terms of the historic agreement and give the Sandinistas every chance to keep faith with Ortega's pledge.

I told him of a report I'd had from Richard Peña, who had attended the press conference Ortega gave upon arriving in Esquipulas. Responding to questions in Spanish, Ortega had been interpreted by Nicaragua's Foreign Minister Miguel D'Escoto. Peña said that while Ortega was reasonably conciliatory in his responses to questions, his statements invariably bore a perceptibly harder line when filtered into English by D'Escoto. Calero picked up on that immediately. He had been present at the very same press conference, he told me, and had observed the same phenomenon.

Only a few minutes passed before the phone rang a third time. This time it was Will Ball, the able State Department official who had sat in on several of our meetings, subbing for George Shultz in the secretary's absence. Will was a specialist in congressional relations and enjoyed the respect of everyone on the Hill. He wanted to confide in me some of the problems that were arising within the administration. He said that a few in administration circles, Secretary Weinberger in particular, were irate over the ninety-day time span allowed for compliance with the Esquipulas agreement. We had suggested sixty days in our bipartisan plan. The Central American presidents had extended that, agreeing that the foreign ministers would meet within fifteen days and set in motion the ninety-day timetable. Weinberger insisted that the United States should summarily repudiate the agreement and refuse to go along with its terms.

"That's just not very sensible, Will," I said. "You remember what George Shultz said only a few days ago when Ortega was demanding that we negotiate directly with him? The secretary wisely told him that we could not sit down and barter away the rights of the other Central American presidents to establish the parameters of any agreement affecting the whole area. Those are their countries, and their people who are dying. Those presidents are the ones who are directly responsible to the people of the region, and we indicated we'd be supportive of any reasonable plan they should evolve.

"Well, they've evolved one, and we'd look foolish to repudiate it now. Nobody who understands the Latin American people could have expected them simply to take our proposal and embrace it in toto without any changes of their own. They have their own pride. It's a darn good agreement, and the difference between sixty and ninety days is not enough to come unglued about. In fact, they may know something we don't know."

Will Ball emphatically agreed. He said he would be carrying that very message to Frank Carlucci, and that official comment from the administration would be supportive of what was done in Esquipulas. He just wanted me to know that there was some internal unhappiness.

The response from other nations in the hemisphere was uniformly good. President Cerezo of Guatemala called the agreement the "most important regional accord in Central American history." President Arias, the plan's principal architect, predicted that world opinion would force the Sandinistas to honor the treaty. The Contra directorate took a publicly supportive stance, vowing to support negotiations, saying they would continue the armed struggle until a cease-fire was in place but expressing willingness to abandon the fighting as soon as there were concrete agreements on amnesty and reconciliation.

There were a few nay-sayers in Congress. Jack Kemp publicly criticized the plan. Senator Ted Kennedy, on the day the president announced the initiative, called it "a sham from beginning to end," but he altered his view as soon as the Central American presidents responded with their own plan. Most others in the House and the Senate were at least tentatively hopeful. Many were enthusiastically supportive.

That same pattern held in the press. Most editorials expressed support, but there were exceptions. On August 11 the *Wall Street Journal* and the *Washington Times* both threw cold water on the plan. The *Journal* proclaimed it "Reagan's Bay of Pigs," while the *Washington Times* warned of what it called "the peace proposal trap." Most papers agreed with the *New York Times,* whose lead editorial was titled "Risks Worth Taking on Nicaragua." The *Oregonian* pleaded "Give Peace a Chance," admonishing President Reagan that if he wanted the peace process to work he must make that clear to his friends at home and to U.S. allies in Central America.

Arturo Cruz, Nicaraguan ambassador after the overthrow of Somoza and an officer at the Inter-American Development Bank since his principled defection from the Sandinista ruling group, wrote an insightful piece in the *Los Angeles Times* of August 20, calling the plan "the best hope for peace" and urging the United States to embrace it, carry it out, and pursue it with great diligence. Lawrence A. Pezzullo, U.S. ambassador to Nicaragua in the early months following the Sandinista takeover, wrote an article urging the president to be wholehearted in his support of this peace effort.

Reagan soon began to feel pressure from his right wing, however. A group of conservative fund-raisers, invited to meet with the president in the White House, failed to applaud him when he was introduced and when he finished his remarks to them. Howard Baker told me this was the very first time, to his knowledge, that this particular president had been treated to calculated rudeness by any group since assuming the presidency.

I mentally flinched for the president. A hostile audience does something to the psyche of any public person, particularly an old thespian like Ronald Reagan.

Meanwhile, the Sandinistas formally began taking steps to implement the Esquipulas agreement. Ortega declared a total amnesty to be effective with the cease-fire. He agreed to sit down and negotiate with someone who would speak on behalf of the Contras, suggesting either the Catholic Church or the Red Cross. He flew to Cuba and talked with Fidel Castro about removing the Cuban presence in Nicaragua. Castro at least publicly embraced that idea and the peace plan itself. The Nicaraguan leader then appointed a reconciliation commission to carry out and oversee such domestic reforms as amnesty, release of prisoners, and reintegration of the armed opposition into civil life with full political rights. In El Salvador, President José Napoleón Duarte was appointing a similar commission and calling on the armed guerrillas of the FMLN (Farabundo Marti National Liberation Front) to come and talk with him at a place of their choice anywhere in the country.

*   *   *

All of this seemed to me an ample cause for optimism. We should have been expressing encouragement and approval. Instead, I began to discern a pattern of negative response from State Department press spokesmen. Phyllis Oakley, in her daily press briefings, disparaged each of these steps. Whatever Ortega agreed to do, the State Department's official reaction seemed to be that it was cosmetic, unimportant, and in any event "not nearly enough."

Finally, I called George Shultz to ask why we weren't being more publicly supportive of the positive developments. He said his deputy for Latin American affairs, Elliott Abrams, simply was not convinced that Ortega was sincere. "We need to make it clear to them that we aren't going to be satisfied with anything less than real performance," he stressed.

As much as I respected George Shultz and admired his integrity, I profoundly disagreed with the psychology of consistent disparagement. "Those people are like people everywhere, George," I said. "They're like you and me. When they do something they think should merit our approval and we scoff at it, it simply makes them less willing to try to please us in the future. Of course, we should disapprove when they violate a commitment. But when they make an honest effort to comply with a commitment, as they seem to be doing now, shouldn't we try to encourage more of that sort of behavior?" Shultz said he agreed in principal but wanted to see more good-faith performance.

One specific comment involved the people appointed by Ortega to the Reconciliation Commission. The Nicaraguan president selected his vice president, Sergio Ramírez, to represent the government and an opposition lawmaker named Mauricio Díaz to speak for the other domestic political parties. He chose Cardinal Miguel Obando y Bravo, clearly the most respected personage in his country, and a Baptist clergyman named Gustavo Parajón to speak for the humanitarian sector. Parajón was also a medical doctor, trained in the United States. He was head of Protestant charities for the country.

With a sweeping dismissal of all the others, Ms. Oakley in a State Department briefing for reporters, pronounced that Cardinal Obando was the only acceptable person in the group.

In mid-August, Philip Habib announced his retirement as our special ambassador to Central America. This was a bombshell. Habib, a good soldier and team player, had tried tirelessly to carry out administration objectives in dealings with the countries of the region.

When the peace plan was announced, he expected to be dispatched immediately to the region where he would ride herd on events daily and enter into talks with each of the countries, including Nicaragua. When it became clear that the administration chose not to pursue these negotiations directly, Habib resigned, leaving a memorandum for the State Department's files. He refused to make a public statement and gave no press interviews. But it was known among Phil's friends that he was deeply disappointed with the administration's failure to pursue the peace opportunity more actively.

In Latin America, however, there was excitement. Governor Rafael Hernández Colón of Puerto Rico called to invite me to speak to a conference of Caribbean basin nations meeting on September 23 in his country. The governor also made a suggestion. Our mutual friend President Oscar Arias would be honored in New York on September 23 preparatory to his trip to receive the Nobel Peace Prize. Raphael thought it would be helpful throughout Latin America if I were to invite Arias to speak to a joint session of the Congress on September 22. That seemed to me a magnificent idea. It would demonstrate our respect for the persistent peacemaker and our commitment to the peace plan.

Immediately I called Howard Baker to set things in motion. Howard said it sounded good, but he wanted to touch some other bases. He told me there were problems in the White House with trying to pacify what he called "the professional conservatives." Certainly we should show our courtesy to President Arias, he agreed. The Nobel Prize was a magnificent honor and this would be a chance to demonstrate our respect. Arias was well known as a staunch anticommunist and should be an acceptable spokesman for the best of what was happening in Central America.

Tony Coelho suggested that the congressional leadership have a lunch for the five ambassadors of the Central American signatory nations. We scheduled it for Tuesday, August 25. All came except the ambassador of Guatemala, who was ill. Fernández of Costa Rica, Tünnermann of Nicaragua, Martínez of Honduras, and Rivas-Gallont of El Salvador came, along with Father Timothy Healey, president of Georgetown University, whom we invited to ask the blessing for our endeavors.

There had been a few disquieting reports that Honduras was under pressure from U.S. spokesmen to delay implementation of the plan. I did not believe those rumors, but Honduras did occupy a special role in the region. It was there that Contra forces trained and bivouacked between armed forays into Nicaragua. It was there also that U.S. National Guard units had gone on training missions, sometimes as a warning to Nicaraguan adventurers. In a recent meeting in Venezuela, the official Honduran representative had expressed concern that full implementation of the Esquipulas plan might cause the Contras all to move into Honduras, which could give that country a major headache. The luncheon would allow the ambassadors a forum for any such concerns. It would also afford congressional leaders an opportunity to express appreciation and support for progress on the peace plan.

We sat at a big round table in the center of the room. I turned to Nicaraguan Ambassador Tünnermann and quipped: "Hey, Carlos, a la mesa de los eguales, usted está a mi izquierda en una dirección, pero quando usted mira a la otra dirección, está a mi derecha" (At a roundtable like this we are all equals; I look in one direction and you are on my right, but in the other direction you are on my left). The often somber Tünnermann grinned broadly, and I knew we were off to a good start.

That lighthearted reference to his supposed left-wing ideology seemed to set everyone at ease. Martínez, the Honduran, was a stocky, completely bald man with a deep voice and roguish twinkle in his dark eyes. His size and appearance reminded me of Sam Rayburn. I told him so and he said many people had remarked on the similarity. "If you will excuse me, Mr. Speaker, usually those who remember Mr. Rayburn are much older people than you." We all laughed at that.

About halfway through the luncheon, Martínez grew mellow. "We are like five fingers of one hand," he philosophized. "Each of us in Central America sometimes thinks of his country as a single unit, but we know we are inseparably tied together. There are five stars in our Honduran flag; they represent the five nations of Central America. There are five stripes in the flag of Costa Rica, and that also represents the five nations." Then he turned with a devilish grin toward his Nicaraguan counterpart. "And there are five volcanoes in Nicaragua. They also may represent the five nations of Central America!"

Tünnermann pledged that his country would faithfully carry out every commitment under the pact. He was sure we'd all be pleased, he said, with the work of the Reconciliation Commission. After lunch, I asked Guido Fernández privately to stop by my office for a separate visit. I had waited several days for a formal reply from the

White House about inviting President Arias to address a joint session. Such invitations come officially from the Congress, of course, but it is customary for the president to request an invitation for a visiting head of state to speak to a joint session. Foreign presidents were often invited, however, to address members in only slightly less formal settings.

Less than a month remained, and I did not want to run a risk of losing the opportunity altogether. I discussed the matter with Fernández that day and he said he was certain that his president would be honored to speak to the members under any circumstances. He did hope it would be in a setting sufficient to accommodate the entire membership, as such an address would be broadcast widely throughout Central America, and he felt it would have a much more powerful impact if it were obviously being delivered before a large live audience of U.S. lawmakers.

Uncertain whether the White House would ask for a formal joint session and unwilling to schedule one in the absence of agreement with the executive branch, I started planning for the next best thing. I asked my party's caucus chairman, Dick Gephardt, to schedule a Democratic Caucus for the morning of September 22. Then I wrote a memorandum to all committee chairmen requesting that they allow no committee meetings prior to noon on that date.

Senate Leader Bob Byrd had already told me he would prefer a 10 o'clock meeting to avoid interfering with afternoon legislative business. I notified Bob of the plan and asked him to spread the word among senators. We would hold the meeting in the House chamber where the Democratic Caucus sometimes meets prior to the convening of the House. If the White House did not want a formal joint session, we would simply invite senators and members of the Republican Conference to join us informally in the House chamber to honor the Nobel Prize winner and chief architect of the Central American peace plan.

President Reagan was in Santa Barbara for the August vacation. Frank Carlucci called from there to ask if I would receive and visit with the members of the Nicaraguan Contra directorate on August 27 after they had talked with President Reagan. The president was at some pains, Carlucci explained, to reassure the resistance forces that we had not forgotten them in our zeal to pave the path to peace. I consented with alacrity. Unlike some Democratic colleagues who dismissed all the Contras as anathema, I knew and liked a number of those people. I particularly respected the Chamorro family, publishers of the closed newspaper *La Prensa*. I always enjoyed visiting with Alfredo César, who once attended the University of Texas, and Alfonso Robelo, whom I met first on my trip to Nicaragua in 1980 following the overthrow of the Somoza regime.

The Contra group arranged to stop off at Dallas–Fort Worth Airport on their way back from Santa Barbara. On the eve of our meeting, the Sandinista government in Managua announced it was inviting back into the country three exiled priests, including Father Carballo and Bishop Vega. The government also spoke of permitting Radio Católico, the daily church broadcast that had been shut down, to recommence its programming.

The Contra directors, on their way to meet with President Reagan, publicly made a concession of their own. They said they would like to see Reagan suspend military aid to them as an act of good faith during the negotiating period. I had heard two days before that President Duarte was urging that course upon the Nicaraguan resistance leaders when they met with him in El Salvador.

The three civilian Contra leaders who met me at the airport on August 27 were Robelo, César, and Aristedes Sánchez. We discussed the idea of some plan to hold military-aid funds in escrow if necessary while the peace process was ongoing. Robelo and César, who both speak excellent English, probed for some creative way to permit their armed forces to receive strictly humanitarian aid—food, shelter, medical supplies—while observing an armistice of several months' possible duration. I had not met Sánchez before that day. He spoke occasionally in Spanish, seemed content to let the other two carry the thrust of the conversation.

The Contra leaders, I noted, seemed more optimistic about the peace process than some of the hard-liners in our own country. They were considerably less critical than Ms. Oakley had been of the personnel appointed by the Sandinistas to the Reconciliation Commission. They acknowledged that Vice President Sergio Ramírez was probably the least doctrinaire of any in the ruling Sandinista junta, and probably the easiest to talk with. They thought him philosophically the most moderate. They agreed that Cardinal Obando would not permit himself to be appointed to the commission unless he expected it to do a fair and honest job. They had nothing negative to say about the evangelical Baptist clergyman Gustavo Parajón.

At the end of our two-hour meeting, the press was ready to pounce on us with questions about what the Contra leaders would do if the peace talks broke down. The Central Americans handled themselves well.

"We hope the talks do not break down," said Alfredo César, "and we are trying to do what we can to assure that they do not break down."

When someone asked if I would favor sending any humanitarian aid to the Contras, or any financial aid to Nicaragua in the future, I said, "I would always rather send the Peace Corps and a literacy corps to teach, and a medical corps to heal. Maybe then we won't have to send the Marine Corps or an army corps!"

Howard Baker finally called back to say the administration did not think we should hold a formal joint session for Arias. "Duarte will be coming in a few months, and we wouldn't want to run a risk of offending him by inviting Arias to address a joint session," he explained.

"That's easy," I answered. "We can invite Duarte to do exactly the same thing when he comes."

Baker said, "Then we might raise similar expectations among all the other presidents in the region."

It was apparent to me that the administration preferred not to have a formal joint session. "Okay, Howard. I'll go along with that. We'll just have him speak to the Democratic Caucus, and we'll invite the Republicans to join us informally as well as all senators who wish to come."

A couple of days later Baker called again. "I understand you're planning to receive President Arias in the House chamber," he began. I told him that was correct. "I wish you'd hold it somewhere else. Why couldn't you do it in the Cannon Caucus Room?"

"Well, for one thing, the House chamber is where the Democratic Caucus always meets. For another, we've already announced it and invited the Republican Conference, and they've voted to accept our invitation."

"We'd like to keep it from assuming too high a profile if possible," he insisted. "We're afraid the House chamber gives it too much the appearance of a formal session. Isn't there some way you could arrange it?"

This was beginning to irritate me. I couldn't understand why the White House would want to downplay the event. Furthermore, it was the Speaker's clear prerogative to invite whomever he wished to address the Democratic Caucus in the House. Finally, I said, "Howard, it's too late to change it. President Arias has already been invited and has accepted our invitation. It would be embarrassing to change the location. People would see it as a deliberate downgrading. Furthermore the Senate is invited and expecting to attend. The Cannon building would be physically inconvenient for them, and there wouldn't be enough room. All things considered, I think it would be an enormous mistake to try to change it now. Let's go through with it, and make a success of it, and give it a high profile, and be proud of it!"

The September 22 event was an unqualified success. President Arias impressed an overflow crowd in the House chamber with his recurring theme, give peace a chance. The Costa Rican president's somber demeanor, the pensive immobility of his facial features, his sad intelligent eyes, and his utter lack of theatrical flourishes gave to his presentation the appeal of unmistakable sincerity. The audience was responsive, eager to break in with applause but restrained by the simple eloquence of understated truth. There were no empty seats either on the House floor or in the galleries. A good cross section of senators was present, and Bob Michel's Republicans turned out. Arias spoke in straightforward, grammatical English. The absence of jingoistic slogans and artfully contrived applause lines lent authenticity to his message.

After the speech, members of Congress retired to a private question-and-answer session across the street in the Cannon Caucus Room. Arias had agreed to this as an addendum to his formal address. He was candid in his responses, acknowledging the difficulties ahead. He admitted that the task required big changes on the part of the Sandinistas, humility and even some luck on the part of Duarte's government, and persistence among the other nations.

"It is my frank opinion," Arias said in answer to one question, "that free elections honestly conducted in an atmosphere of peace will bring about a change in the government in Nicaragua. The Sandinistas are not popular. But the Contras are even more unpopular. Believe me, they are not the solution; they are the problem."

The Costa Rican president's performance apparently won over several Republicans and conservative Democrats who had been on the fence up to that time. Leaving that meeting, I overheard two right-wing devotees of the Contra cause telling the press that they believed Arias to be sincere and thought now that the process had at least an outside chance to work.

We had a luncheon in the House Foreign Affairs Committee room for the Costa Rican delegation. Hosts were the Democratic and Republican leaders of the House and Senate. Some spouses were present. Margarita Arias, the president's beautiful U.S.-educated wife, made a big hit with men and women alike, as did Muini Figueres, the daughter of former President José Figueres, father of modern Costa Rican democracy.

Arias himself, by nature taciturn, was visibly moved by the genuineness of his reception. He twice expressed his gratitude to me privately, and publicly asked me to speak on December 1 in San José to celebrate the thirty-ninth anniversary of the disbanding of the Costa Rican army. I had the disturbing sense that the peace process was getting me committed to more traveling engagements than my schedule could comfortably accommodate. But I said I would try to make it.

In Puerto Rico the following weekend, I visited with José Napoleón Duarte and marveled again at the stubborn integrity of El Salvador's beleaguered leader. In the 1980s, under his patient, determined guidance, that country had experienced a longer stretch of democratic rule than ever before in its five hundred years of blood-splattered history. Duarte was now setting the pace in complying assiduously with the Esquipulas accords and challenging the Sandinista leaders in Nicaragua to match his performance.

The United States did not have a better friend anywhere in the hemisphere, I was convinced, nor democracy a better preceptor. First elected president in 1972, Duarte had been seized, tortured, and deported by a brutal military junta. Not to be denied, he returned to El Salvador and became provisional president when the excesses of the junta drove it from office. Duarte presided over elections of a constituent assembly to write a modern constitution. When in league with a couple of fringe parties Roberto D'Aubuisson's ARENA party outpolled Duarte's Christian Democrats in the 1982 constituent-assembly elections, Duarte turned over the reins of power with dignity. This was the first time in Salvadoran history that political power had passed peacefully from one rival faction to another.

Two years later, in 1984, the short, soft-spoken Notre Dame graduate with the rugged countenance, the slight lisp, and the light blue eyes was again elected president. Close to 80 percent of the people braved threats of violence to stand in long lines, some for hours, to fulfill the privilege of voting, the right casually forgone by so many in our own country. As a witness to that election, I visited five Salvadoran communities that day in 1984, interviewed at random seventy or more people, and came away with a profound conviction of their desire for peace and freedom and the rudiments of social progress.

Now, having pointed the way to democracy, Duarte was trying by example to show a way to peace. He was offering total amnesty to the armed marauders who had made unrelenting guerrilla war against his elected government and some of whose number had recently kidnaped his thirty-five-year-old daughter, Inez, holding her captive for several days. Duarte, just days before our meeting in Puerto Rico, had gone unarmed to a jungle rendezvous with the rebel leaders. It was at that meeting that he offered complete amnesty to the government's enemies if they would lay down their arms and pursue their competition in the electoral arena.

"They asked me just what I meant by amnesty," Duarte told me. "I said I would tell them what amnesty means. 'It means forgiveness,' I said. 'It means that what you have done against us in the past is forgotten. The slate is wiped clean.'

"Then I looked around the circle, and I said, 'I know which ones of you were involved in kidnapping my daughter. It was you—and you—and you.' As I said that, I pointed to the very men who had held my little girl captive while trying to extort concessions from the government. And then I said, 'Amnesty means that your crime is forgiven. Your government forgives you, as I forgive you personally.' "

I wondered, as this unpretentious and uncomplicated man recounted to me that event so hauntingly personal, how few people of my acquaintance could summon such supreme generosity of spirit. Just as war is physical, peace is spiritual. The ingredient it needs most of all, and which is maybe the hardest to come by, is forgiveness.

Not everyone wants to forgive. Perhaps not everyone can. Events were moving, at least, in the direction of peace. From that I took satisfaction. Most Americans approved, according to opinion polls. Most, but not all. A powerful remnant had invested enormous amounts of time, money, and prestige in the effort to overthrow the Nicaraguan government by force of arms. Some of them felt cheated. Assistant Secretary of State Elliott Abrams, following the U.S. assault on Grenada in 1983, had even called for a U.S. military invasion of Nicaragua. Some highly placed people simply did not want a negotiated settlement. I did. After six years of bloodshed I was determined to do what I could to help establish peace in our hemisphere. That course would breed resentment and bring me into unavoidable and increasingly bitter conflict in the months ahead.

CHAPTER 8

Beleaguered Are the Peacemakers

I have never known a peace made, even the most advantageous, that was not censured as inadequate, and the makers condemned as injudicious or corrupt. "Blessed are the peacemakers" is, I suppose, to be understood in the other world; for in this they are frequently cursed.

—Benjamin Franklin

Two problems loomed in the next six weeks. The first involved how much and what kind of aid to continue for the Contras. Many Democrats wanted to abandon the Contra effort entirely. They argued that continuing even economic assistance to the guerrilla forces would violate the spirit of Esquipulas. The administration and most House Republicans fervently insisted that we owed a moral obligation to those whom we had helped recruit and lure into battle. To dismantle the resistance forces, moreover, would remove the major incentive for the Sandinistas to comply with their agreements, conservatives argued.

125

A temporary decision at least had to be faced on September 25, 1987, in the continuing resolution, that short-run, catchall appropriation extending the government's spending authority beyond the September 30 end of the fiscal year. It would stay in effect until the regular departmental funding bills had been signed by the president.

In private talks with Democratic and Republican leaders, I asked support for continuing nonlethal aid—food, shelter, boots, medical supplies, and communications equipment—at the current level of spending. There would be no new money for weapons or ammunition stockpiles, but the estimated ten thousand men who had left their civilian pursuits to join the Contras would not be summarily abandoned. This was the first time the House Democratic leadership had assented formally to assistance of *any* type to the Contra movement. I thought it prudent, even essential, under the circumstances. The United States had indeed helped recruit these naive young men, some no more than twelve and thirteen years of age, into the resistance forces, and we owed them a safer and more orderly return to civilian life in their Nicaraguan homeland than simply to cut off their food and medical supplies without warning.

There was opposition in the Democratic Caucus to even this degree of humanitarian aid. The issue was deeply divisive. With the help of David Bonior, we kept the lid on the bottle of pent-up emotions while Majority Leader Tom Foley presided over daily sessions of House and Senate chairmen struggling with a package to resolve this and other budgetary issues for the full fiscal year.

The second and larger question that plagued peacemakers was just how to negotiate the end of the war in Nicaragua and reconcile the warring factions in a democratic social order. Who would negotiate with whom? A letter from the Nicaraguan ambassador to the United States suggested that the Sandinistas were taking positive steps (the complete original letter can be found in the appendix).

Daniel Ortega had insisted from the beginning that he would talk only with the United States. At one point he had said in scornful derision of the Contras, "It is no good talking to the dogs; one must talk to the owner of the dogs." Our State Department, on the other hand, was intent on giving stature to the resistance. "It is a Nicaraguan problem," George Shultz said, "and it must be settled by Nicaraguans." In other words, Sandinistas must talk to Contras.

Resistance Leader Adolfo Calero, meanwhile, added another caveat. "We will meet Ortega in Managua," he insisted, "and establish the ground rules there in the nation's capital." Ortega rejected both the concept of a direct meeting and Managua as its site. He professed concern that Contra leaders might be attacked by angry crowds if they came into Managua and doubted that the government could give adequate assurance of their safety.

Obviously, someone had to yield. It was apparent to me from the day I met with the Contra leaders at the airport in Texas that a mediator of top standing would have to set the ground rules for negotiation, maybe even recommend some terms of settlement. Only one person came to my mind. Only one had impeccable credentials of both position and personality. Only one was universally respected by Sandinista and Contra sympathizers alike. He was Cardinal Miguel Obando y Bravo, the Catholic prelate of Nicaragua. Cardinal Obando was an unembarrassed critic of the Sandinista regime's authoritarian excesses, as he had been of those practiced earlier by Luis and Anastasio Somoza. His integrity was unimpeachable, his independence unassailable.

On each of my visits to Nicaragua, I had gone for a visit with Father Obando—bishop, archbishop, now cardinal. We would sit in the shade of a banana palm grove at his unpretentious residence on the outskirts of Managua, sipping iced tea flavored faintly with vanilla. He always answered my questions forthrightly. Questions about the people, about their social condition and the state of the economy, about the trustworthiness of the government. In 1979, then Archbishop Obando was the only person with whom I talked who expressed reservations that Sandinista leaders would carry out their pledges of pluralism and political liberty. I trusted him. Now, through September and October 1987, I several times urged Contra and Sandinista leaders alike to agree to a mediation of the issues between them with Cardinal Obando acting as intermediary. Nobody expressed outright disagreement.

On Tuesday, November 5, three Nicaraguans came to see me at my office in the Capitol: Ambassador Tünnermann, Victor Tinoco, and Manuel Cordero. They came to give me a progress report, Tünnermann said, and a preview of what would be asked that afternoon in Managua. At 5 o'clock Nicaragua time, President Ortega would pardon a thousand or more prisoners, including former Somoza national guardsmen, along with militant Contras. Also he would announce a general amnesty to be effective as soon as the International Verification Commission signed a finding that other conditions required in the Treaty of Esquipulas were being met. Perhaps most important, the state of emergency would be lifted. Tünnermann claimed that the Nicaraguan legislature was passing a law to repeal the Emergency Act and thereby reinstate the full range of political freedoms guaranteed in their constitution. The new act would be effective upon the determination of the verification commission that conditions of the treaty "are being met by other countries."

"Wait a minute," I said. "What I think I hear you saying is that amnesty, the repeal of military law, and the restoration of constitutional rights will be effective when the international commission says that the United States has stopped sending military weapons to the Contras. Is that right?"

"That is correct, Mr. Speaker," declared Tinoco. "The twenty-three articles of our constitution which were suspended when we had to adopt the state of emergency will be fully and legally restored."

"As I think you know," I reminded them, "Congress has not authorized any more military money to the Contras, but we're sending them some humanitarian assistance."

"We don't mind the humanitarian assistance at all," replied Tinoco, "but we are concerned that the CIA continues to supply weapons and other military hardware. From August 7, when we signed the Esquipulas agreement, through October 31, there were 137 supply flights."

I asked how he knew the planes carried weapons, not food and medicine. Tinoco said his people had it on good authority that the transports were laden with weapons. He said that 128 of the flights originated in Honduras and 9 in Costa Rica. In addition to these, he stated that the CIA had conducted 136 reconnaissance flights, all personally observed and reported by Nicaraguan ground forces. While doubting the accuracy of the figures, I had no way to disprove them. So I changed the subject.

"Today is November 5," I pointed out. "This is the day the cease-fire was supposed to begin. There has been talk of the need for an intermediary to negotiate and oversee the cease-fire. President Arias has suggested, and I firmly support his suggestion, that the ideal intermediary would be Cardinal Obando, if you can prevail upon him to assume the responsibility. What is your reaction to that?"

Tünnermann broke in to emphasize that indeed there should be an intermediary. He insisted that his government was ready to begin the cease-fire negotiations "immediately" through a proper mediator. He paused briefly continuing. "But it cannot be the cardinal."

"Why not?"

"There are domestic reasons," he said. "Internal reasons in Nicaragua. He would not be acceptable to the public."

"That's ridiculous!" I blurted. "It seems to me that you're not serious. His Eminence is the most respected man in all of Nicaragua, maybe in all of Central America. Everybody respects him for his honesty. He may have enemies that I don't know about, but there is nobody who doesn't respect him. Nobody else could give half as much credibility to your negotiations. Surely both sides trust him as an honest man. You may have some other reason for not wanting him, but to say that he is not acceptable to the public—well, that just isn't believable!"

It was clear from the expression on their faces that the three emissaries had not expected me to become so agitated by their rejection of Obando. The force of my disappointment, in fact, surprised me. In a calmer voice, I continued. "Don't you see what I'm saying? If you aren't willing to engage a credible intermediary, a person of stature, someone who would be acceptable to the other side, then a lot of people in the hemisphere will conclude that you aren't behaving in good faith. In addition to that, you lose credibility here in Congress. People will think you are not serious about a real cease-fire and real restitution of political freedom."

I knew I was coming down hard on these guests, but I was determined to make them understand the importance of this decision. Finally, Victor Tinoco said, "But I am authorized by my government to declare that we *do* want an intermediary who will be credible and acceptable—and I am further authorized to ask *you*, Mr. Speaker, if you will be the intermediary."

I thought I had misunderstood him. "What did you just say?"

He repeated the invitation.

"Me?" I asked. "I *couldn't* be the intermediary. That wouldn't work at all. You honor me by making such a suggestion, but there are many reasons why I couldn't serve in that position. The principal one is that I have a full-time job right here in this office, trying to manage the House of Representatives. We have an enormous set of problems right now. I'm responsible for trying to solve those problems—the budget, welfare reform, the homeless, right here in America. You see, I couldn't possibly leave these problems and go down there and spend a week or more at a time. It simply wouldn't work!"

"Perhaps both we and the Contras could arrange to meet with you here," Tinoco insisted.

"No, no. I *have* a job," I explained. "I can't do justice to all that is required of me now. Furthermore, I wouldn't be qualified. My Spanish isn't good enough to serve in that capacity. You need someone who understands all the nuances of the language. You also need somebody who knows the region better than I do. Suppose both sides agreed to a cease-fire in place. One side might say, 'We control everything up to that ridge.' Then suppose the intermediary goes back and runs into an argument with the other side saying, 'We control everything down to that river.' I wouldn't know who was telling the truth. You need to have someone who understands the terrain, and the language, and the people. It seems to me you need a Central American, preferably a Nicaraguan."

"Nobody in Nicaragua can do it," Tinoco insisted. "Everything has become so polarized that any Nicaraguan is suspect by one side or the other."

If they really had to go outside the region, I suggested, they would need an experienced diplomat, better yet someone with experience in mediation and arbitration. I said if it were to be a North American, and I really didn't think it should be, they might think of someone like Phil Habib, or maybe Sol Linowitz, or perhaps Paul Warnke. I thought of Lawrence Pezzullo and wondered silently about other ambassadors.

Wilson Morris, my quiet and productive aide who sat in on many of my meetings with foreign dignitaries, and almost never spoke during them, leaned over and suggested, "What about Jimmy Carter?"

After the meeting ended and I was en route to other appointments, I thought that a Jimmy Carter–Gerald Ford team would be ideal if indeed it were proper to involve North Americans. I made a note to call former President Carter when I returned to my office and ask his advice on the matter. But I felt sure that neither he nor former President Ford would want to involve themselves unless President Reagan asked them to.

That afternoon I got a call from Miguel D'Escoto, the Sandinista foreign minister. "I've had a report of the meeting this morning," he began, "and I fully understand why you cannot do what was requested."

I felt relieved. At least someone understood. But then he continued. "Why don't you undertake the assignment in name," he said, "and then you can appoint whomever you will to come down and perform the actual work?"

It was a bit exasperating that apparently the Nicaraguans did not understand my limitation under our system. I tried to explain. "Look, Miguel," I said, "I'm a lawmaker. I'm not a diplomat. This would not be compatible with my duties. My responsibility is to the legislative branch. You want another kind of person. There is no reason why you would want me as mediator."

"The reason we would want you is because you have great credibility down here."

"I appreciate your saying that. But you don't want a *norteamericano*. You don't want someone from the U.S. government running that negotiation. That's too much like Yankee imperialism, and that's the very thing you *don't* want!"

"You are the one person that Central Americans do not associate with imperialism," the foreign minister explained. "People in these five countries believe that you are fair."

I thanked him again for the compliment but told him emphatically that I just could not under any circumstances be the mediator.

Finally, he said, "Well, let me come up and talk with you. I will come to your office. I will be in Washington tomorrow night for the OAS meeting that starts on Monday. May I come by and talk? Perhaps we could explore some other ways to conduct the cease-fire talks."

"Okay, Miguel. Come ahead. I'll be glad to see you. But please understand that I can do no more than suggest. You know my suggestion. I think there is one man on whom both sides could agree, and that is Cardinal Obando y Bravo."

"I know your feeling about that," he said. "Let us pray to God that something may happen which will help us work this out to a successful conclusion."

I told him I was leaving town Friday for a trip to the West Coast and would not be back until Sunday night.

"I will come by your office first thing Monday and will wait until you can see me—and I must ask you one other thing, Mr. Speaker. Our president wants to see you. Can President Ortega come up and talk with you? He'll make a special trip to see you," he said.

"He would be welcome if he wishes to come," I responded. "Of course he may come by. I'll be glad to see him, but please explain to him that I cannot take part in any negotiating. I want the process to work. I want the bloodshed to stop. I want to see political liberty restored in your country and elsewhere in our hemisphere. To the extent that I can help, I will, but I still think the cardinal is your very best choice. If not he, you might think of someone like José Figueres or maybe talk to Raul Alfonsin."

One additional reason for trying to get Obando to mediate the cease-fire, I thought as I hung up, was the respect he enjoyed within the Reagan administration. I realized that any of the others whose names had come to me might be suspect to the Elliott Abrams wing in the State Department. The White House would be under pressure to trash any agreement reached by a mediator whom the militant rightists found unacceptable. Even they, as far as I could tell, trusted the stocky little cardinal.

On Friday, I got a happy surprise. I had scheduled an active West Coast weekend—speaking appearances for colleagues in Washington State and California, and a televised guest appearance for Reverend Robert Schuller at his Crystal Cathedral on Sunday. As my plane arrived in Seattle, I was handed an urgent message to call Wilson Morris. Wilson told me President Ortega had just announced in Managua that he was asking Cardinal Obando to mediate the cease-fire. The cardinal had not formally accepted but was requesting permission from his episcopacy to explore the offer. This news was wonderfully hopeful. The Contras surely would not decline to participate in talks moderated by Obando. The offer showed new flexibility on the part of Ortega. Apparently my entreaty had made an impact. I supposed that the White House would be pleased with these developments.

The New York Times, in fact, published a story on November 7 by Special Correspondent Neil A. Lewis with an odd twist on reported White House reaction. "Reagan Administration officials said today that they were pleased by Nicaragua's willingness to negotiate," according to the story, "because it enhanced the political stature of the American-backed rebels." Unnamed officials thought the development "could set the stage for giving additional military aid to the rebels" if the Sandinistas failed to comply. Apparently, as I had earlier feared, there was an element that publicly welcomed the talks but hoped for their breakdown as a prelude to resuming the war.

On Sunday morning I spoke at Dr. Schuller's eleven o'clock service about the chances for peace, both in Central America and with the Soviet Union. Careful to avoid any partisan implication, I told of my trip to the Soviet Union during the preceding Easter recess as head of a bipartisan House delegation. We had met for two hours with President Mikhail Gorbachev. At the conclusion of that meeting, Gorbachev had asked if I would like to speak, via nationwide television, to the Soviet people and answer questions posed by a moderator. I did this in a live broadcast on Good Friday, April 17. Anxious for feedback from average people, I invited personal letters and offered to send each who wrote a small lapel pin featuring the flags of our two countries, like the one provided to members of our delegation by the U.S. State Department. In the next few weeks I received almost three thousand letters from all sorts of people in various parts of that sprawling country. Fully 90 percent of them were friendly and supportive of an end to the arms race. That worship service at the Crystal Cathedral was taped and broadcast nationally three weeks later. This would bring a great many letters of encouragement from Americans interested in the prospects of peace in Central America as well as with the Soviet Union.

Miguel D'Escoto came early on Monday to my office in the Capitol. He said his government's reconciliation group had set up 256 neighborhood "peace commissions," headed for the most part by local clergy. Some 620 people, he reported, had accepted amnesty. He told me of his and Ortega's talks with the cardinal. The prelate had not decided whether to undertake the role of cease-fire intermediary. D'Escoto said Cardinal Obando expressed to him a desire to talk with me before reaching a final decision. I assured him I would be pleased to see the cardinal at any time.

D'Escoto said President Ortega would like to come by my office on Wednesday afternoon, that Cardinal Obando would be arriving in Washington Thursday night, and he wondered if I would be willing to meet with the two of them on Friday morning.

I explained that I would have to leave early Friday afternoon for Fort Worth. My local supporters had scheduled our biennial fundraiser for that evening and had been working for weeks on arrangements. But if Obando wanted to see me prior to noon on Friday, I would make myself available.

Then D'Escoto tried to resume the conversation of the week before. He wondered if I could appoint a congressional group to monitor the peace talks. I said there were limits to our involvement. "That's a job for diplomats," I said. He stressed again the often-stated desire of his government to normalize relations with our country. He told me that in October of 1983 he had come to Washington with a proposed peace treaty in hand to show to Secretary Shultz.

According to his account, he had an appointment to talk with the secretary but was kept waiting for three days and then never permitted to see Shultz.

The day I met with D'Escoto, November 9, President Reagan spoke to the OAS foreign ministers and offered what appeared to be a major concession. He said the United States was ready to negotiate security issues with Nicaragua. It would be done in a regional setting, however, in the presence of representatives from the four other Central American countries. Reagan cuffed the Sandinista government for past transgressions but offered the following olive branch: "When serious negotiations between the Sandinistas and the freedom fighters, under the mediation of Cardinal Obando, are under way, Secretary Shultz will be ready to meet jointly with the foreign ministers of all five Central American nations, including the Sandinistas' representatives."

The next step, obviously, was to persuade Obando to assume the mediator's role.

The season's first snow began to fall early on Wednesday, November 11. Driving to the Capitol on the George Washington Parkway was painfully slow. Fortunate, I thought, that it was Veterans' Day and many government workers would take the day off. By evening there was about twelve inches of snow. Meetings at the OAS were proceeding on schedule, I was told. Ortega was to speak that morning. Shultz had addressed the organization on Tuesday, elaborating on Reagan's theme of Monday. Shultz emphasized that the United States would indeed be prepared to meet with representatives of the Sandinista government if they observed their obligations under the Guatemala accords.

Daniel Ortega, in his speech that morning, vowed that Nicaragua was "ready to comply 100 percent" with the agreements. His country, he reiterated, had asked the cardinal to mediate the cease-fire. He stressed the eagerness of Nicaraguans to meet with the U.S. government. "Nicaragua is not . . . [an] enemy of the United States," Ortega proclaimed. "The United States is the one that has been waging war against the people of Nicaragua."

Two things struck me about Daniel Ortega when he came to my office that snowy November afternoon. The first was that he had matured in the five years since I had last talked with him. He was wearing a gray suit and a brown sweater vest. I had never before seen Ortega in anything but the olive-drab fatigues he always wore in

Nicaragua. He had a haircut and appeared to have trimmed his unruly trademark mustache. My second impression was of his continued unsophistication, even naïveté, despite all his exposure on the world stage. He marveled over the snow. It was the first snowfall he had ever seen, he said. Then he grinned and confessed that it was his forty-second birthday.

Ortega was accompanied by Ambassador Tünnermann and Miguel D'Escoto, whose help I needed to decipher their leader's rapid, staccato Spanish. He was worried about President Reagan, fearful of what he called our chief executive's "obsession" with Nicaragua, apprehensive that Reagan would not let the Contra leadership agree to anything short of the physical removal of the country's public officials and their replacement by people of Reagan's personal choosing.

"That isn't going to happen," I said. "Nobody's talking about anything like that. The Contra directorate in my presence has disavowed any interest in power sharing or forcing a coalition government. What they do insist upon is fair and free elections. In these, they want the right to participate equally, with equal access to the media, and your agreement in advance to honor the results of those elections. That's what the Esquipulas agreement is all about."

"We will do those things!" Ortega said impatiently, his eyes flashing. "We have said repeatedly that we will do those things! We invite international inspection of our elections. We invite the OAS, the UN, the United States, anybody who will send observers. We want the world to know that our election is honest. If the other side wins, I will turn over the presidency to them. I have made this clear! But Mr. Reagan is not interested in elections. Three years ago he talked Arturo Cruz out of running for president. He would not send observers to our elections in 1984, although other countries did. And everyone who came said our election was fair and our count was honest. The opposition got 38 percent of the vote. But Mr. Reagan was not satisfied. He says he wants to make us cry 'Uncle!' "

"That was several years ago, Daniel." I leaned forward, looked him in the eye, and deliberately lowered my voice. "Things have changed. My country is committed to the Esquipulas plan. Stick with that. Get a cease-fire in place. Start sincere talks with the resistance. Make peace. Mr. Reagan was answering questions at a press conference when he made that 'Cry uncle' remark. If the truth were told, he probably regrets having said it just that way. He didn't mean it the way it sounded. I'm reasonably sure of that."

I had been watching his eyes. I could tell that he wanted to believe me but was still skeptical. The destruction of communications and water supplies in his country, the economic embargo, the mining of his nation's harbors, the six years of U.S.-financed bloodshed had left deep scars of disbelief. And some of Reagan's comments at the OAS two days earlier had opened fresh wounds. That morning, in the same forum, Ortega had responded angrily that "the government of the United States must contribute [to the peace effort] because what it is doing at this moment does not contribute." He cited the alleged 140 CIA supply flights of weapons to the "mercenary forces" over the past ninety days.

Finally, I said, "Mr. Reagan is not going to be president forever, Daniel. But he is president for the rest of this year and all of next year. You simply have to recognize that fact. You can't expect to wait until someone replaces Mr. Reagan in office before beginning the cease-fire. I honestly believe President Reagan will have to respect whatever agreements you and the Contras are able to reach, so long as the end result is a free and peaceful electoral process open to all Nicaraguans."

Ortega asked if I could see Cardinal Obando on Friday. The cardinal wanted to come by and talk with me about taking on the mediator's role.

"Of course, he may do that," I replied. "He's welcome to come whenever he will. As I told Miguel D'Escoto, I'll try to make myself available at anytime on Friday morning."

David Bonior and I talked briefly after the Nicaraguans left. Ortega had asked if he could drop by again tomorrow, Thursday, and bring some materials with him. Bonior and I decided we should have at least staff representation from other leadership offices, including Senator Robert Byrd's office.

When Ortega came the next day, Ed King of Senator Byrd's staff joined us. As a retired military officer and a close student of Latin American affairs, King had Byrd's ear and enjoyed the respect of other senators. Also present were Kathy Gille, who followed Central American matters for David Bonior, Wilson Morris of my staff, and Richard Peña. In addition to Miguel D'Escoto and Ambassador Tünnermann, Ortega this time brought Victor Tinoco and Sophia Clarke.

The Nicaraguan leader unrolled a large map of his country on which three irregular circles had been drawn. These were areas, embracing some 10,000 square kilometers, in which he proposed that the Contra military forces could take sanctuary during the cease-fire. Next he handed out sheets of paper on which had been copied a ten-point plan. He said he would offer this to the cardinal as a suggested starting point for discussions with the Contra leaders. His mood was more conciliatory. "This is a *proposal*," he said. "That is the important word. It is not an ultimatum. It is a proposal. We think it is fair, but we are willing to discuss changes. If the Contras do not like it, let them tell us how they would alter it. We will consider whatever they say, but we think this is fair."

The proposal was fairly short, only one page. D'Escoto began reading it, point by point, to the group. Early in the document was a paragraph alleging that the U.S. government had tried to "sabotage" the peace process. I interrupted.

"It isn't really our prerogative to tell you what you should say in your cease-fire proposal," I remarked. "But I just don't see any point in this language accusing my country of sabotaging your effort. In the first place, it isn't going to make you any friends in this country. Furthermore, I don't think the Contras would agree to that language."

"Let's just drop that paragraph," Ortega agreed.

The rest of the proposal seemed mostly constructive. It dealt with the terms of a cease-fire, a means of monitoring compliance, a method by which the mediator could talk to each side in turn, and in somewhat broad language, amnesty for the Contras in the context of their reintegration into the civil life of Nicaragua.

David Bonior spoke up to suggest that the terms of amnesty should be more precisely defined and that a more specific commitment should be made to releasing prisoners held in Nicaragua's jails. "Not only the Contras but the citizens of the United States are interested in that, and they are sure to be insistent on a firm and unequivocal statement in this regard."

I suggested that everyone would be reassured by an unmistakable commitment to lift the state of emergency once the official verification commission certified that the mandates of Esquipulas were being complied with. To our mild surprise, the Sandinista leaders agreed without argument or hesitation. "We will simply add another point— point number eleven—to incorporate the suggestions made by the Speaker and by Mr. Bonior," announced Ortega.

D'Escoto asked if he might consult with Wilson Morris and Richard Peña in drafting the additional language. At this point I began to wonder just how far we should go in trying to perfect the document.

It was, after all, *their* proposal, not ours. But these emissaries were so unexpectedly accommodating it almost seemed they would let us change it in just about any way we chose to specify. I was eager to do anything and everything I could, within proper bounds, to make it work. But just what were those bounds? Clearly, I said, I was not competent to pass judgment on geographic lines of the cease-fire. I did not want anyone to infer that our discussion in any way implied approval of the proposed cease-fire boundaries.

There was a reference in the written proposal that might be interpreted to sanction firing on any forces discovered outside the delineated zones within fifteen days after the cease-fire went into effect. Wilson Morris objected to that provision, and his objection was seconded by Ed King. They suggested that questions of violation, rather than being invitations to open fire, be referred to the verification commission or to the mediator. The Sandinistas offered no major resistance to this. Ultimately, we all shook hands in the hope that this would be a useful step in the path to peace.

As soon as the Nicaraguans left, I was plunged into another maelstrom. Majority Leader Tom Foley, accompanied by House Budget Chairman Bill Gray, came to report on snags they had encountered in budget reconciliation talks with the Senate and the administration. We soon were joined by Leon Panetta of California and Pat Williams of Montana, who had special responsibilities in the budget negotiations for agriculture and education, respectively. Tom Foley, whom I had asked to take personal charge of the heterogeneous collection of bright and determined House leaders involved in the budget summit, was a paragon of patience. Often, my own nerves frayed and exposed like pieces of electric wire with the insulation worn away, I marveled at the outward calm and imperturbability of this big friendly man from Washington.

The negotiators, working feverishly to narrow differences and tie down agreements on dozens of unresolved issues in the big catchall spending bill, had been hard at it for weeks. We talked of the four or five remaining sticking points. I took down the names of four members to whom I would need to make individual pleas for personal concessions aimed at nailing down an agreement. Trying to be a congressional leader, I mused, was like trying to play a game of chess and a game of basketball simultaneously. At the moment, negotiations in Nicaragua seemed more amenable to solution than those on Capitol Hill.

Just as the budget negotiators were leaving, Secretary George Shultz arrived for a 2:30 P.M. appointment he had made that morning. I began to tell him of my visit with Ortega but discovered that his own immediate interest was in the ongoing budget struggle. There just wasn't enough money to spread around, and a whole range of foreign operations for which Shultz had responsibility was being pinched. He had come to ask for my help in restoring some cuts in several State Department programs. It was not a new discussion between us. I sympathized with his position and wanted to help.

"As we discussed earlier this year," the embattled secretary began, "the foreign operations of our government are getting the short end of the stick. Things for which we were able to spend $27 billion annually just a few years ago have been whittled down to a total of about $18 billion this year. That's a darn big cut! We've had to close USIA [U.S. Information Agency] libraries, reduce exchange programs, almost eliminate foreign aid except for three or four countries. We've closed chanceries in some important cities, and I don't know how we're going to keep our embassies operating effectively unless we get some help in this budget."

"I agree with you, Mr. Secretary, and I sympathize with your position," I said. "What an irony! We're spending $18 billion on the *positive* side of U.S. foreign policy and $300 billion on the *negative* side—arms and ammunition. That would be like a pro football coach paying $300,000 salaries for defensive players and only $18,000 salaries for those on his offensive team. He wouldn't put many points on the scoreboard."

I made a note to talk with David Obey of Wisconsin, our tough-minded House subcommittee chairman, and with Appropriations Chairman Jamie Whitten. "I'll do what I can, Mr. Secretary, but I don't have to tell you it's a hard sell!"

With just a few minutes left before Shultz was due for a similar meeting on the Senate side, I tried to tell him briefly of my discussion with Ortega. "I'm told that Cardinal Obando wants to see me, and I expect to be seeing him tomorrow. I'm sure you agree that his taking on the responsibility of intermediary in the cease-fire is the best possible thing for all concerned."

"Yes, I think that would be fine," he agreed. "But Americans are not participants in that negotiation."

Shultz was getting his papers together preparing to leave. His mind was on the budget problems. What I understood him to say was that, yes, we hoped Cardinal Obando would agree to conduct the cease-fire, but that it was between the Sandinistas and the Contras. America was not a party to it. If he was trying to suggest that I should not talk with Obando or try to persuade him to take on the mediator's role, I'm afraid I missed the point entirely. I supposed the cardinal's participation was critically important to us all.

As he was leaving, Secretary Shultz turned around with an after-thought. "I almost forgot," he said. "I wanted to ask your opinion, personally and confidentially, about another matter. As you know, Mr. Gorbachev is coming here in just about one month. There has been some expression of interest in his being invited to address a joint session of Congress. What would be your reaction to that?"

"That's a White House call, Mr. Secretary," I replied, remembering the unexpected flap over my invitation to President Arias. "We'll cooperate fully in any course the administration wishes to pursue. In my opinion, Gorbachev enjoys considerable approval among the American people. If you request it of us, we'll issue him a formal invitation. I believe I can assure you that we'd receive him with courtesy and decorum."

Little did I dream that within less than a week conservative Republican House members would be publicly uttering ugly threats to the White House, vowing to stage a noisy walkout before the television cameras if the Russian leader was invited. Deeply embarrassed by the headline-hungry partisans of its right flank, the White House ultimately had a spokesman call my office to say it would not be pursuing any request for a joint session.

After Shultz left, I started making calls to colleagues in an effort to piece together several budget agreements. Suddenly I looked at the clock and realized how quickly the day was passing. It was November 12, our wedding anniversary, and I had not even picked up a card for Betty. In frantic haste, I summoned my driver Lionel to take me to Trover's on Pennsylvania Avenue. There I picked out an appropriate card to present to my bride at the dinner table that evening, and hurried back to the Capitol in time for my appointment with the Contra leaders.

Wilson Morris popped in briefly to tell me I had been requested by the papal nuncio to come to the official residence on Massachusetts Avenue to meet with Cardinal Obando y Bravo at ten o'clock the following morning.

"I understand the cardinal intends to be in town for only a few hours," said Wilson, "and it'll be a convenience to him if you can meet him there rather than in the Capitol."

"Call and say I'll be glad to come," I said.

The four Contra leaders as they walked into my office presented a visual contrast to Ortega. They were better groomed, more polished, and self-assured. At least three of them were. Aristedes Sánchez, who spoke no English, sometimes seemed a bit self-conscious. But Alfonso Robelo, Alfredo César, and Adolfo Calero were accustomed by now to dealing with U.S. officialdom. While Ortega had come in a tweed suit and sweater, these three were stylishly attired in freshly pressed two-piece suits.

When I told them of my visit with Ortega and my expected meeting with Cardinal Obando the next morning, they affirmed their readiness to negotiate. They also confirmed my earlier impression that they were not interested in discussions over power sharing. When I broached the question of cease-fire zones, César stressed the need to make certain that lanes of supply and resupply remained open during the cessation of hostilities.

It seemed to me that these were realists. They tacitly acknowledged that the time for military aid would be drawing to a close if fighting ended and the cease-fire held while negotiators made progress on the long-term solution—free elections in a democratic environment. The military solution Reagan's right wing had sought, the physical overthrow of the Sandinista regime, would be foreclosed.

Again I sought to reaffirm their endorsement of Obando as the mediator. Before talking with him, I wanted to be certain that he was still acceptable to the resistance leaders. Calero reiterated the long-standing party line about preferring to sit down directly with the Sandinistas rather than talking through any intermediary. "I understand, Adolfo," I said. "That's always been your position and that day will have to come. But you aren't going to let that stand in the way of taking this first necessary step, are you?"

Calero and Sánchez seemed uncertain, but Robelo and César both spoke up immediately to affirm their readiness to begin talks if the cardinal could be persuaded to take on the role of intermediary. I supposed they would leave my office and go directly to the State Department to disclose to Elliott Abrams or someone in his shop the details of our conversation. Dave Bonior and Wilson Morris, who sat through this meeting with me, were certain that a trip to the State

Department had become a routine sequel to the directorate's meeting with House leadership. They resented that, but I didn't. I felt it was a useful way to keep all our lines of communication open.

"Wish me well in my talk with the cardinal tomorrow," I said as they left. They nodded enthusiastically, signaling assent. "Buena suerte!" (Good luck!) said Alfonso Robelo.

Later, after I had left for my anniversary dinner with Betty, Ed Fox called to remonstrate with Richard Peña. Fox was congressional liaison for the State Department, a friendly and competent go-between. I always liked Ed, had taken a number of trips with him, including at least two to Central America. A man of slight build, balding prematurely and with friendly brown eyes, Ed got along well with most of us on the Hill. Richard later reported the conversation to me.

"Why didn't your boss tell the secretary about the meeting with Cardinal Obando tomorrow?" Fox asked him.

"He did tell Secretary Shultz he was expecting to see the cardinal," Richard Peña replied. "He didn't know exactly when and where the meeting would be. The Speaker didn't receive the call from the papal nuncio's office until after the secretary had been here and left."

If I had known anyone in the State Department was complaining to Ed Fox, I would have been on the phone immediately to talk with George Shultz. As it was, I went to dinner happy with the day's events and looking forward to the next morning's meeting. Later that evening, I had a call at home from a friend named Dennis Neil. His message was alarming: "Did you know that Secretary Shultz is refusing to meet with Cardinal Obando because he is meeting with you and Daniel Ortega tomorrow morning?"

"Where did you get that?" I stammered in disbelief.

"From Popio Laghi, the papal nuncio. I'm with him right now," said Neil. I could not believe what he was telling me. I asked to talk with the nuncio. He confirmed the essence of the report.

"Was it George Shultz who told you that, Monsignor?" I asked.

"No, it was not he," replied the nuncio.

"I thought not," I said. "It doesn't sound like something he would say. It sounds like someone else, perhaps like Elliott Abrams."

"That is exactly right," said Laghi. He confirmed that it was Abrams who had called him.

This was infuriating. If Secretary Shultz did not want me to talk with the cardinal about mediating a cease-fire, he had passed up several good opportunities to tell me, I thought. I had told him about it that very afternoon, and he had offered no direct objection. I knew that Abrams resented my efforts to keep the peace plan on track, but I didn't think he would go to the extreme of trying to manipulate the papal representative into calling off the meeting that the cardinal had requested.

I took a deep breath. "Monsignor," I said, "I really don't have to come over there tomorrow. If you think it would be best, I could simply bow out of the meeting. What's your judgment? I want to be helpful if I can be, but I don't want to create problems. Should I come or not?"

"Yes, by all means, I think you should come. You are a catalyst in this matter," said Monsignor Laghi.

Immediately I called George Shultz and told him what I had heard. "I just thought you should know of this, George, and I was very eager to learn if you actually had any such feelings as were attributed—not meeting with Obando if he met with me. I simply couldn't imagine your saying anything of that type."

Shultz replied, "Well you know, of course, that I would not say anything of that kind, Jim. I would never tell anyone that if he saw you, he could not see me. But what we have said is that if the cardinal is used for propaganda purposes by Ortega, we would rather not see him on this trip."

I told Shultz that I had been invited to the papal nuncio's residence for ten o'clock in the morning. The invitation had been issued by the nuncio at the cardinal's request, as I understood it. I thought it was important to persuade Obando if possible to undertake the delicate task of negotiating. I went into greater detail about my conversations with both Ortega and the Contra leaders and said that I believed for once both sides were ready to start serious talks through the good offices of Obando if he could be convinced to take on the job.

"You are free, of course, to see whomever you wish, Mr. Speaker," Shultz said. "As you know, administration policy has been to freeze Ortega out of any official discussions with us. We have simply refused to see him. What worries us about the meeting tomorrow is that we think he might use it for a propaganda advantage."

There it was again. Our president and our State Department met with Gorbachev. They met with the leaders of Communist China and with other communist heads of state. They met Pinochet of Chile. But they drew the line at Ortega. They wouldn't see him, wouldn't hear him. How do you make peace if you don't sit down and talk?

"George, I told them I would come. I know they're expecting me. I think one of us needs to be there to hear what is said and to try to keep things on track. Maybe even to keep Ortega honest. Unless you have a strong personal objection, I think I should go."

And so I went. Wilson Morris, Richard Peña, and I rode together the next morning in the Speaker's car, out Rock Creek Parkway and up the ramp to Massachusetts Avenue. It was a beautiful day. The sun was out and only little patches remained of the snow. The papal nuncio's residence, across the avenue from the stately grounds that had once been the Naval Observatory and where the vice president now resided, loomed in sight.

As we entered the circular driveway, we were suddenly surrounded by cameramen and reporters crowding the entrance to the handsome building. We entered and were ushered up the stairway to a conference room on the second floor overlooking the avenue. The others were there when we arrived at 10:00 A.M. We wasted little time in pleasantries, although I was genuinely glad to see Cardinal Obando. There was something square and solid about him. Despite his lack of physical height, he had an imposing presence. I thought of a comment my father had made many years ago: "Some personalities say 'Here I come.' This is one that says 'Here I am.' "

We sat around a long table, Ortega at one end and the cardinal at the other. I sat beside Monsignor Laghi to Obando's right and Ortega's left. Across the table was Paul Warnke. I supposed he had been invited by the papal nuncio. I summoned Richard Peña for a hurried, whispered question: "I want to be sure I have the title right. I do call him 'Your Eminence,' don't I?" Peña replied, "That's right."

I began with a brief comment to the cardinal about the importance of the moment and the unusual opportunity it provided for service. I said I hoped he would undertake the role being offered him.

The cardinal went immediately to the heart of the matter. He asked the nature of the role itself—whether he would be serving as an actual arbiter or simply a messenger. Ortega's response was not definitive. I stepped in to suggest that for this to work the cardinal would have to be a mediator with the power of originating proposals, and not merely a messenger boy carrying answers back and forth. He would have to be given the latitude to make creative suggestions and expect that those suggestions would be respected, if not always embraced, by both sides. "If I were the cardinal, I would insist on that," I said. Ortega finally nodded assent, saying that would be satisfactory with him. I could tell that this was the answer Obando needed to hear.

Next, the cardinal inquired about the scope of the dialogue. Was he being asked merely to ratify geographic metes and bounds and the timing of a cease-fire, or would the dialogue get into substantive issues like democratization and human rights? Ortega thought the first task had to be the cease-fire. He said it was the necessary prelude to discussions in depth. I mentioned my conversations with the Contras, suggested that they would be interested in guarantees of their freedom of movement and access to communications even during the cease-fire. In addition, however, as the talks matured, I felt sure they would have to deal with political liberty in its totality. Not power sharing, but elections.

The conversation turned to talk of where the meetings should be held and who should be appointed to staff those meetings. It was apparent that President Ortega was trying to lay the grounds for holding them in Washington and staffing them with U.S. personnel, maybe enlisting the help of veteran peace negotiator Warnke as well as senior congressional staffers. I could tell that this raised questions in the cardinal's mind.

Obando said he had some ideas about whom he would like to have assist him. Clearly that was important to him, and he looked at me for a response. Finally, I looked directly toward Ortega and said: "It seems to me that if the cardinal is asked to take on this enormously important job, he must be invested with all the moral authority he needs to carry it out. He should be the one to select the site for meetings and issue invitations. He surely should be accorded the right to choose whomever he wishes to assist him in the endeavor. Congressional personnel probably should not be directly involved. Anything any of the rest of us might do should be, I think, at the cardinal's request."

This was the heart of the matter. If Ortega agreed, he would not be able to surround the cardinal with people of his or any other's choosing. After only brief discussion, Ortega agreed.

That was about all I could do, I decided. I had helped direct the conversation in such a way that Cardinal Obando's principal concerns were resolved in his favor. He said he would want a letter from the government, signed by Ortega, and another from the Contra directorate formally asking him to serve as mediator and outlining the bounds of his authority in the terms we had discussed. He didn't actually say he would do the job, but the expression on his sometimes impassive face seemed positive. Behind the thick-lensed glasses, he smiled.

It was a good time for me to take my leave. I explained I had some work to do at the Capitol before departing at noon for Texas. I thanked Monsignor Laghi for his hospitality, apologized to all present for my departure, and shook hands warmly with the stocky cardinal. "Blessed are the peacemakers," I said.

"Son los hijos del Dios" (They are the children of God), replied Cardinal Obando.

The others walked to the door with me and waved from the portico as I prepared to get in the car. Paul Warnke asked if he might hitch a ride to his office en route to the Capitol. Newsmen pressed around, insisting that I give them a statement.

"It isn't the millennium yet," I said, "but there is movement in the right direction. I see some evidence of good faith on the part of both the Sandinistas and the Contras." Then I left. I did not touch on any of the details of our talks. Better that I leave that to the principals.

On the way back to the Capitol, I turned to Paul Warnke. "I don't think he wants any technical help from us in negotiating the cease-fire. Do you agree?"

"That's exactly the way I read it," he replied.

We were in high spirits as we boarded the plane, dubbed the Cowtown Clipper, for Texas. A lot of people from Washington, including a large contingent of my colleagues, were going to Fort Worth with me for the weekend events held in my honor, at which I would raise funds to assist colleagues in their 1988 reelection efforts. There would be a dinner at the convention center that evening attended by about a thousand people, an informal barbecue for local citizens at Will Rogers Coliseum Saturday afternoon. Despite a touch of fatigue, I was feeling great. Peace seemed nearly within grasp. My spirits soared.

Forgotten for the moment was the date. It was Friday the 13th. Trouble was brewing.

When we landed at Meacham Field in Fort Worth, people from my office ran up the boarding stairs to tell me they were being swamped by press requests. Dan Rather wanted to interview me live in one hour for his evening news. Tom Brokaw would be on the air in five minutes, and arrangements had already been made for me to take his questions from an office in the terminal building there at Meacham. And there were others who wanted to talk. Apparently someone in the State Department had been criticizing my presence at the meeting in the papal embassy. What would I say?

I agreed to the interviews with NBC and CBS. Brokaw wanted to know if I thought I should have permission from the State Department before talking with foreigners on a matter of this kind. I mentally tried to calculate how many dozens of heads of state I had met, how many scores, maybe even hundreds, of conversations I'd had with foreign leaders, always in the interest of U.S. policy as I understood it. Never had I criticized a U.S. president in the presence of foreigners. But did I need *permission?* The suggestion was downright demeaning. I said the lawmaking branch was not "subservient" to the executive and that I didn't need "permission" to talk with anyone.

By the time I reached the Mallick Building in downtown Fort Worth, which housed the remote broadcasting setup for the local CBS affiliate, I was calmer and had thought out a more patiently worded statement. Brokaw's question had caught me off guard. I had let it upset me and was afraid that that had been noticeable.

The dinner that evening went like clockwork. Dick Gephardt said a few words in behalf of the contingent of colleagues from outside Texas. The enthusiasm was contagious. Everyone seemed joyous that peace was coming at last to Central America.

The next morning I had breakfast with a number of the out-of-towners. John Silber, president of Boston University, a friend of mine since he was a dean at the University of Texas, offered an invitation to his campus if I needed a forum in which to state my views on the propriety of congressional involvement in foreign affairs. I thanked him, but decided I would use the afternoon crowd to answer the attacks being launched against me. Obviously, someone was orchestrating those attacks.

Some criticism came from identifiable sources, although the most unfair remarks were from unidentified people. State Department and White House Spokesmen Charles Redman and Marlin Fitzwater led the attack. Their principal theme was that I was "interfering" in foreign policy, "usurping" the role of the executive branch. But other quoted comments were more personal. One unnamed source called me an "egomaniac" for presuming the right to work for peace.

That afternoon, before seven thousand people in the tall-ceilinged coliseum in western Fort Worth, in the room where the annual rodeo performance and the Shrine Circus played each year, where the State Golden Gloves Championships were held, I talked of peace. I spelled out the situation of the past few days and asked the audience if they thought I should have gone to the meeting on Massachusetts Avenue. The crowd roared its approval. I felt magnificently well as I left the cavernous coliseum, the hearty approbation of the home folks— those who had known me longest and knew me best—reverberating in my head.

It was late, maybe nine that evening, when a reporter from the Fort Worth *Star-Telegram*, David Montgomery, called. I had seen him at the afternoon event, had talked with him in a brief interview. Now he was on another story. "My editors have an advance on a story which will appear in the *New York Times* tomorrow saying that you and the president really don't like each other. They want me to round that out and do a similar story for tomorrow's *Star-Telegram*." My heart sank. With all the positive comments and reaction from the afternoon's highly successful public event from which to draw a colorful story, the local newspaper would turn instead to what the *Times* was headlining as a "feud" between Reagan and Wright.

The subtitle of the *Times* piece, written by Steven Roberts for Sunday, November 15, was "Issues Remain Unresolved as Powerful Leaders Battle." The relationship between Reagan and me, Roberts wrote, had "deteriorated so badly that it is complicating efforts to arrange compromises on domestic and foreign policy." The story said I had "virtually ignored the White House while consulting with President Daniel Ortega Saavedra of Nicaragua"—no reference to Cardinal Obando or the aim of my consultation. According to unnamed White House aides, the president regarded me as "an egotistical and untrustworthy congressional leader who sees himself incorrectly as a co-equal of the President."

The story went on to quote a joke supposedly making the rounds of the White House: "Where are President Ortega and Nicaraguan rebels going to meet?" The answer: "Speaker Wright's embassy."

The *Times* story referred to my "contempt" for the president's "ideological fixations." It said I considered the president a person with whom you "could not discuss serious issues seriously." The worst part of it was that, in a moment of frustration, I had said that. I wished now that I had not. It served no purpose to make such a statement publicly. And I certainly had never said that I held the president in "contempt." I had told Steve Roberts that Reagan was a delightful raconteur and that I enjoyed his company.

(More than four years later I would read Haynes Johnson's book, *Sleepwalking Through History*, and would come upon a description of President Reagan that could have been taken almost verbatim from my off-the-cuff comments to Steve Roberts. The quote said that Reagan could be thrillingly eloquent but was "not intellectually curious. . . . I think he deeply believes everything he says. That doesn't mean it's always right or that it's all that carefully thought out . . . and he can rationalize why a tax increase is not a tax increase." That analysis, so nearly identical to mine, was attributed in the book by Johnson to my then-colleague Republican Dick Cheney. I had not intended to demean the president, just as Cheney certainly had not. But I wished now, in mid-November of 1987, that I had not even consented to the Roberts interview.)

The *Washington Post* on the same Sunday, November 15, had carried an even more stinging story, right on the top of page one. By John Goshko, it quoted "a senior administration official" as describing my effort to help in the peace process as "unbelievable melodrama" and an "exercise in guerrilla theater" that dealt "a serious setback" to the regional peace process. The official declined to be identified, but Goshko wrote that "he has a major role in planning and executing administration foreign policy." The story spoke of "the anger building inside the administration over the Speaker's efforts to prod it into a more active role in Central America." Goshko noted that I was "in Texas yesterday and could not be reached for comment."

Quite obviously, key elements inside the administration were deeply angered by what was happening in the peace talks. They blamed me in a vicious, highly coordinated attack meant to discredit me.

The unnamed source of Goshko's story falsely claimed that I had "dragged in Paul C. Warnke." But I'd had nothing whatever to do with the invitation list. The story's source, obviously, was Assistant Secretary of State Elliott Abrams, who disliked Warnke and was increasingly demonstrating personal disdain for me. On Monday, in a news conference in the presence of Goshko, I would say when asked about the story, "The unnamed source was not proud enough of his opinions to identify himself with them. I will name him, however. It was Elliott Abrams. The author of the article is present and if he can deny the truth of what I have just said, I will apologize both to him and to Mr. Abrams." John Goshko simply stared at the floor and said nothing.

Perhaps that was unnecessarily abrasive of me. It may have been a breach of some unwritten etiquette. I had made no public attack on Abrams, but I was getting fed up with his sniping at Congress, particularly at me.

My first reaction to the Sunday story was outrage. My second, following immediately on its heels, was to try to patch things up. I called Howard Baker and asked for an appointment Monday morning with the president and Secretary Shultz. I wanted to tell them exactly what had happened at the meeting Friday and to request that we talk directly to one another and not through unnamed sources in the newspaper columns. "If you people have something to say to me, please say it to my face," I told Howard.

Now it was Monday. On my way to an early interview on "Good Morning America," I read a highly critical editorial in the *Washington Post* accusing me of "intervention" in the running of foreign policy. Abrams and the White House hard-liners had done their work, all right. Strange, I thought, that the *Post* would hasten to editorial judgment without hearing any part of my side or giving me a chance to tell my story.

On "Good Morning America" I tried to be conciliatory. Disagree though we might on policy, I did not want an open rift with the White House. That would serve no good purpose. I extended an olive branch. I hoped the president and George Shultz were listening. We would talk personally in a couple of hours.

At the White House Lionel Lawson, my driver, brought the car to the southwest entrance, which is almost always free of reporters. We pulled in as unobtrusively as possible between the White House and the old Executive Office Building. I got out and quickly entered the building. I didn't want to run the press gauntlet before talking directly with President Reagan. I felt certain that once Reagan and Shultz understood what I was trying to achieve—what I believed I *had* achieved—they would approve and appreciate my efforts.

The two were waiting for me in the Oval Office. Reagan was angrier than I had ever seen him, stiff and unbending. He castigated Ortega as a chronic liar and scathingly remarked that in place of the Wright-Reagan plan, "we now have the Wright-Ortega plan."

I braced myself, stunned. That was a needless blow, I thought. I swallowed hard. "Mr. President, I'd like to tell you about that meeting—what I did and why I did it. Some of the things that have been said aren't right, and they aren't healthy."

Reagan was implacable that day. I felt I made no headway with him. Soon he excused himself and left. He had another appointment, he explained. So I turned to George Shultz and tried again: "We say that we want peace, and I believe that I have moved events one small step in that direction." Secretary Shultz indicated that he wasn't sure if it was progress or retreat.

"Whether we agree on that or not," I said, "there's no justification for leaking vicious diatribes against one another. I think we both know it was Elliott Abrams who gave that story to John Goshko. If a member of my staff ever leaked a story like that about *you*, Mr. Secretary, I'd fire his ass." Shultz did not respond.

I wondered why he had so long tolerated, even patronized Abrams. I recalled that day at the new members' reception just the previous spring—it seemed now like an age—when Shultz had called me aside and asked me to see if I couldn't get Abrams back in the good graces of the House committees. In his appearance before the Iran-Contra committee, Abrams had admitted deliberately lying to the Congress in earlier testimony. He hadn't even seemed contrite. "I wasn't authorized to tell the truth," he had said. Several House committees had immediately sent word that Abrams would not be welcome to testify before them in the future except under oath. That was a tough, almost unprecedented action. I had tried to open the door for a new start but without success. When I asked George Crockett, chairman of the Foreign Affairs Subcommittee on Latin America, if he would relent, he had shown me a news story quoting a more recent attack by Abrams on the Congress. My entreaty on that occasion had gone nowhere, and I had reported my findings to Shultz (the complete original note can be found in the appendix).

Colin Powell and Frank Carlucci, who had joined us in the Oval Office, repeated the president's charge about Ortega. You couldn't count on anything he said or did unless you had him at the end of a bayonet, they concluded. They said the Contras had need for an additional $30 million in military aid and wanted to know if I could help them get it. It was an astounding request following the personal attacks that had been launched against me. I told them I was having a hard enough time getting approval for humanitarian aid—food, clothing, and medicine. Democratic liberals were criticizing me for trying to get even that. I didn't believe I could persuade a majority to vote for a renewal of military assistance even if I thought it the solution, which I didn't.

*   *   *

That night, as a guest on the "MacNeil-Lehrer News Hour," I discussed the need for cooperation in foreign affairs, the powers and limits of the executive and legislative branches. I had worked with this president, as I had with six of his predecessors, to develop and carry out a bipartisan foreign policy. I explained that the legislative branch also had responsibilities to the nation, that the public expected more of us than blind acquiescence to predetermined policy. People wanted *us* to be creative, too, and involved. That's what they hired us for.

I also spoke of the need to keep an open door, to be available, particularly to our neighbors in Latin America. When we loftily refused to see them or even hear their opinions, it created a damaging impression of presumed superiority. That attitude was hurting us with our neighbors to the south, I explained.

Apparently what I said touched a responsive chord with viewers. The next day I was deluged with calls and telegrams agreeing with my position on Central America and on the role of Congress.

The next night, on "Larry King Live," I stressed many of the same points and answered questions from viewers. I pointed out that I had been invited to join with President Reagan in the peace effort; I had not invited myself. I had kept Secretary Shultz informed of my actions at every juncture and he had not discouraged them. I said, "I hope that we're on the same team, that we both have the same objective, which is peace in the hemisphere."

More favorable reaction from the public poured in, more telephone calls, telegrams, assurances of support. Almost all my Democratic colleagues were rallying around. Ironically, among the most supportive were many of those who had tried initially to discourage me from getting involved in this process with Reagan back in July.

But, while I was winning the battle for public support, the sentiment was not universal. The issue of Central America, which had polarized Congress for years, which during the summer had seemed on the verge of a consensus, was now being used to split the parties again. Congressmen and senators returned from trips to the region with their own preconceptions reconfirmed. "There's a genuine sense of optimism," reported Democratic Senator Chris Dodd of Connecticut, while Republican Senator Steve Symms of Idaho said dismissively, "I don't see where there's progress."

Now Senator John McCain, conservative Arizona Republican, joined the chorus attacking me. My role, he declared, was "at best unseemly and at worst unconstitutional." McCain charged me with acting as "mediator of the Sandinista government." Nancy Kassebaum of Kansas wondered aloud if I should be involved so actively. Mickey Edwards, Republican from my neighboring state of Oklahoma, told the press I was "trying to curry favor" with my "liberal colleagues." But what I heard from the public at large was comforting.

People seemed to understand that I was trying to encourage peace, sticking to the course we had set in July, and most people approved of that. Most rejoiced that the Central Americans themselves were actually making some progress toward a peaceful settlement. They felt we ought to assist that movement, not try to sabotage it. Colleagues understood that I was faithfully pursuing our government's publicly announced policy even as elements with close ties to the White House were trying to undermine it. I was comfortable in the conviction that my position was both right and in harmony with what most Americans wanted.

I didn't want the peace effort to degenerate into an even more partisan conflict, certainly not into a personal tug of war between me and the president. Bob Strauss was worried about the same thing. He called to say that he and George Shultz were together at lunch. Shultz had written some thoughts out on a piece of paper. He wanted a detente. Would it be alright for Shultz to come by my office and discuss it? "Certainly," I said. "Both of you come. I'll be expecting you."

There were six points in Secretary Shultz's brief memorandum. They spoke of our goals in Central America, peace and democracy. They extolled the value of bipartisanship in foreign policy. They acknowledged that both Congress and the executive branch had important roles to play. I agreed with every bit of that.

If this was an olive branch, I wasn't going to snatch it away from the secretary and switch him across the face with it. I offered a reciprocal gesture. "Mr. Secretary, I mentioned to you several days ago that I had been invited to speak at the ceremony commemorating the thirty-ninth anniversary of Costa Rica's abolition of its army. President Arias asked me to come. It will be on December 1. If you think it would be helpful for me to get out of that engagement so as to avoid the appearance of intruding upon diplomatic prerogatives, I'll do that. But I'd need to call Oscar Arias right away, out of courtesy to him, and make my excuses in time for him to make other arrangements."

Shultz said no, by all means I should go. It would be very useful for me to do that, he said.

Then the three of us went together to the House press gallery. Shultz read three of the six points in our common declaration, and I read the other three. Someone asked if this meant I would thereafter cease talking with foreign leaders, and I said no. It meant we would act out of mutual respect, not attack one another in the press, and try where possible to move in the same direction (the complete original statement can be found in the appendix).

It was a worthy effort. Each of us felt we had to make it. To keep the level of partisanship and personal sniping down would be difficult. We both knew this. Neither of us could control all the others on our respective teams.

On the trip to San José, Costa Rica, I made a special point to take along a bipartisan delegation. There were five Republicans and four Democrats. We were hospitably welcomed by the people of that beautiful little country. I spoke in Spanish, praising Costa Ricans for their leadership in literacy, in cultural and social development, and in setting an example of peaceful civility for the rest of the hemisphere.

Oscar Arias believed that the destiny of all the countries in Central America must be to follow the trail blazed by Costa Rica when it abolished its army. Basking in the easy ambience of its friendly society, one found it hard to disagree. In El Salvador, fear stalked the streets almost daily. The U.S. embassy was like an armed fortress. Nicaragua, beset by a decade of armed conflict, had taken on the habiliments of a police state. But here in Costa Rica, what a contrast! How relaxed, how happy, how free of fear everyone seemed.

Following a mass at the cathedral in downtown San José, Cardinal John O'Connor and our congressional delegation joined President and Mrs. Arias, former President José Figueres, and other Costa Rican dignitaries in a public procession. The crowds that had lined the sidewalks eight and ten deep now closed in, joyously festive, moving toward the middle of the thoroughfare. People tugged at the president, clasping him in the physical *abrazo*. Both men and women approached the first lady directly to kiss her cheek.

Such a scene anywhere in the United States would have been an absolute nightmare to those charged with the first family's security. But here in Costa Rica people trusted one another. Trying to clear a modest path for the president's party through the teeming crowd was a tiny, fragile-looking lady in an immaculate white dress. "Por favor," she repeated pleasantly. At her smiling request, the crowd parted politely.

Upon our return to Washington at least four Republicans—Marge Roukema and Matt Rinaldo, both of New Jersey, John Kasich of Ohio and Sherwood Boehlert of New York—gave glowing public statements about the trip, the ceremonies, and my efforts in promoting good relations with Arias and this exemplary democracy.

The flower of bipartisanship is delicate. Sometimes it gets choked out by the weeds of unrelated controversies. I was driving hard to adopt a domestic agenda that I had announced early in the year. We had overridden presidential vetoes on the clean water bill and the highway bill, had virtually rammed legislation for the homeless down the throats of the Republicans. We had passed our budget resolution without any help from the opposition, and I had been hardheaded in my insistence that Congress provide new revenues—translate, "taxes"—to hold the deficit in check. We had got through a massive trade bill with several controversial features that GOP leaders had wanted stripped out.

Worst of all, from the Republican point of view, I had employed a little-used parliamentary device—adjourning and reconvening in the same afternoon for a second "legislative day"—to get the reconciliation bill passed with the taxes intact. I had been hard driving in domestic policy, too insistent perhaps, even abrasive at times—like sandpaper on a sunburned nose. Now I was trying to be bipartisan in foreign policy. It wasn't easy to separate the two functions, and some were perfectly willing not to. In six years the Nicaraguan war had become a litmus test for ideologues of both persuasions. Tom Foley's heroic efforts to patch together a broad mosaic of budget compromises almost came to a shattering crash over the issue of Contra aid.

Die-hard conservatives, playing upon the nervous jitters that always accompany the frantic last-minute maneuvers before end-of-the-year adjournment, threatened to bring down the continuing resolution that funded the entire government unless it contained some promise of renewed military aid for the Contras. Liberals were equally determined that the Contra forces must not get any new military aid. The result was a compromise that nobody really liked. It contained a complicated delivery system for humanitarian and other nonlethal aid, and authorized no new lethal aid but permitted delivery of weapons and ammunition already paid for and in the pipeline. It also guaranteed a straight up-or-down vote on Contra aid in the House on February 3, 1988.

This was the price now being demanded by the administration. It was a stopgap measure that in effect postponed the critical decision. The package was negotiated during many late-night sessions between House and Senate leaders of both parties in meetings with White House emissaries Jim Baker, Howard Baker, and Office of Management and Budget Director Jim Miller.

The continuing resolution with these mammoth provisions finally came to a vote in the House at almost midnight on December 23. The Democratic Study Group officially denounced the package because of the Contra aid issue. A vocal group of Democrats led by lanky, Lincolnesque Robert Mrazsek of New York, condemned the proposal, warning of a fatal breakdown in the peace talks if military aid were resumed in February. Thus the biggest bill of the session, on the last night of the session, almost broke apart on the rocky shoals of the Contra issue. It finally passed by a one-vote margin, with 128 Democrats voting against it.

More battles lay ahead.

CHAPTER 9

Bipartisanship Buried

The whole history of the progress of human liberty shows that all concessions yet made to her august claims have been born of earnest struggle. . . . If there is no struggle, there is no progress.

—Frederick Douglas

The stage was set for the major confrontation on military aid for the Contras. It would come in February 1988. The razor-thin closeness of the December 23 vote, and the willingness of partisans in both camps to march to the edge of the cliff over this issue, put everyone on notice and heightened tensions. White House insistence on another military aid vote told me that, for all the official platitudes endorsing the peace process, there were some high-ranking people in this administration who really did not want it to work. They had no faith in democratization, reconciliation, elections. They wanted whatever excuse they might seize upon to reignite the war in hopes of physically overthrowing the Sandinista regime, the goal that six years of bloodshed had failed to achieve.

I still did not believe, perhaps because I did not want to believe, that President Reagan was firmly entrenched in the camp of those who wanted the peace talks to fail. His statements, surely enough,

had been ambivalent. It was true that he had failed in early December
to take up an initiative by Gorbachev to discuss withdrawal of Soviet
military advisers from Nicaragua. It was true also that President
Daniel Ortega had written Mr. Reagan a long personal letter—and
another long letter to the *New York Times*—asking for bilateral
talks. The letters firmly asserted his willingness to accept specific
limits on the size of Nicaragua's armed forces, to banish all foreign
military advisers and forbid foreign military bases, and to guarantee
that his country would not be used to launch subversion against its
neighbors. The Ortega letters also pledged that forthcoming elections
would be free and fair. If the Sandinista Party should lose, he promised, it would willingly relinquish power.

President Reagan ignored the letters, their pledges, and their appeal for diplomatic conversations. Instead, as though to impeach the
validity of all Nicaraguan concessions, both actual and promised, the
CIA produced Major Roger Miranda, a military officer newly de-
fected from the Sandinista regime. Major Miranda publicly declared
that the Managua government was actually planning to raise an army
of 600,000 men, to obtain MiGs and other advanced weapons from
the Soviet Union, and to build bases that would threaten the security
of the United States.

These statements, trumpeted to newsmen and members of Congress, seemed wholly implausible. Nicaragua could not afford an
army of 600,000; it could not even afford the force, roughly one-
tenth that size, that it now maintained. If anyone in that small country had even a contingency plan remotely approaching that scope, it
would have to contemplate a suicidal last-ditch melodrama in response to an outright U.S. invasion, which some Nicaraguans still
feared. Moreover, Gorbachev was clearly trying to conciliate the
United States. Surely he would not deliberately irritate us by sending
Nicaragua an armada of weapons that menaced our military security.
As a serious prospect, the story lacked credibility.

Still, the lurid threats reported by Major Miranda were enough to
send tremors through moderate ranks in Congress. Some conservatives welcomed and publicized the Miranda story. It confirmed what
they had been saying all along about the Sandinista threat to the
United States. Most liberals scoffed at the tale, branding it invention
and hyperbole.

In the middle of a polarized Congress were thirty-five or forty
swing votes. Mostly moderate, Southern and Midwestern Democrats, these members could go either way. In past votes, they had

provided the margin of victory both for and against Contra aid. Some of them were troubled by the Miranda statements. Even if they didn't believe them, they guessed that their constituents might. To oppose a renewed installment of military aid for the Contras in light of the highly publicized Miranda charge could subject them to bitter criticism at home, quite possibly to active opposition at the polls.

Then I learned a startling fact. During my years as majority leader I had served as an ex-officio member of the House Intelligence Committee, to which the CIA and all other government intelligence agencies were required to report. As Speaker I had appointed the current chairman, Louis Stokes of Ohio, and other Democratic members to this blue-ribbon panel. When troubled over some unusual disclosure or uncertain how to proceed, these members would occasionally seek a private audience with me to discuss the problem. Because of the classified nature of the information, these conversations were always conducted in strict confidence.

At the height of the Miranda fanfare, one of these colleagues came to me privately with a shocking disclosure. Major Miranda, it turned out, had been given a $500,000 cash bonus, up front, by the CIA. In addition to that, he was given a pledge of something like $45,000 a year for five years, and on top of that was paid about $92,000 to help him move and find housing in the United States. The total package, according to the information I was provided, came to more than three-quarters of a million dollars in taxpayers' money. I was stunned. To a product of Nicaragua's impoverished economy, a sum of such magnitude would represent riches undreamed of. Couldn't it tempt a witness to perjury? Surely this had been paid to Miranda to compensate him for coming to Washington and lobbying Congress for more Contra military aid.

This news put me on the horns of a moral dilemma. I agonized over what I should do, recording my private thoughts in the oral history I was preserving. Here is what I said into the tape recorder at the time:

> This strikes me as a dangerous practice. If we are going down there and recruiting people for such sums as that to come here and give testimony and lobby Congress, it casts a big question mark over the validity of their testimony. . . . In addition, I think there is a strong impropriety in using taxpayers' money to pursue that result. All of this is classified

information. I am wrestling right now with a big question of conscience as to whether the public needs to know that. It seems to me that the public's right to know on a matter of this kind is very important. On the other hand, of course, those who serve on the Intelligence Committee are sworn to secrecy and this is classified information. This is a problem I have to resolve in my own mind.

I resolved it for the time being by not divulging anything publicly about the clandestine payments to Miranda. I was fully aware that members of Congress, in both houses and in both political parties, had blown the whistle on other questionable CIA practices. They included archetypal conservative Senator Barry Goldwater and the first chairman of the House Intelligence Committee, Representative Eddie Boland of Massachusetts.

Congressmen had publicly denounced such covert activities as the mining of the Nicaraguan harbors and the distribution of assassination manuals. Republican senators had condemned a bombing of a civilian airport, which they laid at the agency's door. But feeling ran so high over the Contra aid question at this moment in late January of 1988, and people on both sides were so eager to attribute bad faith to their ideological adversaries, that I chose not to add unnecessary fuel to those flames.

Instead, I tried to tone down the intensity of anger and harsh rhetoric that was beginning to rise on both sides. As Speaker, I had certain responsibilities distinct from those of a party leader. On the evening of Saturday, January 30, I sat beside President Reagan at the Alfalfa Club dinner and engaged in a surprisingly pleasant conversation for two hours without discussing the upcoming vote. He knew where I was on the issue and I knew where he was. Reagan believed that only military might, guns staring down their throats, could force the Sandinistas to keep the pledges they had made at Esquipulas and subsequently. I was fully convinced that a renewal of belligerent threats backed by new weapons shipments could do nothing but shatter the peace effort. The elected presidents of the Central American democracies agreed with me. There was no point in discussing it. The Alfalfa dinner was for laughter and fellowship.

In mid-January, the five Central American presidents met to review the progress of the peace accord. Congressman David Bonior at my request had led a delegation of members to observe the talks and hear the views of leaders as they carried out their role. At the start of these meetings there had been a sense of pessimism about the future of the process. But the impasse was broken when President Ortega agreed to hold *direct* negotiations with the Contras, something the Nicaraguan government had sworn it would never do. Bonior and the others came back with renewed hope.

Nevertheless, President Reagan asked for a new $38-million package for the Contras, including military aid. In submitting his request, he asserted that the talks had failed and that the blame for that failure lay directly with the Sandinistas, that they had not negotiated in good faith.

On Monday, February 1, I met with a group of my fellow Democrats to plan an alternative offering in case Reagan's proposition was voted down. A large number of moderate Democrats wanted to offer a sensible program of humanitarian aid to permit the Contras at least to hold their heads high during the peace talks and, when those negotiations brought peace, to withdraw with dignity, either reintegrating themselves into Nicaraguan society and participating freely in the political life there or resettling themselves elsewhere in Central America if they chose.

Dave Bonior, aided by his excellent research assistant, Kathy Gille, was liked and trusted by a broad cross section of the members. I asked him to put together a task force including liberals, moderates, and conservatives to fashion a package of humanitarian assistance. We let it be known that such a package would be offered in case the military aid were rejected on Wednesday.

The next day, Tuesday, I held a luncheon honoring Bob Michel, my Republican opposite number. Bob now liked being called the *Republican* leader rather than by his official title, minority leader. Over the years I had known him, Bob's instincts had been to cooperate and conciliate. Now he was being driven by an insistent, vocal band of mostly younger Republican members to act in a more vigorously partisan way. I always felt it went against the grain of his nature, but he had been slowly yielding to their demands with increasingly forceful and partisan public statements.

My goal at the luncheon was to abate the rising hostility and search for some area of common ground. In the Speaker's private dining room, its north wall decorated with a newly borrowed Frederic Remington painting entitled "The Parley," we broke out the finest china and sought to build new bonds of fellowship among the thirty-five or so top Democratic and Republican House leaders. From the League of Women Voters I had ordered unique neckties, adorned with drawings of a donkey and an elephant in friendly conversation. I gave a tie to everyone present and asked for ideas about how we could nurture a spirit of amity and genuine bipartisanship in the new year.

Some interesting ideas surfaced. Some Republicans felt we should bring their leaders into our confidence before rules of debate were determined in the Rules Committee for major bills. They felt Republican members had been cheated of the right to offer serious amendments on recent occasions. I made a mental note to try and consult more with them and be more considerate of their wishes regarding amendments.

Then I said, "All of us know that the Contra vote tomorrow will be very close. Regardless of how it goes, let's all vow not to let it spoil our personal relationships. There's no need to impugn one another's motives. Let's all try to recognize that the fellows on the other side are just as sincere as we are." At that point I divulged my strategy and made a further plea: "If the president's military aid proposal goes down, I intend to offer a rather broad *humanitarian* aid package for the Contras. It really should be a bipartisan package. Dave Bonior is my chairman of the task force to draft such a proposal, and I will ask him to work with the Republican leadership. I know our Republican colleagues are concentrating now on trying to pass the president's military aid package tomorrow. You may succeed, but I just want you to know that, in case you do not, we are eager to have your help in preparing a mutually acceptable alternative approach."

We talked about a lot of other bills, including the trade bill and a possible new omnibus antidrug initiative. I told the group of my earnest desire to pass all of the appropriations bills, on time, to have them through the House before the August recess and on the president's desk before the beginning of the fiscal year at the end of September. This was something that had not been done in twenty-eight years. Republicans agreed to cooperate on a timetable aimed at this objective. Deadlines were accepted for committees to report major authorizations and appropriation bills.

When the meeting ended I tried to assess the gain. Marginal at best, I decided. Collegial spirit had been damaged by the harshness of some of the things said in the Contra debate. At least I had made a start. Perhaps we could build on it.

*   *   *

That same day, a Washington-based group calling itself the Council for Inter-American Security published a full-page ad in the *Mid-Cities Daily News,* the paper with the second-largest circulation in my Texas congressional district. The ad attacked me for my efforts in the Central American imbroglio and urged constituents to "Call Jim Wright today!" and register their "support for the anti-Communist Freedom Fighters in Nicaragua." In big block letters, the paid advertisement asked "WHO DOES HE SPEAK FOR?" then offered the following simplified choice: "Communist Dictator Daniel Ortega of Nicaragua? Or the People of Texas and the United States?" The advertisement accused me of using my "powerful position as Speaker of the House to appease the Communist leadership of Nicaragua." It threw in a new charge: "Yes, that's the same Jim Wright who tried to arrange for Soviet leader Gorbachev to address a joint session of Congress." (This claim, of course, was wholly unfounded. The overture had come from the White House. I had merely expressed my willingness to cooperate.)

Now the gloves were off. It would be brass knuckles from this point on, and no Marquis of Queensberry rules. The gaggle of right-wing groups that supported the war in Nicaragua, the ones who had plotted the sale of weapons to Iran to finance their illegal war, had now targeted me for political extinction. Attacks on the personal character and patriotism of those with whom they disagreed were hallmarks of their technique.

Within days this same right-wing group, with a cover letter signed by L. Francis Bouchey, president of the Council for Inter-American Security, sent copies of that ad to a nationwide mailing list asking for contributions to finance more such ads. The letter also begged for signatures on a "demand petition" addressed to the House Ethics Committee insisting on "an investigation of Speaker Wright." The letter began on a note of hyperbole: "I want to alert you to a growing scandal in Congress." It declared that I had "broken the law" by conducting "direct negotiations with the brutal Nicaraguan Communist government. Our sworn enemies." Then it pleaded for donations to "stop Jim Wright," saying that I had done more than any other person "to help the Communists in Central America."

On the eve of the February 3 vote, President Reagan made an emotional appeal over Cable News Network. He raised the level of rhetoric, accusing the Soviet Union of sending big shipments of military aid to Nicaragua for a communist takeover of Central America. He represented this as a threat to the United States. He said he had not become president to preside over the communization of Central America. That latter comment, I decided, expressed the central core of our disagreement.

In my speech closing House debate on the highly charged issue, I pointed out that six years of bloody warfare had won not one single concession from the Sandinista government. But in only six months, I explained, their neighbors under the Esquipulas accords had elicited many significant concessions—the reopening of newspapers and radio stations, the release of hundreds of political prisoners, the appointment of Cardinal Obando as head of the Reconciliation Commission, the repeal of the emergency act, the agreement now to negotiate directly with the Contra forces, the promise of free and fair elections, and the pledge by Ortega "that if the opposition wins the election, we will turn over the government to them. . . . We are prepared to become the loyal opposition if that is what the Nicaraguan people decide.

"I do not know," I continued, "whether you can trust that or not. I am not telling you that you can. But I think you have to test it. And surely the way to test it is by sitting down at the negotiating table and following the process of peace."

Finally, I spoke of the fact that other people value their pride and dignity just as Americans do, that we must treat our Latin American neighbors as equals and assume their good faith while negotiating with them in good faith. I referred to President Reagan's paraphrase of Winston Churchill's comment that he had not become "His Majesty's First Minister to preside over the liquidation of the British Empire." Reagan had said he did not come to Washington "to preside over the Communization of Central America." To this I made the following response:

Well, of course he did not. He does not want that result. None of us wants that result. None of us came to Washington for that result. But there is an important point to make, and that is that neither Mr. Reagan nor any of us came to Washington to *preside* over Central America in any sense. We came to Washington to preside over the United States. . . . The people of Central America elect their own leaders to speak for their own countries. The five Central American presidents have joined together and have asked us not to send any more destructive weapons into their region. There have been enough deaths. . . . They have asked us to desist from sending aid to irregular forces trying to topple and overthrow governments in their region. Let us heed their plea. Let us accord them the respect that is due them . . . the right of local, nonviolent self-determination. . . . Let us join with them—not against them—in seeking an avenue of peace and democracy and justice with dignity.

By a vote of 219 to 211, the House defeated the administration's request for a renewal of military funding. Now it was up to the leadership to produce an alternative.

That task was made infinitely more difficult by the polarization of the House. Charges and countercharges continued to reverberate in newspapers and on talk shows. An increasingly shrill group of activists militantly promoted their separate sides of the issue throughout the country. During debate on February 3 the House galleries teemed with partisan onlookers. Several times fans on both sides had to be called down for violating House rules by breaking into voluble applause for statements made by a spokesman for one side or the other. At one point, a group of anti-Contra enthusiasts disrupted proceedings with shouts of "No Contra aid!" and "End the war now!" They also unfurled a paper banner with large blue letters reading, "Obey the World Court!" (This referred to the decision, mentioned earlier, by the International Court of Justice ruling against the United States over the CIA's covert mining of Nicaraguan harbors in 1984. The official administration position had been to defy the court and ignore its jurisdiction.)

The bitterness engendered by this issue was not confined within U.S. borders. The public would not discover for almost two more years that one branch of the publicly financed National Endowment for Democracy, at the urging of Republican Party representatives to that agency, was violating the basic premise of the law by financing Costa Rican publications attacking the leadership of President Oscar Arias in his own country. There was increasing resentment of Arias in White House and administration circles.

At about this time, it became apparent to me that American personnel in Nicaragua were actively encouraging and even helping organize public demonstrations against the Sandinista government. CIA officials, when asked about this, said they were trying to "test the limits of pluralism," to embarrass the Managua administration by goading it into some repressive action. This was exactly what a former senior analyst for the CIA had testified to under oath before the World Court in 1986.

Now, however, that practice ran directly against the grain of stated U.S. policy. Our State Department was paying at least official lip service to the peace process; the continued practice of stirring up domestic opposition to the government and trying to bait local officials into a repressive response seemed counter to our announced purpose. Chairman Louis Stokes of the House Intelligence Committee agreed with me that this was bad practice, contrary to official policy. He said he intended to discuss it with CIA officials.

Meanwhile in the United States, propagandists were turning up the heat, unleashing their arsenals of negative attacks on members of Congress who voted contrary to their wishes on the question of military aid to the Contras. This was not confined to the pro-Contra ideologues. Anti-Contra activists were busy too, particularly on college campuses.

On February 6, three days after the vote, the Fort Worth *Star-Telegram* published a bitter tirade by a new columnist named Bill Thompson. "Chalk up a victory," it announced, "for Commie sympathizers, shortsighted pacifists, left-wing nitwits and Jim Wright's pal, Daniel Ortega." In thirty-three years of serving the Fort Worth district in Congress, I had often run afoul of editorial writers. But never before had a columnist or editorialist in my hometown newspaper attacked my motives or questioned my basic integrity. Now, spurred by the hysteria of the moment, the paper's new pundit pulled out all the stops. "Don't be fooled by Wright's cover-our-tail proposal to provide the contras with humanitarian aid. . . . And don't be fooled by the Speaker's conciliatory rhetoric . . . if Wright truly wanted to work in harmony . . . the Speaker would have supported the President's $36.2 million contra aid package. . . . He clearly intends to settle for wrecking Reagan's policy."

Who was this Bill Thompson, I wondered, and how did he come to be working for the Fort Worth newspaper? He had evidently been in direct touch with David Hirschmann, identified in the column as director of research for the Council for Inter-American Security, the propaganda and fund-raising group that had run the ad against me in the other newspaper. Thompson quoted Hirschmann as saying that any proposal the Democratic leadership supported would be only a "cleverly disguised method of killing the contras," and that "if the contras are abandoned, the options are U.S. military involvement or learning to live with a Communist regime in Nicaragua." No hope at all, in other words, for any negotiated settlement. It was strictly us against the Commies!

In this atmosphere of rhetorical overkill going on across the country and in other congressional districts, our job in putting together a bipartisan alternative for humanitarian assistance was a steep uphill climb. Republican leaders shied away from sitting down with us to try and craft a joint position on Contra aid. In rejecting my invitation to the Republicans to join in constructing a package, Bob Michel apologetically explained that he had been unable to stir up any enthusiasm among fellow Republicans for a joint effort. "Golly darn, Jim, there's still just too much anger over the defeat of Reagan's plan," he explained. "Our guys are still mad about it, and these outside groups keep stirring them up."

There was something more personal, too. Failure must seek out a scapegoat. People who had poured energy and conviction and money into the Contra effort for six years were angry. Their war was going down the drain, and they deeply distrusted the peace process. It was natural for such people to lash out and blame me.

News articles and editorials began appearing with stunning frequency in the *Wall Street Journal* and *Washington Times* castigating me for my position on Contra aid and for a catalogue of other real and imagined sins. A few questioned my patriotism.

House Republicans, in the minority for thirty-four years, had additional frustrations. Thus far in the 100th Congress they had not prevailed on a single significant vote. The old Dixiecrat coalition, so successfully remobilized in the early Reagan years, wasn't working for them now. From their point of view, it was my fault. That sometimes the votes were close, as on February 3, simply sharpened their dismay. In a meeting of the Republican Conference, according to reports brought to me by Republican friends, militant younger members were advocating a strategy: Discredit Wright! Sack the quarterback!

It seemed as though good things often soon followed bad. On the morning after the vote, February 4, Daniel Ortega telephoned and suggested the vote was a vote for peace. He expressed interest in the negotiations on a cease-fire and concerns over the development of verification procedures. My memorandum of our conversation was soon sent to the White House and Secretary Shultz (the complete original memo can be found in the appendix).

Soon after the vote I wrote President Reagan and Secretary Shultz assuring them of our desire to work with their people in developing a constructive program of humanitarian aid. I invited whatever suggestions the administration desired to offer (the complete original letters can be found in the appendix). There was no direct reply. Informally I heard what the White House attitude was: The Speaker said he'd produce a bill, let's see him do it (the complete original reply from the president can be found in the appendix).

But could it be done by Democrats alone?

Denied any input from the Republican side, Dave Bonior convened a working group of moderate, liberal, and conservative Democrats to fashion an assistance package that would support and strengthen the peace process. A series of meetings came together during the weeks of February 15 and 22. Many members stayed in Washington and canceled appointments in their home districts during the official Presidents' Day recess in order to continue work on the proposal. The critical issue was how to craft a package that would provide incentives to keep *both* the Contras and the Sandinistas at the negotiating table.

A crucial question arose over who should deliver the aid. Liberals opposed any U.S. government involvement and wanted an international agency to take over the task of dispensing humane assistance as stipulated in the Esquipulas II accord. Moderates would have accepted that solution. But no international agency would accept the task of delivering aid to an army in the field, and at the moment there still was no official cease-fire.

Finally, the task force decided that deliveries should be made by the Department of Defense until a cease-fire was formally declared, whereupon delivery would be turned over to the International Red Cross or some other international agency.

Addressing the needs of the war's *victims* for the first time, the Bonior group agreed to include several million dollars for "children's survival assistance." Among other things, this would finance medical care, surgery, and prosthetic devices for children with arms and legs blown off during six years of war.

All in all, it was a creditable package. Its compassionate and creative features were immediately embraced by Latin American leaders. We mounted an all-out effort to gain domestic public support for the proposal. Outside church groups and others who had never supported a dime of assistance to the Contras endorsed the measure. The Democratic Study Group, which had opposed the continuing resolution in December, now came on board. We scheduled the vote for March 3, exactly one month following the defeat of the president's military aid proposal.

In spite of an energetic effort on the part of Bonior's task force and the active assistance of most members of the Democratic whip's organization, led by Tony Coelho, the package was narrowly defeated on March 3. It went down, the victim of an odd-couple coalition— some arch liberals who refused to vote for *any* kind of aid to the Contras, joining almost all of the Republicans, some openly willing to do whatever it took to embarrass the Democrats, even if that meant letting the Contras hang out to dry without needed food, clothing, or other rudiments of survival during the cease-fire.

The vote against the bill was 216 to 208. It drew only five Republican votes.

This was the low point. Discouraged but unwilling to leave affairs in such an indecisive state, some of us assembled the day after the vote and began planning for another try. Some of my more partisan Democratic colleagues suggested that we simply let the matter drop. "The Republicans have outsmarted themselves," one Democrat crowed. "*They've* killed the Contras! Let them stew in their own juice!"

Within a very few days, some in the Republican leadership realized the naked vulnerability of their position. Bob Michel came by to see if we could work together to salvage something. "Sure, Bob. Of course we can," I said.

This time, the package came together quickly. Republican hardliners had their pound of flesh. They had embarrassed the Democratic leadership by making us swallow a defeat on the floor. There was no need for further recalcitrance. So far as I was concerned there was no profit in gloating over their discomfort by delaying a solution and blaming them for the Contras' demise. What I had hoped for in the first place was a bipartisan solution. Now we would have one.

David Bonior agreed to take the lead again for the Democratic side. Congressman Dick Cheney of Wyoming (a year later to be made secretary of defense) and Mickey Edwards of Oklahoma were anointed by Michel to represent Republicans in the joint effort.

*   *   *

But progress, even now, was not to come easily. Contra leaders were refusing to attend meetings to discuss a cease-fire. Some of them were talking publicly of raising private funds to renew the war. I heard directly from one member of the Contra directorate that two of the five designated spokesmen were for pursuing the peace opening, two favored starting the war anew, and one was under great pressure from Elliott Abrams to join the holdouts and try again for a military solution.

Richard Peña, my personal emissary to the Esquipulas meetings, now returned from a trip to Costa Rica and told me of a long visit he'd had with President Oscar Arias. Arias directly confirmed the story I had heard. Contra leaders had told him of enormous personal pressure from Abrams and one or two others in the administration whose names Arias could not recall. Clearly, forces presuming to speak for the White House were doing everything within their power to make the peace talks break down.

Upon learning this, I went to George Shultz. I told him the good faith of the Contras was at stake as well as the good faith of the administration. Shultz said he had no personal knowledge of anyone in his department deliberately dissuading attendance at the talks. But he began to espouse the same shibboleths that had characterized earlier administration statements. "We feel the military pressure of the freedom fighters is all that will bring about any agreement on the part of the Sandinistas to do anything," he said. I tried to point out that we had financially supported military pressure for many years without any result, and that the results we now saw had come about through the initiation of the peace talks.

"Well, before we have a cease-fire," the secretary said, "we have to know what is going to happen after the cease-fire. It would be unwise for the freedom fighters to engage in a cease-fire until they know first what the cease-fire will produce."

"But doesn't the cease-fire itself provide the calmer atmosphere in which to sit down and unravel the problems that lie in the future?" I asked. The sheer military impracticality of the secretary's position became clear to me. "Look, Mr. Secretary, the Contras don't have any legal source now for any more weapons or ammunition. Wouldn't they be better off to go into a cease-fire and conserve what ammunition they have just in the event the cease-fire should break down and hostilities resume? Right now, as long as the shooting continues, they're burning up ammunition without knowing where, or if, they'll be able to get any more."

Shultz had no immediate response to that. Finally, he said, "Your opinion is always a matter of importance to us, and I always get something of value when I talk with you."

I tried one more tack. "Your diligent efforts in the Middle East are certainly commendable, Mr. Secretary. That is an almost intractable situation. By contrast, I sense that the Central American situation is much closer to a solution. With just a little effort, with a little creativity of the type we're investing in search of a solution for the Middle East, we just might hit pay dirt in Central America!"

George Shultz's expression was, as usual, inscrutable. I went on: "The White House is unwilling to talk with the Sandinista government. You and others at State have refused to talk with Ortega. Your official position has been that he must talk directly with the resistance leaders. Now, finally, he has agreed to do that. What excuse can we have if now we dissuade even them from seeking a negotiated solution?"

On Tuesday, March 15, the bipartisan congressional leadership was asked to meet with the president at the White House. Discussion ranged over situations across the globe. We discussed Noriega's intransigence in Panama. We heard a glowing report about the fortieth anniversary celebration of NATO. Senators Cranston and Simpson reported on recent meetings in Moscow. They seemed hopeful that things were on the verge of working out in Afghanistan.

Then President Reagan began a doleful forecast of how bad things seemed in Central America. He said the cessation of humanitarian aid had created a critical need among Contra families for the most basic necessities. He could not understand, he said, why Congress had refused to continue even humanitarian assistance of the most elemental type. I was perplexed. Could he conceivably be *unaware* that the Democratic leadership had tried earnestly just two weeks earlier to do exactly what he seemed now to be asking and had encountered a solid phalanx of Republican opposition!

Now General Colin Powell, the new national security adviser, was talking. He said the Contra forces were "at end game." Virtually all aspects of the situation in Nicaragua, he stated, were "in crisis or on the verge of collapse." Food for Contra families in southern Honduras would run out on April 1 and the number of rebels in Nicaragua would fall to about three thousand unless something was done swiftly. The whole aid program was "drying up and dying before our eyes," Powell said. Then he disclosed that the Nicaraguan government was putting together what appeared to be a major offensive. Our intelligence people had been monitoring it for about ten days. Powell distributed pictures of helicopters delivering goods to advanced Sandinista army positions in the north of the country where government army forces were pushing the Contras back into Honduras.

"The resistance forces and their families need help," said Powell. "We tried to get it from Congress in February and failed. We tried again in March, and that wasn't successful."

I could no longer remain silent. "Look, General, I don't understand this. If you've been monitoring this advance of troops, if you've been anticipating the exhaustion of food supplies for the Contras and their families, you surely should have been able to foresee that development on March 3 when we tried to keep the flow of humanitarian aid alive."

As I warmed to the subject, the sheer injustice of the White House position came pouring out of me. "With just five or six more votes for the humanitarian-aid package two weeks ago, we wouldn't be facing this dire disaster that you describe. Instead, the administration encouraged all Republicans to vote *against* the program, and President Reagan expressed *pleasure* at the time over the fact that it was defeated."

Turning to the president, I tried reason. "If the resistance forces are in as bad a shape as you and General Powell say they are, Mr. President, it seems to me they would be attending the talks aimed at producing a cease-fire. At least that would give them a breathing spell and stop the Sandinista advance. We're trying now to revive the humanitarian-aid package. With some bipartisan effort, that can be done."

"What good is it to feed people if they're going to be dead?" asked the president. Apparently he still entertained hopes of a Contra military victory.

Mickey Edwards, the conservative Oklahoma Republican, spoke up. "Mr. President, we simply don't have the votes for military aid. The Speaker is offering to help produce a substantial amount of humanitarian aid. Surely that is better than nothing. We need to be talking about the achievable."

Edwards had been very partisan, highly critical of Democratic efforts in the past. He was as good a soldier as Ronald Reagan had in the House. Seizing upon his opening, I told the president and General

Powell that if we could all work together quickly, we could produce a bill before April 1. But we would all have to be working with the same goals in mind—a cease-fire, a peace settlement, and democratization through negotiation, not warfare.

Senate Majority Leader Byrd had been sitting silently. Now he spoke up. "Mr. President, you negotiate with the Russians. Just last December you talked at length with Mr. Gorbachev. Why don't you just sit down and try to talk with these people in Nicaragua? I have a feeling that's all it would take to get this whole thing settled."

President Reagan replied that we should not engage in any such talks. To do so, he said, would make us look like "the Yankee behemoth to the north." Apparently it did not occur to him at all, I was thinking, that sending military weapons and financing an army in an effort to overthrow a Latin government made us look more like a Yankee behemoth than sitting down and talking would.

But I did not press the point. Polemics were less important at this point than the fact that Mickey Edwards and Republican Whip Trent Lott sought me out at the meeting's end and pledged their active help in putting together a package.

The Sandinista military did advance to the Honduran border. Immediately I asked Wilson Morris to inform Paul Reichler, a Washington lawyer who represented the Sandinista government, that it would be an extremely serious offense if Nicaraguan troops entered Honduras. Congress would look unfavorably on even an unintentional crossing, I wanted the Sandinista government to know.

Soon I got a telephone call from Nicaraguan Foreign Minister D'Escoto. I told him our Congress and our administration would view with great seriousness any invasion by armed forces into any neighboring country. He said there had been heavy fighting in the area of the border town of Bocay, but that President Ortega had been in direct contact by telephone with President Azcona of Honduras four times on Tuesday and Wednesday, assuring and reassuring him that Nicaraguan troops had no designs whatsoever on his country. Ortega, the foreign minister said, was proposing a direct meeting that very day with Azcona and, as a precaution, had ordered Nicaraguan troops to withdraw well into Nicaraguan territory, away from the international line.

D'Escoto further said that Ortega was calling on the secretary general of the UN to send a technical commission to inspect the situation on the ground and verify that no troops were on the wrong side of the border, as well as to make recommendations for sealing off that border as a cordon sanitaire.

Soon I received another call, this one from Alfredo César. He told me the logjam had been broken among leaders in the Contra directorate. Participation in cease-fire talks had been authorized in spite of Elliott Abrams's objections. César and Adolfo Calero would attend a meeting on Monday with Sandinista leaders at a place called Sapoa and would try to get a cease-fire agreement.

The next day, Howard Baker asked if I would set up a meeting for him and Powell to brief the joint House leadership on the situation in Nicaragua. I supposed that they knew of the agreement to begin serious talks and might want to discuss the new humanitarian-aid package. We set the meeting in the Speaker's dining room and I invited all the Democratic and Republican leaders.

The White House contingent arrived, and with them George Shultz. It quickly became apparent that the purpose of the meeting was not what I had supposed. Rather, Secretary Shultz wanted to discuss what he described as "a grave threat to our national security." He referred to the reported incursion across the borders into Honduras. When I told Shultz of the conversation I had just had that morning with D'Escoto and the assurances I had been given, he seemed unwilling to hear it. He discounted its importance, did not even say that it was interesting or that he was glad to hear that the Nicaraguans had been ordered away from the border. He seemed, if anything, disappointed that some of us in Congress had been talking at all with the people in the region.

The purpose of the meeting, it became clear, was to incite us against a Sandinista "invasion" and perhaps to prepare us for the announcement of the subsequent day that the administration was sending 3,200 airborne troops to Honduras. Or perhaps that decision was made later. I cannot be sure.

We were told at the meeting, in response to a question, that President Azcona had *not* asked for military assistance. General Powell even cautioned us against false reports. He said we might hear that the 82d Airborne was on its way, but that this was not correct. These comments were given to us at about three-thirty in the afternoon of March 16, 1988. But I heard later that evening that a decision to send troops had been made in the White House at eleven that morning, and that it was based on a request from President Azcona of the previous day, March 15. Certainly these new notifications directly contradicted what General Powell had told us just hours earlier. In any case, the 82d Airborne *was* ordered to Honduras. Clearly, whatever the official rationale, it was a decision hastily made and hastily carried out.

This U.S. military response had all the earmarks of an effort to escalate tensions, to magnify the image of the Sandinistas as inherently bad, irredeemable, and dangerous to U.S. interests. The maneuver seemed one last desperate effort to revive the prospect of military aid to the Contra forces.

All this was nullified, however, by the Nicaraguan Contras and Sandinistas themselves. On March 23 the government and the resistance, meeting in the little town of Sapoa, Nicaragua, entered into a now-historic agreement. There would be a sixty-day cease-fire. Contras would be free to receive humanitarian aid from the United States, including communications equipment. This could be delivered by any neutral international profit or nonprofit agency. Future meetings would ratify specific steps to internal democratic reforms, the release of prisoners, and eventual elections.

The two delegations, leaders of forces that until now had been killing one another, stood and smiled for photographs together. So standing, they joined in singing Nicaragua's national anthem.

The Sapoa agreement, more than anything else, made a bipartisan package of assistance possible. The resulting legislation provided that the assistance be administered by AID, with actual distribution to units in the field handled by neutral organizations in a manner compatible with provisions of a cease-fire agreement. The Sapoa accord called for monitoring of its terms by a verification commission to ensure that the aid was being administered and disbursed in keeping with the agreement's terms.

Some Republican members were nervous about what might happen if the peace process broke down entirely. Might they then have a chance for a new look, and a new vote? Would we agree to an "expedited procedure" by which the president could craft a new package and send it to the House for an up-or-down vote, with no amendments allowed, on a day of his choice?

No, I replied, there would be no end-runs around congressional prerogatives. But, as long as I remained Speaker, there would indeed be a chance for a decisive vote. Whenever the President made a proposal concerning Contra aid, I declared, it would be referred to the appropriate committees with my instructions to report their recommendations—not necessarily the president's—promptly to the House. An early vote would be scheduled. But we would follow due process, regular procedure. The House would have all its options open to amend, modify, or alter in such ways as a majority of the members might choose.

There was a certain amount of grumbling. Senator McCain of Arizona asserted that he did not trust the Speaker of the House. I could sense the depth of hostility that my efforts in behalf of peace had engendered in some quarters. In thirty-three years as a member of the House, my word had never before been questioned. But I swallowed my pride, made no public reply. The result was more important than my personal feelings. In the end, the voluntary agreement I offered was accepted.

On March 28 and 29, the senior members of the two parties met in my offices in the Capitol and carefully discussed every provision—every line, in fact—of a bill that ultimately filled ten typed pages. Our bipartisan drafting group even called in the Contra directorate at one point to ask their specific suggestions. We also consulted with the secretary general of the OAS, João Clemente Baena Soares, concerning the verification commission that he and Cardinal Obando were jointly to head.

The result of these labors was a bill remarkably similar to the one the House had rejected on March 3. But this time there was a major difference: Republicans, sensing that this just might be the last train out of the station, were on board.

On March 30, the bill passed the House with a preponderant margin of 345 to 70. The next day the Senate adopted it without change, 87 to 7. We had completed the job as I had promised, by April 1, the day on which President Reagan signed it. I sent the president a letter outlining our procedure for requesting renewal of military aid to the Contras (the complete original letter can be found in the appendix).

Spring was in the air. We'd had a good couple of weeks. I was almost euphoric. Riding into work one morning, I spoke into the tape recorder:

Now I feel very good . . . the peace process has become almost inexorable. It still could be upset and reversed, but . . . with any good fortune at all we should see an end to hostilities in Nicaragua and turn our attention to El Salvador. . . .

Then maybe we can begin a process of benign and active involvement with Central America. It's a wonderful thought on a morning like this as I pass broad vistas of green dotted with the yellow daffodils, and the buds in the trees beginning to color the boughs, and the white blossoms on the ornamental fruit trees. . . . As new life springs from the old earth, maybe we do dare to hope. . . . Peace can spring from the crust of the ground where heroes and martyrs and simple people lie buried who have died in its pursuit.

Ernesto Rivas-Gallont, the dapper ambassador from El Salvador, came by my office that day. His country was conducting its fifth consecutive election. The current decade marked El Salvador's longest continuous stretch of democracy. Under José Napoleón Duarte's prodding and insistence, the people had gone to the polls on five occasions and chosen a constituent assembly, a president, and now municipal officers. They had voted in impressive numbers, the more impressive considering persistent violent efforts by antigovernment guerrilla forces to break up and discredit the elections.

Rivas and I reminisced. Twice I had been to his country on election day. Both visits had produced unforgettable memories. In March of 1982, FMLN armed insurgents had published death threats in a forceful but utterly ineffective effort to discourage voter participation. Undaunted, Salvadoran peasants flooded the polling places. Thousands walked for many miles in the hot sun and through jungle trails. Many stood in long lines for hours to cast their ballots. In the backcountry I saw pregnant women and landless farmers without shoes brave the guerrillas' taunts to assert the precious right so long denied them by a succession of military governments. The vote that day went against the party of President Duarte and Ambassador Rivas, electing a constituent assembly that tilted toward the charismatic anticommunist militancy of Roberto D'Aubuisson.

Two years later, in 1984, the electorate reversed itself to reelect Duarte. Again almost 80 percent of the qualified citizenry turned out to vote. This time the guerrilla movement, embarrassed and blistered by public opinion in 1982, made no threats of violence against voters. But by cutting transmission lines it produced a power blackout in San Salvador on the morning of election day. Like others in the party of congressional observers, I shaved and showered and dressed in the dark. Along with U.S. Ambassador Deane Hinton, I visited five communities and talked with voters. I asked what they hoped their votes might achieve. "Espero que traera la paz," (I hope it will bring peace,) many responded. Some said, "Una democracia, exactamente como ustedes tienen en su país" (A democracy just as you have in your country). For me, that day was a deeply emotional experience.

Rivas reminded me that the helicopter carrying Ambassador Hinton and me had lost power, forcing an emergency landing at a remote hydroelectric power dam somewhere between San Miguel and San Salvador. Of course I remembered. How could I forget it? "You never knew how close you and the ambassador were that day to the leftist guerrilla forces in the hills around that dam," Rivas smiled.

"I'm glad *they* didn't know who was in that crippled chopper," I laughed. Then I reminded him that a corpse had been thrown out of a speeding car the night before election day onto the sidewalk directly in front of a San Salvador restaurant where some of the American contingent were eating. "Our embassy had told us that restaurant was one of the safest places in your city," I chided Rivas.

"No place is wholly safe, Mr. Speaker, but there is something you can do which may help make things safer."

"Tell me what, and I'll try."

The ambassador thought it would encourage the people of his embattled land if Congress would pass a resolution formally commending the people of El Salvador for their dedication to the ballot box. I called in Foreign Affairs Committee Chairman Dante Fascell. He brought Spencer Oliver, a top member of the committee staff. We drafted the resolution. Fascell gained committee approval, and it passed unanimously on the House floor.

Here at least was consensus on one issue, elections. That was the heart of the matter. People were entitled to choose their own leaders. Even the Nicaraguan government had finally embraced that principle in terms strong enough to be accepted by its domestic opposition. In the March 23 agreement at Sapoa, the Sandinistas had agreed to recognize the Contras as a legitimate political force with all rights to compete in elections inside Nicaragua.

That pledge was specific and unequivocal. Nicaraguans who had left the country "for political or for any other reasons" were invited to return and incorporate themselves into the political life of the country. They "will not be tried, punished or persecuted for any political-military activities they might have engaged in." They would be expected only to abide by the laws.

Senate Majority Leader Byrd, encouraged by this visible progress, was calling for a meeting between the United States and Nicaragua to work out other agreements, including dissolution of the Soviet military presence and ironclad protection against infiltration of weapons from Nicaragua to Salvadoran rebels. "Let's give U.S. diplomacy a chance," Byrd pleaded.

Senator Tom Harkin of Iowa called for lifting our long-standing trade embargo against Nicaragua as a first step to better understanding. The Sandinistas themselves renewed that oft-repeated plea. All they wanted in addition to peace with their neighbors and internal democracy, they insisted, were direct talks and normalized relations with the United States.

And Senator Bill Bradley of New Jersey, who long had wanted to implement the positive recommendations of the Kissinger Commission, now introduced a bill to authorize about $500 million in trade and economic benefits for Central American countries. Nicaragua would not be eligible to participate initially but could qualify for trade concessions and needed debt relief by faithfully carrying out its leaders' pledges of political reform.

There were holdouts. Hard-liners shared none of the ebullience. John Felton, writing in *Congressional Quarterly* on April 2, quoted Jesse Helms of North Carolina as calling the humanitarian-aid bill "too little, too late, too limited, too loaded with the stench of betrayal . . . blood money, pure and simple."

Other parties had their hard-liners, too. On a Sunday television talk show, Nicaraguan Resistance Leader Adolfo Calero seemed to have second thoughts about the agreements he had entered into at Sapoa. And top Contra general Enrique Bermúdez was soon working a deal with the U.S. branch of AID to let Contra military commanders collect and disburse the "humanitarian aid" in cash. Instead of foodstuffs and medicines being delivered by a neutral agency, as contemplated in the legislation, AID administrators would meet a military officer of the Contra forces at the Honduran border and hand him, in Nicaraguan cordobas, the cash equivalent of fifty cents a day for each of the men he claimed under his command—multiplied by thirty days for a month's rations. Thus if an officer said he commanded 200 men, he would get $3,000. It was up to him to spend it in the interest of his troops as he saw fit. Accounting was impossible.

We learned of this from civilian leaders of the resistance. On May 5 a small group came to complain that approximately $17.7 million of the humanitarian aid we had authorized was simply not getting into the hands of those for whom it was intended. This highlighted a long-smoldering split within the top Contra ranks. For years there had been friction between the civilian spokesmen, represented by Alfonso Robelo and Alfredo César, and the military contingent headed by Bermúdez. Calero often sided with the military faction, but occasionally he and Bermúdez clashed privately.

From the beginning, internal tension existed between those who had been associated with Somoza before his downfall and those who had helped overthrow him in 1979, who had joined the resistance only after deciding that the revolution's goals had been betrayed by the Sandinistas. Enrique Bermúdez had been a Somocista, a partisan of the late dictator, a colonel in the national guard. Calero was a successful businessman in Managua. Others such as Robelo, César, banker Arturo Cruz, and the Chamorro newspaper family, including Violeta, widow of La Prensa's martyred publisher, and their son Pedro Joaquín, had been outspokenly anti-Somoza.

The Reagan administration had tended all along to favor the old Somoza element, composed mainly of former national guardsmen based in Honduras. There was bitterness among the moderates that this fact played into the hands of the Sandinistas by allowing them to associate the Contras in the public mind with Somoza.

Clearly the resistance leader most popular with the people was Edén Pastora, "Commander Zero," a fabled hero of the revolution. He might have been a focal point behind which the people would rally. Pastora left Nicaragua, publicly denounced the Sandinistas, and in April of 1982 began to organize a political countermovement. When he expressed moderate economic opinions and refused to collaborate with former Somoza national guardsmen, however, U.S. officialdom quickly lost interest in him and attempted to stifle his activities.

Denied U.S. help, Pastora tried to set up an independent resistance movement along the Costa Rican border. One day an explosion ripped through his camp, injuring the charismatic leader. Clearly it was a case of sabotage. The bomb had been planted by someone who knew exactly where Pastora would be. Some of the hero's followers believed the bomb was set by the CIA. Disillusioned by this and by the attitude of the United States, Pastora announced that he was giving up the revolution and returning to his old trade as a commercial fisherman.

Now, with U.S. humanitarian-aid money going directly into the hands of military officers, civilian moderates saw the reins of their movement's leadership slipping to the control of those who, like Bermúdez, mistrusted the peace talks and still wanted a military victory. Regardless of the internal politics of the matter, the method of distribution was sloppy. Moreover, it failed to carry out the unmistakable intent of the law and of the Sapoa agreement.

The legislative craftsmen of the bill called top AID administrators into a meeting. Wasn't there a better way to distribute the assistance? we asked. We pointed to the provisions of the law. They simply were not being followed. Finally it was agreed that an agency of the OAS might undertake delivery in the field. João Clemente Baena Soares, cherubic secretary-general of the OAS, was eager to help. But weeks dragged on without a clearcut modus operandi. Our agreement was not being put into effect.

The AID people were much more demanding of strict accounting from the OAS than they had been with the Contra military officers. To be fair to AID, its administrators never had wanted the role we assigned them. To make matters worse, embarrassingly worse for the OAS, the United States was behind in its dues to that regional organization.

And in Managua, Interior Minister Tomás Borge, the rigid leftist ideologue, was finding it harder and harder to tolerate the growing waves of dissent. The CIA, we had learned, was drilling people in the local political opposition on how to put on protest demonstrations— the bigger and noisier, the better. Emboldened now by the abolition of the Emergency Act, the reappearance of *La Prensa,* and by the government's promises of political liberty, recruits were easier to rally for an antigovernment march. Several times the Sandinista faithful organized their own counterdemonstrations to protest the protesters. On a number of occasions, rival mobs clashed in a shoving contest. Tension mounted.

Throughout the late spring and summer of 1988, I was preoccupied with the domestic agenda of Congress. My hands were full. We passed an education bill, reversing the years of decline in our commitment to the nation's schools. We overrode the president's veto of a civil rights bill and extended Medicare coverage for catastrophic illnesses. This was the first major expansion of Medicare since its inception in 1965. And we were well on our way, for the first time in modern memory, to passing *all* appropriations bills *before* the start of the fiscal year. The landmark trade bill we had sent from the House in April of the previous year worked its way through the

Senate, along with a provision requiring management to notify employees before closing industrial plants. We Democrats were on a roll, reversing the domestic priorities of the Reagan years.

This legislative agenda, added to what many critics saw as my "intrusion" into foreign affairs, was infuriating the political right wing. Like angry bees, the hive of conservative Washington propagandists, journalists, and politicians began to swarm. Increasingly I was the object of personal attacks. I tried to shake them off, but they stung. Nobody likes to have his patriotism or his personal honor impugned. I have often wondered how nature ever indulged in such profligate waste as to create the rhinoceros with a hide two feet thick and no apparent interest in politics!

Richard Cheney was chosen to fill the void in House Republican leadership as caucus Chairman Jack Kemp sought the GOP presidential nomination. A few years earlier Cheney had collaborated with his wife Lynn in writing a book entitled *Kings of the Hill.* The book glorifies the few truly powerful Speakers of the House. Thomas B. Reed of Maine, Cheney's clear favorite, virtually disenfranchised Democrats by his artful, often autocratic interpretation of House rules, once saying that the only "function" of the Democratic minority was "to make a quorum" and its only "right" was to draw its pay. Cheney's book, which I had read and enjoyed, also contained a glowing chapter on Henry Clay who, as Speaker, spearheaded the effort to get our country into a war with Great Britain. Later, at President Madison's request, Speaker Clay personally negotiated the peace treaty with the English foe.

Now, to my surprise, Cheney was accusing me of intrusion into foreign affairs and the abusive exercise of power. As noted in John Barry's book, *The Ambition and the Power,* Cheney said of my effort to keep the peace momentum alive, "He's a heavy-handed son of a bitch!" On May 24, 1988, he and other GOP stalwarts joined in a series of floor speeches complaining about the way I was conducting the House. Cheney and those who participated with him were implacable supporters of the Contra military effort.

Newt Gingrich of Georgia, who in the previous Congress had repeatedly attacked Speaker O'Neill as "corrupt," now went after me with a vengeance. After weeks of press conferences and verbal assaults, Gingrich filed formal charges accusing me of violating House rules in my personal finances. His specific charges, which relied on old newspaper stories going back eight and ten years, were ultimately dismissed.

Before he filed them on May 26, the complaints already had been written off by House Republican lawyers as groundless. At party leader Bob Michel's request, GOP stalwarts Robert Livingston of Louisiana and James Sensenbrenner of Wisconsin along with three staff attorneys had spent several weeks reviewing all of Gingrich's allegations. Their unanimous verdict: not worthy of pursuing.

Specifically, Gingrich charged that I had (1) acted improperly once in 1980 by writing the Department of Interior on behalf of a Texas drilling company in which I allegedly owned $15,000 worth of stock (I had never owned a penny's worth of stock in the company); (2) written the Egyptian government in 1979 on behalf of another Texas company that had drilled wells in the Sinai for the Israelis and now wanted to do the same for Egypt (I had done so very openly as an act of legitimate constituent representation); (3) received higher than usual royalties from a book of my essays published in 1984 by a Fort Worth printer (the little book sold for $5.95, I got no advance, and my royalties could not be compared to contracts with big commercial firms that then marketed books for several times that price and gave huge advance payments to Washington authors); (4) possibly used the book to convert campaign funds to personal use (no campaign funds were involved); and (5) interceded with savings and loan officials on behalf of Texas borrowers (I had twice called Bank Board chairman Ed Gray on behalf of delinquent borrowers who told me they needed extensions of time to avoid bankruptcy).

Many of the complaints involved services for constituents, the sorts of intercessions most congressmen routinely make for private citizens ensnarled in the coils of bureaucracy. My colleagues understood this. Before a weekly meeting of the Democratic whips, David Obey of Wisconsin said, "The Wall Street Journal is after your economics, Mr. Speaker, not your ethics. Newt Gingrich is after your effectiveness, not your ethics." In The Ambition and the Power, Barry quotes Gingrich as telling him, "This is not about ethics; it's about power."

The time it took to research each of these charges factually and refute them formally distracted me from my primary responsibilities. That is what I resented most. Wanting to clear up these matters once and for all, I publicly asked the House Ethics Committee, composed of six Democrats and six Republicans, to conduct a complete inquiry into the charges and report their findings. Naively, I supposed it would take the committee three or four weeks, a month at most, to dispose of what I knew were spurious allegations. Meanwhile, I would go about my business of leading the House. At that time in late May and early June of 1988, we were passing the thirteen annual appropriations bills.

Little did I dream that ranking committee Republican John Myers would insist on hiring an outside counsel, a politically ambitious Chicago lawyer named Richard Phelan, who would see his job as that of a special prosecutor, expanding the inquiry far beyond these complaints to investigate many facets of my private and political life going back as far as 1948. Instead of the few weeks I had anticipated, the publicly financed inquiry would extend for a full year. While Phelan's firm was being paid by the taxpayers to search for any wrongdoing in my history, I eventually would have to raise more than half a million dollars for legal fees in my own defense.

This was no polite exercise in polemics. The right wing was out for blood. A man named Peter Flaherty, who ran a Washington-based operation called Citizens for Reagan, circularized Republican national mailing lists with a series of letters viciously upbraiding me for "open and repeated cooperation with the Communists" in Nicaragua. I was, one mailing asserted, "guided by greed for money" and "willing to do Ortega's bidding." My speakership, the piece contended, had been "marked by dishonesty, lying, intimidation."

Tom Foley, whom I had appointed earlier in the year to represent the leadership on the Iran-Contra investigating committee, recognized Flaherty's name. It had surfaced a time or two, Tom said, in the course of the Iran-Contra hearings. Flaherty had been a member of the cabal trying to funnel money to the Contras. Now whatever money he managed was dedicated to the destruction of my political career and my personal reputation.

One of the Flaherty mailings asked for everyone receiving it to write letters denouncing me to the House Ethics Committee and the newspapers. "HERE IS YOUR CHANCE TO HELP GET RID OF WRIGHT," the written appeal concluded. "WE CAN'T LET ORTEGA AND WRIGHT RUIN THE HEMISPHERE." In another, even more audacious mail-out, Flaherty declared that I had "provided aid and comfort to the Communist Sandinista regime" and pleaded, "HELP PUT JIM WRIGHT ON TRIAL!" The letter urged recipients to sign a petition to the attorney general of the United States to "insure that Jim Wright is brought to justice"— presumably for treason.

The National Right to Work Committee, in a July 25 mailing to a nationwide list of employers, branded me its "#1 enemy in Congress" and asked businessmen to telegraph their representatives "so that every Congressman—Democrat and Republican—will feel the heat to censure Speaker Wright." A group called Free the Eagle mailed in August, charging among other things that I had "threatened America's national security," and urged readers to write their congressmen demanding "that Congress force Jim Wright to step down as Speaker."

Reading all this I marveled at the reckless lack of restraint of some of those who seemed so determined to revive the Nicaraguan war and at their readiness to destroy the reputation and honor of anyone who stood between them and that objective. Were they simply cynical and calloused? Or true believers pursuing their private vision of Armageddon? Some of both, most likely. I remembered something my Texas colleague Jack Brooks had said one day as we told old war stories. The talk had turned to Central America. "Isn't it strange," Jack mused, "how patriotic some people can be with other people's lives?"

Then, whimsically, I recalled that evening just about a year before when Tom Loeffler and Richard Peña and I had sat outside on the deck of my house in McLean, surveying the prospects for a bipartisan approach and a breakthrough at Esquipulas. Tom was expansive in the long summer twilight. "Sure, there are some who'll resent it and try to torpedo the effort, but we Republicans just have to recognize and live with the fact that Democrats are likely to be in power in Congress for a long time to come." I replied, just partly in jest, "Yes, Tom, the Democrats can probably stay in the majority, but I might not be Speaker if this thing goes wrong." I had known all along that it was a personal risk, but I had not become Speaker just to bask in the title. I would have traded the job if that were the price required by some cosmic equation to end the senseless killing that had claimed so many thousands of lives. Of course, I never imagined it would come to that. In contrast to the mounting right-wing drumbeat for my scalp, back home in Fort Worth the local Republicans chose for the first time in fourteen years not even to run a candidate against me in the November election. I felt good about that.

Behind the scenes in Congress, another battle was in progress. This involved the proper role of the U.S. government in the internal political affairs of other countries. Specifically, did the United States have the right to employ covert means to weaken and destabilize governments in our hemisphere? Should the CIA, or any other U.S. agency, carry out clandestine schemes inside other countries to undermine duly elected governments or to influence the course of domestic politics? Was it proper to spend U.S. tax dollars to help one political party against another in foreign elections, or to promote or instigate public incidents deliberately intended to embarrass a government with which we maintained diplomatic relations?

These questions had surfaced in March when the bipartisan task force was putting together the humanitarian-aid package for the Contras. Dick Cheney had wanted to earmark some of that tax money for "political activity" inside Nicaragua. I had argued that this would be a big mistake. It could be seen as an open violation of the Rio Treaty and the OAS charter. Those agreements provide for political self-determination for each member country and commit their signatories to nonintervention in the domestic affairs of others. Besides, I said, it could be absolutely counterproductive. It could give the most anti-U.S. elements in Nicaragua a whipping boy against which to rally public opinion. "How would we feel," I asked, "if another nation—let's say Japan, for example—were to appropriate money in their national budget to influence politics in the United States? Wouldn't the American people resent the hell out of that?"

Cheney quickly dropped the proposal. He saw, I think, that it would be futile to press for political money in the humanitarian-aid bill. But he did not drop the basic idea of U.S. political intervention, as I was later to discover.

David Bonior and I discussed with Cheney and Mickey Edwards the basic philosophical difference between a CIA operation and something like the National Endowment for Democracy, which conducted its business openly and supposedly in a bipartisan way. I did not know at the time that one wing of the NED had donated money to a political magazine in Costa Rica that published harsh attacks on President Oscar Arias. If I had known this, I would have objected vigorously. Perhaps naively, I supposed that the NED's efforts were confined to helping other countries promote such basically impartial activities as voter registration and election-day turnout.

Nor could I have foretold that seventeen months later, in October of 1989, Congress would appropriate $9 million, much of it to assist directly and indirectly in the campaign of an opposition coalition in Nicaragua to elect Violeta Chamorro as president over Daniel Ortega. (It would be illegal under U.S. law for Nicaragua or any other country to contribute money to our Democratic or Republican party.) A former Contra leader named Edgar Chamorro, describing himself as a "non-Sandinista Nicaraguan," was to blast the $9 million U.S. financing of opposition parties on October 25, 1989, as an effort to "buy votes." By the standards of Nicaragua's impoverished economy, he contended, the sum could be the equivalent of a $2 billion foreign intrusion into a U.S. election.

But at least efforts of this type were out in the open. They were not undercover operations like those conducted by the CIA. Ironically, Edgar Chamorro acknowledged that he worked with the CIA from 1982 to 1984 as director of communications for the Contras, until disillusioned by what he described as efforts by the U.S. agency to use his office to plant false and misleading propaganda. He claimed, for example, that CIA officials as early as 1982 were assuring Contra leaders privately that they had official U.S. government backing to "march into Managua" and seize power, but insisting, however, that Contra spokesmen should publicly disavow any such intention. As press spokesman for the resistance, Chamorro had done as instructed.

On September 5, 1985, the same Edgar Chamorro gave an affidavit to the World Court in the case concerning the CIA's mining of Nicaraguan harbors. The deputy station chief for the CIA, Chamorro testified, had awakened him at his home at 2:00 A.M. on January 5, 1984 (following public discovery of the mining), and handed him a press release "in excellent Spanish." The CIA agent instructed him to broadcast the statement over a Contra radio station claiming that the *Contras*—not the CIA—had mined the harbors. In his sworn statement Chamorro declared:

> I was surprised to read that we—the FDN [Nicaraguan Democratic Front]—were taking credit for having mined several Nicaraguan harbors. . . . The truth is that we played no role in the mining of the harbors. But we did as instructed and broadcast the communiqué about the mining.

Former CIA senior analyst David MacMichael, in sworn testimony to the World Court on September 16, 1985, revealed the outlines of an agency plan to employ both paramilitary and political means in an effort to goad the Nicaraguan government into an overreactive and politically self-destructive response. The purpose was "to weaken, even destabilize" the government, according to MacMichael, and to discredit the Sandinista leaders in the eyes of Congress:

> The principal actions . . . were paramilitary which hopefully would provoke cross-border attacks by Nicaraguan forces and thus serve to demonstrate Nicaragua's aggressive nature.

... It was hoped that the Nicaraguan government would clamp down on civil liberties within Nicaragua itself, arresting its opposition, demonstrating its allegedly inherent totalitarian nature ... and further that there would be reaction against United States citizens ... within Nicaragua and thus serve to demonstrate the hostility of Nicaragua towards the United States.

As I said earlier, none of these activities was in keeping with official U.S. policy. No such thing had been authorized by Congress. The nation's laws, in fact, expressly disallowed such clandestine forays into ad hoc policy-making.

Yet, according to an August 7, 1988, United Press International report, the CIA was spending money from a secret $10 to $12 million "political" account earmarked for Nicaragua's internal opposition. Agency and State Department officials acknowledged that they had encouraged internal opposition groups to take "a bolder approach to test the limits of pluralism." A bolder approach? Test the limits? In other words, see what it takes to provoke the government into clamping down? But these were the very things for which the House Intelligence Committee chairman had so recently admonished top CIA officials! The agency had been told that it was *not* supposed to instigate or promote incidents to disrupt the peace process. I mistakenly took Richard Cheney's withdrawal in the humanitarian-aid mark-up sessions as tacit acceptance that the CIA's role in initiating policy was limited now that formal negotiations were ongoing.

We heard reports that CIA spokesmen were pressuring the Contra directorate to follow the leadership of Colonel Enrique Bermúdez in the current internal struggle between the movement's civilian and military factions. According to a story in the *Miami Herald* of May 18, a CIA agent harangued a meeting of the political directors for twenty minutes through a remote telephone hookup on Bermúdez's behalf. The agency spokesman had reportedly called one of the directors "an imbecile" for proposing that the former Somoza guardsman be replaced.

A few days later, Congress decisively resolved one part of this question. The issue came to a head on the House floor on May 26 when Cheney and white-maned Illinois Republican Henry Hyde in a surprise move actually attempted to expand the involvement of the CIA in Central America.

The annual authorization of funds for intelligence activities was up for consideration. Most members expected routine passage. The bill this year was considered relatively noncontroversial. In previous years it had ignited partisan battles, and it had been the vehicle for the original Boland Amendment and its successors prohibiting expenditure of public funds to attempt the overthrow of the Nicaraguan government. This year, Intelligence Committee Chairman Louis Stokes thought he had ironed out all problems within the committee. He thought there was bipartisan agreement. Republican leaders on the panel had told him they did not expect to offer any major amendment.

Then, apparently, a decision was made overnight in House GOP circles to go all out for a wider CIA role. Cheney and Hyde sprang a surprise amendment on the House floor, broadening the powers of the covert agency to undertake secret initiatives on its own. The amendment would have permitted the CIA to determine on an ad hoc basis what was in the public interest. Debate was intense.

Henry Hyde is a large man with a smooth, handsome face and an abundance of silver hair. He is an orator who speaks with patriotic zeal. Sometimes, particularly when inveighing against social evils like drugs and abortion, he makes the rafters ring in a manner that reminds listeners of an old-time evangelist. On this day, Hyde sought to assuage Chairman Stokes's anguish over having been lulled into a state of unpreparedness. "Nothing has been more painful in my congressional career," the Illinois Republican intoned, "than not to inform Mr. Stokes of this amendment." But the matter of triumphing over communist influences in Central America and the Western Hemisphere was so supremely important, he concluded, that it overrode questions of normal legislative courtesy.

Other spokesmen picked up the theme that the United States was in a death struggle in Central America and needed every available weapon, fair or foul, in its arsenal. An enticing argument, but it rang hollow to a majority of the members. Many felt we had been embarrassed too often in learning after the fact of CIA involvement, at first officially denied and then grudgingly acknowledged as true, in activities of which Congress actively disapproved. Like mining the harbors, bombing civilian airfields, distributing assassination manuals, selling arms to the Ayatollah.

When the tally came, the amendment was rejected by a vote of 214 to 190. Congress would still make the policy, and it would not be second-guessed and secretly countermanded by the CIA. The restrictions remained intact on covert activity.

But any lingering hope of bipartisanship was dead. Hyde's maneuver, and Cheney's vocal support, sent an unmistakable message: The militants had taken command of House Republican ranks. So far as Central America was concerned, and maybe in other matters as well, the spirit of comity had fallen victim to ideology. Things would not be the same again.

CHAPTER 10

So Near, So Far

Swimming in the waters of this sea and that sea ...
We knew that the islands were beautiful
Somewhere round about here where we're groping—
A little nearer or a little farther ...

—Antoine de Saint-Exupéry

As May of 1988 ended, I was saddened by my
inability to create a bipartisan consensus in Congress but heartened
by success in our Democratic domestic legislative program and by
new developments that seemed to be bringing the Contras and the
Sandinistas nearer to agreement. Regarding the former, I ruefully
accepted reality. Congressional Republicans were reflecting the White
House. The dominant personalities in the administration did not
want consensus with Congress except on their terms. They resented
my efforts to participate actively in the search for policy. Their idea
of a bipartisan compromise was a plan initiated by the White House
and supported by congressional Democrats, not the other way
around. And they really believed that they, not the Central Americans, should decide the fate of that region.

Considering the past ten months, I now could see a lot of things

191

more clearly in the rearview mirror. In spite of Tom Loeffler's best intentions, people who drove Central American policy in the White House did not really expect the Wright-Reagan plan to produce a peace agreement. They thought the Esquipulas meeting would break up in a squabble. They would blame the failure on Nicaraguan intransigence and use that to justify accelerating the war. Their real goal continued to be the military overthrow of the government in Managua.

My friend Arkansas Congressman Bill Alexander came by my office after the vote defeating the Hyde amendment. Bill had spent a lot of time in Latin America. He was with me in Nicaragua in 1980, in El Salvador and Nicaragua in 1982, in Venezuela in 1985. Bill had a keen, long-term interest in the region and had made a lot of friends there.

"Did you know that Elliott Abrams and General Powell went to Central America last January?" he asked.

"Yes, Bill, I knew about that."

"Did you know they went personally to see every president, except Ortega?"

"Yes, but it didn't surprise me. That's their policy. Don't ask me why. I disagree with it. I think it's childish, petty. But that *is* administration policy," I said.

"Did you know that they tried to get each of the other Central American presidents to denounce Ortega personally and to claim that Nicaragua was violating the peace agreements?"

"Yes, I heard that."

"Well, did you know that they hinted very strongly that foreign aid to each of those countries would depend upon whether its president fell in line with their demands?"

"I heard that, Bill, but I'm not sure I buy it. I find it hard to believe they'd be that crude."

"Well, it's true!" he declared. "I have it on excellent authority. It happened. These people are trying every weapon in their arsenal to break up the peace process."

"I guess the important thing is that they haven't succeeded," I replied. "The Central American presidents didn't take the bait. Anyway, Abrams and Powell couldn't deliver on that kind of threat, even if they tried, Bill. The Central Americans probably know that. Furthermore, they're endeavoring earnestly, eagerly to make the peace process work. They wouldn't fall in line with any ploy to blow it up now, after all the effort they've put into it."

"Jim, I know those people as well as you do," Bill said, a faint hint of impatience in his voice. "What you say is true. But you're over-looking one important ingredient."

"What's that?"

"You, Mr. Speaker. Yourself. The Central Americans will not be bullied because they think you'll protect them."

"Damn thin reed to lean on," I snorted. "I can't even seem to protect myself these days. The whole right wing is up in arms and after my scalp like the Sioux after Custer's."

"I'm telling you the perception in Latin America, Mr. Speaker. Why do you think the right wing hates your guts? It's because when-ever the Latin Americans come to town they want to see you. The White House ignores them. Abrams lectures and threatens them. The Latin Americans think you're the only one who'll listen to what *they're* saying. That's why they'll do almost anything you ask them to do. And that undercuts the hell out of Abrams." Alexander was looking intently at me.

"I really didn't want to undercut anybody, Bill," I mused. "I just wanted to help. They came and signed me on as copilot for a journey to peace. But once we were off the runway, half the crew started bailing out. Now even the pilot has bailed out."

"That's right," Bill laughed, building on the allegory. "And that leaves you in the copilot's seat with the stick in your hand and your feet on the rudders. We're still on course but there's a helluva head wind."

"Yeah. So what do I do, Navigator? Do I find a corn field for an emergency landing? Or do I stay on course and hope we get there before we run out of fuel?"

"I know what you're *going* to do," Bill Alexander said after a brief hesitation. "You're going to keep on seeing these guys. And you're going to try to keep them on course. Just like you did a few days ago when Ramírez came by. I'll bet you're the only official person in Washington who agreed to see him."

Bill Alexander might have been right. Truth was that I had talked with both Sergio Ramírez and a group from the Contra directorate in the past week. Both sides had sought me out, asked to come by my office. I felt, in fact, that I helped engineer a minor breakthrough.

Sandinista Vice President Ramírez listened sympathetically as I described the difficulties we were encountering in channeling human-itarian aid to the resistance forces bivouacked in his country. I told him we wanted our shipments to comply with the Sapoa accord. The OAS had agreed to perform delivery through its Pan-American Development Foundation, but only if that were acceptable to both sides. The Contra directorate had agreed. We needed the assent of the Nicaraguan government. The vice president promised to take it up with the other members of his country's governing junta and get back to me.

On May 24, two days before the floor fight over the Hyde amendment, Ramírez called from Managua. His government had agreed formally to permit delivery by the OAS to its idled military adversaries in Nicaragua. The agency also might contract with private deliverers if it desired.

Ramírez continued. A meeting with the Contras was scheduled for Thursday in Managua. He told me his government would make it clear that Contra representatives attending the sessions were free to meet privately with the news media, including *La Prensa*. He said they would also be given the time and opportunity to meet separately with Cardinal Obando and with domestic religious and political groups opposed to the Sandinistas.

"That is what the Contra leaders said they would like to do," Ramírez told me. "Time ran out and they didn't get to do this last time they were in Managua. We are trying to show them that we want to be fair and considerate of their wishes."

Later that afternoon, I met with four of the Contra directors. Alfredo César was their principal spokesman. He was accompanied by Pedro Joaquín Chamorro, Aristedes Sánchez, and a Mrs. Azucena Ferrey. There had been a dichotomy in the directorate. Some were willing to go through with the meetings scheduled to begin on Thursday in Managua. Others were insisting they should refuse the invitation to return to Managua, cancel the meeting, and hold out instead for a meeting in Sapoa.

That surprised me. "Why *not* Managua?" I asked. "Isn't that where your group has insisted all along on meeting?"

"Well, yes," replied César, "but some feel there are too many distractions in Managua, and too many government people hovering around all the time. Some of our group feel that they would have more time to devote to the substance of things if we scheduled a meeting in Sapoa instead of Managua."

César, it seemed to me, was talking for the benefit of some others in the room. His heart was not really in this argument. Perhaps

Abrams or some other U.S. official was putting pressure on some of the Contras to stall by finding a pretext to delay the meetings.

"Well, I don't care where you meet, Alfredo," I blurted, not entirely concealing my exasperation. "You have to work that out among yourselves. For Pete's sake, it's beginning to remind me of the endless and pointless and fruitless talks that went on for months among the Vietnamese about the shape of the table!"

Later that day, César called and asked Wilson Morris to tell me they would be going to Managua on Wednesday. The directorate had voted to go ahead with the meetings as scheduled. Three members had been present. The vote was two to one. César was to lead the negotiations. The resistance would propose to lay down their arms in August. They would end the war, contingent upon the government's agreeing to a specific date for elections and a firm pledge to disassociate the army from the Sandinista political party. They would want some guarantees about private property, César indicated, but the main consideration was the army. It must be an instrument of the government, not in any way affiliated with a political party.

Things were looking up. My disappointment over the domestic political scene was somewhat assuaged by these developments. If the political establishment at home seemed more polarized than before, the Central Americans seemed to be coming together.

During the first week in June, I received dismaying news about my friend President José Napoleón Duarte of El Salvador. He had abdominal cancer and was at Walter Reed Army Hospital in Washington for evaluation and treatment. I drove out to see him.

Duarte, clad in an oversized robe, rose from a chair and came forward to great me. I felt a sudden shock. He seemed drawn and diminished in stature. Only his luminous eyes showed the undaunted fire of life. My own eyes watered over uncontrollably and my Adam's apple felt like a hard baseball in my throat, as he clasped me in a warm *abrazo*, that Latin equivalent of a handshake between friends.

Duarte told me of the medical diagnosis—the cancer had spread to his liver—and of his personal choice to submit to treatment that, while not ending the cancer, might prolong for some months his capability to be active. It was important to the embattled president of El Salvador that he live out his term of office to oversee the election in the coming year and the peaceful transition of power to his successor, whether of his own Christian Democratic party or of the rival, more conservative ARENA faction.

He had been eager to see me, he said, to discuss the content of two letters he was carefully composing during his hospitalization. They might be, he speculated, the most important epistles of his career. One was to the army. Duarte was writing what he hoped would become a document of lasting inspiration to present and future Salvadoran military officers. He wanted to commit them, enduringly, to the principle of subordination to a constitutionally elected civilian leadership and to the abiding duty to protect—never violate—the civil rights of private citizens.

"I have worked especially hard with the military people, Jimmy," he said. "For a long time there was a vestige of men, a holdover from the old days, who secretly worked with the death squads. Never in uniform, never openly, but like a secret society. They carried out clandestine executions. I knew in my mind that some of those people were military people. I knew it but could not prove it. It was like what I have read about the Ku Klux Klan in your country after the Civil War. These are the wicked people who slew Bishop Romero and murdered the nuns from the United States. I talked and I talked with our military leaders, and I think we have slowly weeded out this lawless element. We must never let it infest our army again!"

We discussed this for a long while. Thirty minutes passed. An hour. The ailing president asked me how I thought the United States had succeeded for two hundred years in preventing the military from usurping power. Did I have suggestions or thoughts he might include in the letter to the army? It was a hard question. Our national traditions, our histories were so different. This brave man, facing a stark personal crisis, was poignantly determined to leave a legacy of political freedom to his country.

A second letter Duarte was composing would be addressed to his party. He hoped the epistle would serve as a compass for the Christian Democrats. It would recite the underlying thesis that had driven this determined man: Political liberty is a tree that fulfills its destiny only if it produces the fruit of economic justice—land for the landless, work for the jobless, education and opportunity for those who have lost hope.

In 1981, Duarte had forced upon a reluctant oligarchy a measure of land reform in which the government exercised eminent domain to buy many small, family-sized tracts from the big *latifundias* and encouraged peasant farmers to settle and cultivate them. The experiment had been only a partial success. The bureaucracy was slow in delivering land titles, and in numerous cases large plantation owners had strong-armed worker families off the land.

Now, pressing his point, Duarte said with intensity, "You remember what I told you, Jimmy, when you and Mr. Kissinger came to see us in 1983. There are two distinct societies in El Salvador. Ten percent of our people still own 90 percent of all our land and property. Ninety percent still have nothing. The 90 percent are gambling on democracy to help balance the scales. If we cannot show some real progress, their disillusionment will be a terrible thing to see."

But Duarte was determined that his followers must not abandon faith in the process. This letter would also stress the imperative of respect for the political system, including a willing and peaceful abidance by electoral results even when they go against the party's wishes.

I had been waiting for a chance to tell the president of a visit I'd had a few days earlier from Guillermo Ungo, political spokesman for the FMLN, the Salvadoran rebel force. Ungo had been elected vice president under Duarte in 1972. After the brutal military overthrow of their administration, the two had gone separate ways. While Duarte persevered to restore the system, Ungo had despaired and joined with the guerrilla forces.

"Ungo came to see me, Nappy," I said, using Duarte's nickname.

"I heard he was in Washington. What did he say?"

"He said he was trying to persuade others in the FMLN to rejoin the political system. He would like for them to participate in the elections next spring. At least that's what he said to me."

"I think it is possible he may feel that way personally," Duarte mused. "I have told them that they should renounce terror and run as a political party. That way we will see just how many people they really speak for."

"Exactly. That's exactly what I said to him. He seems to be hanging back for fear their entering the political contest might split enough people from your left flank to tilt the balance toward the ARENA party. He thinks D'Aubuisson and his people then would set out a reign of terror that would doom any prospects for peace."

Duarte seemed thoughtful. "What did you say to him about that?" he finally asked.

"I told him if that were his chief concern, he ought to rejoin the Christian Democrats and bring as many of the resistance with him as he could to ensure that what he fears doesn't occur. He seemed unable to agree to that course, and that's about where we left it. But

I did plead with him to drop the war and return to the political process."

"Of course what you told him is what he should do," Duarte agreed, "but Villalobos and the other guerrilla commanders do not seem ready to go along that route. At least, not yet. But, thanks to the peace effort, they have stopped the killing for a time now. And Ungo —well, he doesn't want the most left-wing elements in their movement to be attacking him, I suppose. It will come, I know. It will take time, but it will come."

Time was running out for my friend, but he had sublime faith that what he had set in motion would triumph.

Duarte said he had received a call earlier in the day from Daniel Ortega. "Daniel had learned of my cancer. He was very gentle. We have not been friends, you know—not before Esquipulas. He showed courage at Esquipulas. He challenged the radical wing of his party. If only he will stick with what he pledged! I reminded him again today to remember what we both promised our people."

As I was leaving, Duarte said, "I hope you know I will always remember, Jimmy, if it had not been for you—you standing by us so strongly in Congress—my country would not have had a chance at democracy."

Suddenly I was embarrassed by the sincerity of this good man, and shamed that I had begun to grow weary in the struggle. "What I did was just words, Nappy," I replied. "*You're* the one who put his life on the line. You've held the nation together through eight years of civil war. In my opinion, you're the Abraham Lincoln of El Salvador."

On the drive back to the Hill from Walter Reed Hospital, I thought about leadership. Over the past thirty-four years I had met many foreign leaders. Forty or fifty heads of state, I reckoned, maybe more. A few stood out, separate and distinct in character. These were the ones with the big dream, willing to take a chance and risk all on the rightness of their conviction, ready to blaze a new trail in uncharted territory, to swim upstream if necessary against the sullen tide of their nation's history.

Anwar Sadat was one of those. A warrior who despaired of killing, he turned in midcareer to make peace with the ancient foe whom his people had been taught through centuries of preachments to hate. It cost him his life. Gorbachev, I thought, might be another. I had met and talked with him in Moscow in April of the previous year and been impressed with his boldness, his sincerity of purpose, his willingness to lead the USSR in an entirely new direction, to take big risks for peace. And Duarte. In his own obscure time and place, José Napoleón Duarte. Bucking four hundred years of ingrained tradition to promote peace and democracy in Latin America's bloodiest and most authoritarian country, Duarte had earned a place in my personal pantheon of courageous leaders.

In the second week of June, the Contras walked away from the peace talks. The Bermúdez faction, the military commanders, had gained ascendancy for a time over the civilian leadership. (On July 1, with the sixty-day cease-fire expiring, Ortega was to announce that his government would unilaterally extend its observance. The Sandinistas were to do so, in thirty-day increments, until November 1, 1989.) Our group in Congress tried to learn just what had happened. We got lengthy verbal reports from Alfredo César and OAS Secretary-General Baena Soares, who had sat in on some of the talks in Managua. The two accounts coincided.

Apparently for several days in early June, a rapid succession of agreements had appeared to be moving the peace talks toward closure on all issues. Negotiators had resolved sixteen separate agenda items. On six of nine written points involving democratization and political pluralism, they had reached verbatim agreement. They had united on language guaranteeing separation of the judiciary from the executive and legislative branches. They had signed off on provisions granting a full range of human rights and equal treatment for all political parties.

Only two sticking points remained. The Contra draftsmen wanted to include language specifically denouncing the use of "coercive force" to oblige citizens to join the Sandinista Party. The government bridled at the phrase. It could be interpreted, the Sandinista leaders said, as a confession that they had in fact employed coercive force to build party ranks. They suggested instead a verbal affirmation of the right and privilege to belong to any party a citizen might choose. This did not satisfy spokesmen for the resistance.

The other unresolved point involved disengaging the army and the police from any association with the ruling political party. Negotiators came very close to conceptual agreement but could not find mutually acceptable language in which to couch it. The Contras wanted a provision referring specifically to the army and the police.

The Sandinistas were insisting on broader language to the effect that "all institutions and organs of the government" would be totally disassociated from political parties.

Our group in Congress learned all this on June 15. That day Alfredo César, chief negotiator for the resistance, came by for a long talk. He seemed more frank in one-on-one conversations than when he was speaking formally for a delegation. I had always considered him both an adroit political maneuverer and a constructive force.

Alfredo discussed the meetings, the near agreement, the nuances of the two unresolved differences, the hardening on both sides. The peace talks had broken down, I gathered, when extremists and hardliners on both sides began to balk, each insisting on positions calculated to stiffen resistance on the other side. For the first several sessions César, with the backing of the more moderate Contra faction—including Pedro Chamorro and Mrs. Ferrey—was able to patch together positions that he successfully sold to the Sandinista majority. For a time both delegations were led by their more conciliatory elements.

As agreement neared, however, the most conservative faction of the Contras and the most radical element of the Sandinista delegation started digging in their heels. The degree to which this hardening of positions might have been influenced by outside agitators, or by public opinion in Nicaragua, is unknown to me. It might simply have been a product of the political chemistry, each side panicky about or suspicious of the prospect of a too-easy agreement and bending over backward to avoid the appearance of "caving in" to the other. Whatever the rationale, the militant wing of the Contras gained ascendancy within the delegation and broke off the talks. César would not disclose the internal business of his group, and I did not ask him to do so. But I suspect he might have been, at the last minute, outvoted.

A few hours later, Baena Soares of the OAS came to the Capitol and gave an essentially identical description to Tom Foley, Tony Coelho, David Bonior, Dante Fascell, and me, along with members of our staffs. Baena Soares narrated the series of events leading up to the very doorway of a settlement, and described the slamming of the door. After giving his report to the group, Baena Soares whispered that he would like to talk with me privately. Back in my working office, the OAS leader told me his perception of the problem. It boiled down, he said, to pressures set in motion outside the negotiating room by rival military and police factions under the command of Colonel Bermúdez on one side and Sandinista Secretary of the Interior Tomás Borge on the other. Borge controlled the police. The noncompromising extremists on both sides shared a mutual goal: to torpedo the peace talks.

Baena Soares described the following scenario: The Sandinista moderates at the negotiating table would be making concession after concession. The Contras would be responding with reciprocal gestures of conciliation. Then Borge, a rigid ideologue unhappy with these developments, would send out the police to arrest some domestic political opponent of the government on a thin pretext. This would outrage the Contras (a response clearly intended by Borge) and immediately escalate the temperature of the dialogue in the negotiating room.

In retaliation, antigovernment forces—with suspected outside encouragement—would stage a massive protest. On signal, someone would begin hurling insults at peasant youngsters in police uniform. Goaded, a policeman would respond with a blustery threat. Shouting matches would ensue. Someone would shove. Fighting would erupt on the edge of the crowd. Police would arrest two or three of the more vocal agitators. Their friends would respond with cries of "brutality!" Extremists in both camps would fan indignation among their followers. Those on each side who wanted to stall negotiations would have a good excuse to do so.

What a damn shame, I thought, that the confrontationists almost always have the advantage. Ill will is more easily created than good. I thought of the old aphorism that Sam Rayburn so often quoted: "Any jackass can kick down a barn, but it takes a skilled carpenter to build one."

On July 5, *Newsday* carried an article headlined "Contra Peace-Talks Ploy Disclosed." The story quoted a "top contra leader" to the effect that his group had deliberately broken off the talks in order to seek a new dose of military aid. The unidentified source had told a reporter, "So long as we were talking, we had no chance of revival of military aid. Now we may."

Someone who had been monitoring the talks told David Bonior that the last Contra proposal laid on the table departed sharply and harshly from anything previously offered. It included demands that the entire Nicaraguan Supreme Court resign and that the military draft be eliminated immediately.

The hardening of the Contra bargaining position and the escalation of demands coincided with the increasing role of Colonel Enrique Bermúdez, the first active military commander ever named to the Contra directorate. Bermúdez had publicly criticized the Sapoa agreement, calling it "poorly negotiated," and fired the two Contra commanders who signed it.

Following Bermúdez's election to the directorate and the simultaneous dropping of Pedro Joaquín Chamorro from the negotiating team, seven commanders of the Contras' southern front had quit in disgust. They told the press that moving Bermúdez forth into the negotiator's role marked "a steady and pronounced shift to the extreme right." Always controversial, Bermúdez was regarded by the moderate Contra wing as a throwback to the Somoza days. Now word came that the colonel, along with Aristedes Sánchez, had played a key role in preventing a permanent cease-fire agreement. They wanted to throw the dice one more time in a desperate effort to revive military aid and renew the war.

Reagan regulars were searching for ways to resume the flow of arms. Senate Republican Leader Bob Dole drafted a proposal to add $20 million in new military aid and funnel a residue of some $18 million more in previously appropriated weapons money to the Contras. He also wanted to authorize unspecified amounts for radar-jamming equipment and indemnification money for leased aircraft.

On July 12 the *Miami Herald* quoted a Bermúdez threat that an end to military funding would bring on a new Contra strategy featuring terrorism and assassination of Sandinista leaders. This almost surely stoked flames from the embers of hostility still smoldering in Managua.

During the breakdown in talks, the level of violence rose. An organization called Witness for Peace reported that independent sources confirmed the killing of at least five civilians and the kidnapping of more than seventy by Contra field forces. And on July 4 seven civilians and five Contra soldiers died when road mines blew up two vehicles in which they were riding. As sporadic acts of terror increased, so did the political rhetoric. On July 10, in the town of Nandaime, anti-Sandinista demonstrators began throwing rocks. Government police used tear gas and clubs to break up the riot and arrested more than forty people. The government and the opposition blamed the violence on each other.

The next day, the government ordered *La Prensa* closed for fifteen days on grounds of inciting violence. U.S. Ambassador Richard Melton was expelled, along with seven other embassy officials. The Sandinistas claimed that U.S. officials were personally coordinating the antigoverment demonstrations. They accused the U.S. embassy of distributing $180,000 among opposition groups to foment demonstrations, and said that American officials had been directly involved in the Nandaime riots.

President Reagan retaliated by expelling Ambassador Tünnermann and seven other officials of the Nicaraguan embassy in Washington. Citing no specifics, the State Department issued a formal charge claiming that Tünnermann "engaged in activities that constitute an abuse of his privilege of residence in the United States."

Reporters importuned me for a comment and I declined. I knew nothing of the circumstances. I knew only that, prior to being named ambassador, Melton had served under Elliott Abrams as director of the State Department's Central American affairs office. During the Iran-Contra hearings, witnesses had identified him as Abrams's intermediary with retired General John Singlaub, a supporter of a military solution in Nicaragua. Melton, interviewed by *Newsweek* for its July 25, 1988, issue, acknowledged "extensive meetings with the opposition." The article's authors called Melton's appointment the previous April "a switch in U.S. strategy" and concluded that senior officials had "encouraged the internal opposition to test the limits" of Sandinista tolerance. "They hoped to either weaken Sandinista control, or provoke a clampdown that might win new votes for military aid."

Here again were the words CIA spokesmen had recited earlier to House Intelligence Committee members: "To test the limits." And here, publicly renewed, was the admission of direct U.S. instigation of the protest. The real purpose, obviously, was that statement of purpose to which former CIA official David MacMichael and former Contra contact Edgar Chamorro had testified in 1985 before the World Court. The tacit purpose of testing the limits was to "provoke a clampdown," and the reason for that was "to win new votes [in Congress] for military aid."

There seemed to be one subtle difference now. The CIA, following its assurances to Chairman Lou Stokes, was apparently not the principal choreographer of the public agitation. Others, perhaps including embassy personnel, seemed to be taking over much of that task. On August 7, Brian Barger wrote a lengthy story for United Press International in which he quoted "State Department and CIA officials" as acknowledging that they had been "encouraging internal opposition groups to take a bolder approach." These same officials told Barger that the CIA was spending money from a $10 to $12 million "political account" earmarked for Nicaragua's internal opposition. And David Jessup of the American Institute for Free Labor Development, which had been helping moderate Nicaraguan labor groups to organize unions, told Barger of seeing demonstrators come out of a park to a rally "carrying clubs, sticks, rocks and chunks of concrete."

The situation was clearly deteriorating. Chances for peace looked grim. Busily engaged daily in plans for the Democratic National Convention over which I was to preside, and committed to passing all thirteen appropriations bills in the House before the August 1988 recess, I was pressed for time. With such a heavy domestic agenda, I was powerless to make any constructive contribution to reversing the downhill path of events in Central America.

On August 10, the Senate approved a $633 million supplemental spending bill to which Republican Leader Dole attempted to attach his amendment for new Contra arms aid. The amendment was defeated on a fifty-seven to thirty-nine vote. This clear rejection apparently had a chilling effect on Contra hard-liners and renewed the hopes, and influence, of moderates who wanted to negotiate a settlement.

Late one morning during the week of September 12, a group from the Contra leadership came by my office unexpectedly. They had made no appointment, and my schedule was jammed. I was gasping for time like a beached fish gasps for oxygen, but I managed to squeeze them in. The group included moderates and hard-liners. Alfredo César was the principal spokesman. With him, as best I can recall, were Colonel Bermúdez, Mrs. Ferrey, Aristedes Sánchez, Pedro Joaquín Chamorro, and a few others, some of whom I had not previously met.

Members of this group had been in touch with the Sandinistas, I was told, and wanted to renew negotiations. The two sides had a tentative agreement for an informal exploratory meeting in Guatemala on Monday. The climate for fruitful talks, they said, would be improved greatly if the Nicaraguan government could be persuaded to pardon the prisoners they had taken at Nandaime. They wondered if I could help persuade Ortega's government to grant pardons.

"I'll do the best I can," I said, "but I don't know how much effect it will have. Both ambassadors, as you know, have been recalled. We can't go through them. Frankly, I don't know any channels of communication that would be particularly effective." The only thing I could think of was to call and try to appeal to Ortega or maybe D'Escoto personally. I hadn't been in touch with either of them for weeks. Looking directly at César, I said, "I suppose our State Department is aware of what you're asking."

"Oh, yes," replied César. "They know we're here."

That confirmed one thing for me. These people would feel they needed to get the State Department's blessing for a renewal of talks. But what César pointedly did not say made me almost as sure of a second fact: Renewing the talks was his idea, not State's.

César had believed all along that the negotiating process would work. He now held the upper hand, at least temporarily, in the internal Contra power struggle. I did not know how long he could keep it, and neither did he.

Guessing that this little group would be going to Elliott Abrams's office as soon as they left me, I decided to give them the best and straightest advice I could. "Alfredo, my friend," I began, "I'll do what I can about the prisoners, but I frankly doubt that it will be very effective. I'm glad you want to renew the peace talks. But I want to give you some free advice.

"The on-again-off-again nature of those talks has created a lot of disillusionment. If you go back to the table, go with a determination to make it work this time! I'll say that very same thing to the Sandinistas. Don't go back into negotiations looking for some convenient excuse to break them off again. If that's in the minds of any of your negotiating team, you'd be better off not even to begin the charade in the first place!"

While saying these words, I was trying to look at each member of that team and size up their reactions. The faces of Bermúdez and Sánchez were like masks. Sánchez probably did not understand the English clearly. I thought César, Chamorro, and one or two of the others were glad I had said what I did.

"There's one more thing," I plunged ahead. "Don't go into these talks with the idea that the CIA is going to foment demonstrations and push the Sandinistas into overreacting. I've been assured that they are *not* going to do that! So don't be counting on anything of that sort as an excuse to break off the talks."

This message was delivered for the benefit of Bermúdez and Sánchez. I could tell that it had sunk in with some of the others. The conversation ended and the group left.

* * *

Still determined to dissolve the bitterness and break down the barriers of partisan ideology in the House, I tried a new gambit in personal diplomacy. Monday, September 19, was the day set aside for the annual Democratic golf tournament to which members invited political supporters. In a gesture of goodwill, I invited Republican leader Bob Michel to join us for the day's outing, followed by a dinner at which he was made a special honoree. Everybody was surprised. Nothing like this had been done before. Bob, whose appetite for golf was legendary in Washington, accepted the invitation. He seemed to enjoy the day and its relaxed banter. At the dinner that night, I expressed the hope that Michel's presence at our sporting events would become a tradition.

It doesn't cost anything to be gracious to one's political adversaries, I was thinking. The Republicans must have realized following the Senate rejection of Dole's amendment that they had lost the Contra battle. To be gracious in victory, one only has to be a gentleman, I mused. To be gracious in defeat was the harder task. Maybe, just maybe. . . .

Tuesday, September 20, set in motion a chain of events that shattered my optimism and plunged me into the icy stream of reality. As the press corps crowded in for my daily pre-session conference, the mood was upbeat. We had passed the appropriations bills and the landmark trade bill. The agenda I had announced in my televised response to the president's State of the Union message in January was almost complete. I reported the day's schedule for the House and asked for questions.

Into a wide-ranging discussion of such things as interest rates, taxes, textile duties and appropriations bills, an unfamiliar young man suddenly threw a verbal grenade. His question put a bizarre and unexpected twist on my recent private comments to the Contra directors. "Several sources," according to the questioner, had told him that at a recent meeting I blamed the jailing of protesters at Nandaime on "CIA provocation." He claimed these sources further said I told them I was "not willing to offer assistance to get the opposition leaders out of jail." The statement shocked me. I did not recognize the reporter, an apparent newcomer to the daily press conference.

"Would you identify yourself?" I asked.

"Pete La Barbera, *Washington Times*."

So that's it, I thought. The *Times* is trying to bait me. The reporter

was obviously referring to my private meeting with the Contra leaders of the previous week. How would he know about it? I had thought
that conversation was in confidence. All such previous meetings had
been.

Besides, this young reporter had the message badly garbled. He
quoted me as saying the exact reverse of what I actually had said. I
flushed with anger. "The several sources whom you cite were not
present at the meeting, or else they were not listening," I began. "I
said I *was* encouraging the government in Nicaragua to release the
prisoners, and anyone who heard anything different than that was
not listening or was inventing. . . . It is a false story."

The truth was that, at my request, Wilson Morris of my staff
had made a personal trip to New York where he appealed directly
on behalf of the prisoners to Nicaraguan Foreign Minister Miguel
D'Escoto, who was attending meetings at the UN. D'Escoto heard
him out and immediately relayed the entreaty by phone to Daniel
Ortega. At the end of the conversation, he shook his head sadly and
explained to Morris that the Nicaraguan president simply refused to
intercede. "He believes it would encourage more riots and more
violence," D'Escoto said. "They will be released in due time."

As for the other statement attributed to me, that also was incor-
rect. What I had told the group was that the CIA would *not* be
involved in fomenting riots. I had not said that our agents caused the
trouble at Nandaime, although U.S. embassy personnel had indeed
helped organize the demonstration that provoked the riot and the
arrests, and the Contra leaders quite probably were aware of that
fact.

Dismay at the obvious attempt to entrap me and resentment over
the distortion of my words were boiling up inside. The nerve of these
bastards, I thought!

"We had seen clear testimony from CIA people that they have
deliberately done things to provoke an overreaction on the part of
the government in Nicaragua," I stated. They were not supposed to
do that, in fact, had been counseled against it by our intelligence
committees, and I had been assured quite recently that they were not
going to do that anymore.

The testimony to which I referred was that of CIA analyst David
MacMichael, who swore under oath to the World Court that CIA
actions against Nicaragua were performed in the hope that "the
Nicaraguan government would clamp down on civil liberties within
Nicaragua, arresting its opposition." I also was thinking of a similar

affidavit by Edgar Chamorro, who operated under CIA direction while affiliated with the Contra movement.

The effect of this brief discussion on my listeners was riveting. Some of the reporters present knew of past CIA involvement. Some had written stories about the mining of the Nicaraguan harbors and about the assassination manual that advised "the selective use of violence" to "neutralize" judges, police agents, and state security officials. Some knew that our government had assisted in organizing demonstrations to provoke arrests in Nicaragua and stall the peace process. This, apparently, was the first time the provocation of arrests had been discussed in so public a forum.

Lest anyone misunderstand, I emphasized that I had stressed in every conversation or communication I'd had with Sandinista officials the importance our government attaches to free speech, free assembly, and genuine democratization. I simply did not believe it was the proper role of our government "to try to provoke riots or deliberately try to antagonize the governing officials to provoke foolish overreactions.

"We should be using the influence of the United States to encourage the peace process, not to discourage it" (the complete text of that portion of the press conference can be found in the appendix).

The reaction from the White House and from congressional Republicans was swift and explosive. It was almost as though statements of condemnation had been prewritten in anticipation of my statement. Angrily, administration officials ripped into me, accusing me of revealing classified information based on secret briefings. One even charged that I had "jeopardized the lives of Nicaraguan dissidents" and placed the lives of jailed protesters "in serious jeopardy."

Peter La Barbera, writing with Bill Gertz in the *Washington Times* the next day, declared that the CIA and the NSC regarded the "leak" as a "very serious" matter. Those officials, the *Washington Times* story announced, said my information had come from "highly classified House testimony."

Quickly, House Republican leaders filed a formal complaint, publicly demanding a full-scale ethics committee investigation and suggesting that I had violated House rules by bringing the CIA practice to light. To my great surprise, the hastily drawn complaint was filed with great fanfare by Dick Cheney and Bob Michel, who did not even bother to come by and ask exactly what I had said or learn anything of the circumstances surrounding my statement before acting. I soon wrote a letter to the Chairman of the House Ethics Committee, Julian Dixon, volunteering to come before his committee on this matter. The committee did not pursue this inquiry (the complete original letter can be found in the appendix).

Much later I would learn that Cheney had drafted the complaint and pressured Michel into joining him. Bob later expressed his personal regrets to me privately, but the damage was done.

The episode bore all the identifying marks of a setup. The Contras had gone directly from my office to Elliott Abrams's shop in the Reagan State Department. After they reported our conversation, some of them were persuaded by personnel there to "leak" the distorted version of what I had said to the *Washington Times*. Dan Wattenberg, a State Department political appointee, called and made the appointment with the *Times* editorial staff for two of the Contras to come over and give the paper the manufactured story, along with the highly doctored version of my private comments.

This sorry episode was ferreted out by newsman Roy Gutman, who revealed its details in the September 23 issue of *Newsday*. Citing an admission by a senior State Department official, Gutman wrote that Wattenberg, in "an effort to embarrass the Speaker and revive the bitter clash of past months," encouraged Contra officials "to leak a portion of their private conversation with Wright."

The grand irony was that it was people in our own State Department, not I, who had contrived to get the whole thing into print. If classified information had been involved, it was *they* who deliberately catapulted it onto the pages of the *Washington Times*. In spite of the wails of protest over the unauthorized "leak" of sensitive information, those who placed and baited the trap were less interested in protecting government "secrets" than they were in embarrassing the Speaker of the House. That much was certain.

President Reagan joined the chorus, pontificating to the press that I had violated secrecy rules. As noted in the September 24 *Congressional Quarterly* piece by John Felton, White House Spokesman Marlin Fitzwater launched a vicious attack implying that I had been doing favors for the Sandinistas. "The Speaker has always been more than eager to take the position of the Ortega government," he charged.

Bill Gertz and Peter La Barbera reported in the September 21 *Washington Times* that a group of House Republicans held a press conference condemning me for "aiding and abetting the communist dictatorship" in Nicaragua and for spilling official secrets. Jack Kemp said what I had done was "shocking." Henry Hyde called my statement "irresponsible and appalling" and said I should have brought my concerns to the House Intelligence Committee "for investigation before making such serious charges." Apparently Hyde was unaware that I had done precisely that with committee Chairman Stokes several months previously.

Significantly, not one of my detractors denied the basic premise. Nobody said the CIA or other government agencies had *not* tried to provoke a Sandinista overreaction.

Without raising the question of its truth, several newspapers, including the respected *Washington Post,* took umbrage at my statement on grounds that it might constitute unauthorized disclosure. Ever since taking the initiative to get peace talks under way, I had grown accustomed to occasional critical commentary from the *Post,* with some of whose writers Abrams enjoyed a close working relationship. I regretted the sour relationship with the *Post.* Numerous efforts to cultivate a better understanding with the *Post*'s writers and editorial staff came to nothing. I had written personally to Meg Greenfield in May, appealing for an opportunity to sit down and discuss questions directly before the writing of hostile editorials. Those efforts had not borne fruit (the complete original letter can be found in the appendix).

The *Washington Times* was another matter entirely. While treating its writers with courtesy, I knew all along that its reporting was predetermined by a staunchly conservative editorial staff hired by Korean religionist Sun Myung Moon.

David Bonior and Tony Coelho, who had been present at the disputed meeting with the Contras, sent out exhaustive statements on Thursday, September 22, agreeing absolutely with my version of what had been said. They also pointed out that the testimony to which I referred was in the permanent record of the World Court and had been reported on various occasions in news stories. In other words, I was not disclosing secret testimony, and I wasn't revealing anything that had not previously been sworn to and published.

My friend Bob Strauss called to talk. Before almost anyone else, he had warned me of the desperate determination of our country's militant right wing to undermine my leadership in Congress. "They aren't just out to embarrass and discredit you, Jim," he had said more than a year earlier, "they're out to *destroy* you."

Jesse Jackson called. "My brother," he began, "let me tell you what you need to be saying."

"What should I be saying, Jesse?"

"You need to make it real plain. You were acting legally and overtly to make peace. Those others were acting illegally and covertly to make war. Just tell the people that and let them choose!" I smiled as the conversation ended, wishing I had Jesse's winsome way with words.

Whenever I went on the House floor, I was surrounded by well-wishing colleagues expressing their indignation over the attacks. Some of them—Jim Oberstar, Dave Nagle, Bill Richardson, Barbara Kennelly, and Marcy Kaptur—seethed with anger. Jack Brooks, Martin Frost, and others in the Texas delegation wanted to retaliate. Former Speaker Tip O'Neill called to assure me of his support.

House Budget Committee Chairman Bill Gray dropped by my office. Bill was minister of a large church in Philadelphia and still conducted services there on most Sundays. "This is not a political visitation," Bill joked. "This is a pastoral visitation. I was making my hospital calls and wanted to see if you were wrapped in bandages."

"No bandages," I said. "Just a bruised ego and a fractured reputation."

"Remember when I said they were playing sack-the-quarterback and trying to knock you out of the game?"

"Of course I remember. You called that one right!"

"No, I called it wrong. They're not just trying to sideline you for the rest of the game. They want you crippled for the rest of the season—or maybe the rest of your life!" Beneath the mock joviality, I could sense that there was, with Bill and with some of the others, growing concern—both for me as a person and for the House as an institution. The charge that I had betrayed government secrets marked a dramatic escalation in verbal hostilities.

My sister, Mary Connell, came by to share some information she had gathered about the "Mooney" organization that controlled the *Washington Times.* "Do you know how heavily subsidized that shameless rag is?"

"No, Mary, but it must require financial subsidy. My friend Joe Albritton couldn't make a go of the *Washington Star,* and it was a far better paper in my opinion."

"Would it surprise you that Reverend Moon or somebody in his behalf has poured millions of dollars into that paper since 1982?"

"Yes, that would surprise me. Where did you hear that?"

"I didn't hear it. I read it. I've read it more than once. There's a book called *Inside the League* that claims that Reverend Moon was in trouble with our Internal Revenue people and returned to South Korea, but he gives millions of dollars to all sorts of right-wing causes. I read that he paid millions for Richard Viguery's building and set him up to raise money to support Oliver North and campaign against Dukakis. So when does this 'church' cease to be church and become a political organization? And why are these Korean nationals so interested in our political campaigns, anyway? Why doesn't this guy stick to *Korean* politics? And where is he getting all this money?"

"Beats me! Where do you think he gets his money?"

Mary confessed no certain knowledge but advanced a number of theories. She also wanted me to press for an inquiry into the propriety of Reverend Moon's political activities. "If a foreign national is prohibited from giving hundreds of millions of dollars to a political campaign," she asked, "why is it permissible to spend the same amount of money influencing public opinion on domestic political issues and against American candidates for public office?"

The argument was too abstract to command my immediate attention. Furthermore, I felt it involved a constitutional issue. But it showed how a personal attack so often provokes the thirst for a personal counterattack. Political life is especially hard on family members, who can suffer terrible frustration and helplessness in the effort to defend a loved one against vilification. It was that way with my wife, Betty. Hurt and angered at the suddenly increasing attacks on my character, she felt the undeniable instinct of wanting to strike back. "They shouldn't be allowed to get away with this, Jim!" she exclaimed.

It was ironic that I would be portrayed as an enemy of our country's intelligence apparatus. I had always supported the CIA in the performance of its thoroughly legitimate role—gathering intelligence, not overthrowing governments. A Texas colleague of mine, well-known cold-war hawk Charlie Wilson, reminded me that I had personally championed legislation protecting our government's agents: It was my bill, in the late 1970s, that put a stop to the sinister and deadly perfidy of the handful of rogue former agents who had been publishing names and descriptions of CIA operatives. This law makes it a federally punishable crime to publicize the identity of an on-duty secret intelligence agent of the United States.

But there was no doubt that the agency had on occasion been

misused to carry out unauthorized operations in other countries, and that its misuse had cost us goodwill throughout Latin America. It was necessary that I clarify the issue as precisely as I could.

On Friday, September 23, I tried to get the matter into proper focus. At my news conference, I handed out copies of a statement I had prepared in longhand. It read in part as follows:

> The question of greatest importance is not what I said and whether I should have said it. The question is what our government has done, and whether we should be doing it. The CIA was created to gather intelligence, not to make policy. That is the role of Congress. Congress is not subservient to the CIA or any other agency, nor dependent upon their permission to speak. It is the responsibility of Congress to speak out whenever it discovers any agency of government, financed by the taxpayer's money, is operating contrary to established public policy. . . .
>
> It is unfortunately true that while our government has pursued a public policy of supporting the peace talks in Central America, agents of our government have engaged in efforts to destabilize the Nicaraguan government and to produce incidents . . . calculated to be disruptive to the peace talks. . . .
>
> The United States should not say one thing publicly and do another privately. That is unworthy of our nation. We will not be trusted or respected by others if we do.
>
> I have said these things privately to members of the administration. I regret the necessity to say them publicly. But I believe they need to be said.

This statement, so far as I was concerned, defined the terms of the debate (the complete original statement can be found in the appendix). Sensing the raw truth, several important news journals within the next few days were identifying with my position. The *Boston Globe* of September 23 said I deserved "a decoration for candor" and that White House "screeches indicate the policy persists." Trying to invoke secrecy over the matter, the *Globe* wrote, simply had insulated the machinations "not from the attention of Nicaraguans, but from debate by Americans."

The *Los Angeles Times* on September 25 opined that "Wright's decision to go public may well have been necessary. . . . If Wright prevents the Reaganites from further sabotaging the tentative steps

that are now being taken toward peace in Central America, his out-
burst will have been worthwhile." On September 26, a *Newsday*
editorial regretted that "the debate has focused on Wright instead of
on a stupid and cynical policy that was bound to backfire eventually." The *Baltimore Sun* reported on September 25 that the administration's comments made it clear that "some in the Administration
wanted the failure of peace talks."

Even the *Wall Street Journal*, which had been consistently critical
of my position, published on September 29 an editorial commentary
by Alexander Cockburn that described my September 23 declaration
as an "eloquent statement of political and moral principle" and said
the "genuine issue" was either "accountability" or a "secret government." And Robert Pear, writing in the *New York Times* on September 25, quoted unnamed American officials as saying that I gave a
"generally accurate description" of our secret policy when I said that
support for opposition demonstrations had been based on "hopes of
provoking an overreaction by the Sandinistas."

Back home in Fort Worth, my friends had begun circling the wagons. Mayor Bob Bolen and two local businessmen decided one day to
throw a barbecue in my honor. The idea spread like prairie fire in dry
stubble. Within two days, the "sponsoring committee" had grown to
a list of three hundred, which included twelve suburban mayors and
a cross section of business, labor, and civic leaders. Enthusiasm for
the event was surprisingly bipartisan. Republican Governor Bill
Clements called from Austin and said he would like to come. Crusty,
plainspoken Bill and I—often at odds on political issues—had developed a friendship while working together on projects for the state.

The event was set for Tuesday, October 11. The committee booked
the auditorium of Will Rogers Coliseum. It holds ten thousand. As
the date drew near, Governor Mario Cuomo of New York accepted
the committee's invitation to participate in the evening's tribute. It
was not a fundraiser, just a country-style barbecue and welcome-
home party. Admission was free.

On the night of the eleventh, every seat in the auditorium was
filled. Governor Clements made some homey, down-to-earth comments. Governor Cuomo stirred the crowd with an eloquent appeal
to the social conscience of the community. Texans lapped up the New
Yorker's erudite phrases as though they were cornmeal grits and
redeye gravy!

It was for me an emotional experience. For too many days my nervous system had been subjected to the unforgiving schedule and unremitting pressures of Washington. My feelings were too close to the surface, and I had a hard time speaking. It was hard not to show all the emotion I felt. For a few minutes I reminisced. I talked about Fort Worth and home and our common Western tradition, and thirty-four years of working together.

Looking into the audience, I saw whites and blacks and Hispanics, often side by side, in the packed rows and standing aisles of the auditorium. That was a scene I would not have witnessed at the beginning of my career. "I am a populist and an egalitarian," I said. "I believe in the brotherhood of man—and woman—not as an abstract theory, but as a reality. When I was very young, my father told me never to look down on anyone—and never to let anyone look down on me. That is my heritage. It is Texas, the heritage of the plains. I think it is quintessentially American."

Savoring a moment of nostalgia, I spoke of the Depression, and of World War II. "Yes, I've known war. I've made war and hated it. I am not unacquainted with its pain . . . and I want to devote a portion of what remains in my life to making peace."

Then, trying to compress words, I talked of the strains in our current struggle:

> In Central America poverty reigns and streets have been turned into rivers of blood. War and economic blockade have brought near starvation. Children go hungry and fear for their lives when rifles ring out and machine guns begin their frenzied chatter. People deserve better than that.
>
> In Nicaragua the guns were silenced and six years of pointless bloodshed have been replaced by a truce. Neither side is blameless. But I think we must *keep trying* for peace and democracy in our hemisphere.
>
> There are some in our government who do not want a negotiated peace. They are out to undermine the peace process. They want the war to resume in the vain hope of a military settlement, bought by our money and other people's blood and established upon the graves of more innocent victims of both sides.
>
> Yet I seek no quarrel, nor partisan political advantage, in a matter of foreign affairs. I extend the olive branch to those in

our executive department and offer my respect to those who disagree with me. I offer my friendship, my help and honest counsel to the new president, whoever he may be. . . . But I cannot pretend publicly to things that are not so.

With less than a month until election day, I thought I knew who that new president would be.

CHAPTER 11

"Kinder, Gentler"

*Nothing worth doing is completed in our lifetime; therefore, we
must be saved by hope. Nothing true or beautiful or good makes
complete sense in any immediate context of history; therefore,
we must be saved by faith. Nothing we do, however virtuous,
can be accomplished alone; therefore, we are saved by love.*

—Reinhold Niebuhr

To nobody's surprise, George Bush won a land-
slide victory over Michael Dukakis for the presidency. In other elections throughout the country, we Democrats held our own. We had
actually increased our House majority by four seats and our Senate
majority by one. It was the first time in eighty years that one political
party had captured the White House while the other was increasing
its majority in both House and Senate and in the ranks of the nation's
governors.

Republicans had gained no political advantage in Congress
through the right wing's efforts to identify Democrats with leftist
causes in Central America. Our calculations told us we had not lost
one House seat over that issue and might have picked up four or five
in areas where the question of Central American policy was debated.

It was impossible to conclude definitely that this was the case, how-ever, since other questions were involved in those debates as well.

Ronald Reagan's eight years were drawing to a close. His obsessive desire for a military solution in Nicaragua had not borne fruit, except in the deaths of some thirty thousand Nicaraguans. Neither, though, had the tree of peace taken firm root in Central America's rocky soil. We had made a beginning. In Nicaragua and El Salvador, rival groups had stacked their rifles at the door and were talking. George Bush had said next to nothing about the region's problems. He was, to many observers, an enigma.

Two days after the election, I was having breakfast with Bob Strauss in the hideaway office just off the Capitol's Grand Rotunda. "Have you called to congratulate George Bush?" Bob asked.

"No, I haven't called. I sent a telegram yesterday morning."

"Why don't you call?" Bob insisted. "George Bush would love to hear from you. He needs your help and you need his. This is a critical time for getting things started in the right direction. I even have a number at which I think you could reach him."

"There's no time like the present." I got up abruptly and moved across a corner of the room to the telephone.

George Bush came on the line immediately. "I'm awfully glad you called," said the president-elect. "I'd like to come up and talk with you. Could we have lunch together up there someday very soon?"

"Mr. Vice President, I'll be more than glad to, wherever you say. You have a plateful of problems and more things to do than any one man can perform. You just tell me where, and I'll serve your conve-nience."

"I want to come up there, Jim. Could we have lunch in your office? Just the two of us, with no staff or anybody else around?"

"You name the day. What would you like to eat?"

"I'd like a steak, if you won't tell Barbara."

On Friday, November 18, I was standing at the door that enters the first floor of the Capitol beneath the House steps when the presiden-tial limousine arrived.

"Have you met John Sununu?" the president-elect asked. I shook hands with his newly appointed chief of staff. "We'll be at least a couple of hours," said Bush. Sununu returned to the limousine.

Bush entered the downstairs hall where he answered questions from a waiting group of reporters. "We have great respect for the Congress and great personal respect for the Speaker," he declared.

"We're just going to have a private lunch and a friendly, informal

discussion," I said in response to a question. "We'll talk about whatever our president-elect wishes to talk about."

We had steaks and salad and coffee on a small, round antique table
that Betty and her friend Joan Bailey of Fort Worth had bought for
the Speaker's office. There was no broccoli. Bush insisted mainly on
listening. He wanted to know where I saw areas of common agreement. I told him we were anxious to add the flesh and blood of
legislation and funding to his skeletal call for a "kinder, gentler nation." Frankly, I could not foresee just how the pledges of major
improvement in education, the environment, child care, and other
areas could be accommodated within the pledge of "no new taxes,"
but I assured him that we were eager to hear his recommendations.

Then I mentioned Mexico and Central America. Bush said he
would be meeting Tuesday with newly elected Mexican President
Carlos Salinas de Gortari. I told him what I knew of Salinas and his
moderate economic inclinations. We spoke of the staggering level of
debt that buckled the knees of the whole Mexican economy. I said
somehow lenders would have to accept substantial reductions in
principal, extend the terms, and slash oppressive rates of interest by
significant amounts. Only in this way could Mexico's suffocating
economy get any oxygen into its lungs.

George Bush listened, seemed aware that I had discussed this matter
several times in the previous year with Nicholas Brady and Jim Baker.
"I think we're going to be able to work something out," he said.

Then I brought up Central America. "This has been the most
implacable issue of the last eight years," I declared. "Also the most
politically polarizing and personally divisive question on the entire
agenda."

"I agree," said Bush.

"In fact, it's our only major foreign policy disagreement. It would
be good for all concerned if we could find some common ground."

Bush nodded his head. "I know," he said. "What do you think we
might be able to agree upon?"

"The starting place is to substitute diplomacy for military action,"
I said. "We're talking with Gorbachev and getting some good results.
The Nicaraguans and Salvadorans are many times worse off financially than the Russians are. If we'd sit down and talk with them, we
might make more progress than we have."

"Would you be willing to work with Jim Baker on trying to search
out the ingredients of a common policy?" Bush proposed.

"Of course I will," I replied.

*   *   *

George Bush's attitude was friendly and open. He seemed sincerely to want a compatible relationship with Congress. I hoped at first that I might be a catalyst for that. After years of hard-fought battles and harsh recriminations in which I had been point man—first as majority leader and then as Speaker—in opposition to most of President Reagan's domestic agenda, it would be nice to work constructively again with a president. Of course, we wouldn't agree on economic priorities. Maybe in international affairs . . .

But my candle was burning out. The flame that had lighted my singleminded pursuit of political office for more than fifty years—since my junior year in high school—flickered now. I was tired. Physically and mentally exhausted. Congress wasn't fun anymore. The old, easy ambience that let ideological competitors trust and respect and joke with one another was vanishing if not already gone.

After winning eighteen consecutive terms in Congress and making countless appearances in behalf of other candidates, I was weary to the bone with campaigning. The pursuit of elective office had grown increasingly venal. Political campaigns, resorting to quick thirty-second commercials, were brutalizing and trivializing an honored profession. In the arena where Lincoln and Douglas once debated important issues, ghostwriters now spun vapid prose and ad writers hawked candidates like so many boxes of corn flakes or tubes of toothpaste. More and more it was a contest to see which side could raise the money for a last-minute negative TV blitz against the other.

Another thing contributed to the decision taking shape in my mind. Attacks on my personal character intensified. Determined at first not to be distracted by the calculated harassments, I had ignored them. But they mounted. Every facet of my life for the past forty years was coming under attack. Every detail of my personal finances, to which I had paid so little attention, was a subject of scrutiny.

Bad enough to have to divert precious time from important tasks to dig among old files and answer first for one and then for another newsman questions with which I had dealt ten and twelve years before. Worse that a determined claque kept planting questions designed to impugn my motives for such things as modest personal investments over the years in speculative Texas oil and gas wells, helping to get federal grants for restoration projects on the historic old north side of Fort Worth, and trying to intercede with regulators of lending institutions in an effort to avoid a rash of bankruptcies in my state. All of this, none of it ever secret, was now portrayed as sinister.

For thirty-four years I had lived in the goldfish bowl that is public office. I knew my personal conduct was subject to constant inspection. I expected my political judgments to be debated, disputed, disagreed with, and criticized vigorously. What I experienced now was entirely different. Now people who disagreed with my political judgments were attacking my honor, trying to impeach my integrity and my patriotism.

In the middle of the night I would wake up, tossing and turning, outraged by the indignities heaped on my name and frustrated by my inability, for the first time in my life, to cope effectively with a personal crisis. The harder I tried to satisfy the media, the more impossible that task seemed. My blood pressure went up and would not respond to medication. For years I had been able to think myself into a tranquil frame of mind before a blood-pressure test in order to pass it. Now that technique was not working. Capitol physicians William Narva and Robert Krasner changed the medications and remonstrated with me: "Get more exercise. Play golf. Take long walks. Get more rest."

Fine, but when? My schedule was jammed every waking hour.

"One more thing," Doctor Krasner admonished, with a wicked twinkle in his eye. "Avoid stress!"

The people in my hometown, almost universally supportive, were increasingly puzzled and angered by the barrage of artfully planted negative stories suddenly appearing in the news media. My family and close friends began to be targeted. My wife Betty made it clear she would share whatever came, but more than once I saw tears of anger in her eyes.

Before our marriage in 1972, Betty had enjoyed a career in business, employed at different times by a St. Louis publishing firm, a Fort Worth hotel, and a Texas manufacturing enterprise. When we married, she held a responsible job on the staff of the House Public Works Committee. She continued working, which was perfectly permissible under the antinepotism law because her public employment predated our marriage by a number of years. But when I was elected House majority leader in 1976, Betty voluntarily left her job to avoid any possible criticism of me for our both holding government jobs.

Wanting to make some contribution to the family finances and to stay mentally active, Betty helped organize a small family-owned investment corporation. I transferred to the corporation $58,000 worth of stocks, mostly in Texas-based corporations, that I had purchased over the years. Also included was $10,000 worth of stock in the First National Bank of Weatherford, inherited from my mother's estate. Our personal friends, George and Marlene Mallick, contributed an amount of cash equivalent to the market value of the stocks. Joining the names Mallick and Wright, we named the little corporation Mallightco. Since George was largely occupied with two apartment complexes and two office buildings he owned, Marlene was raising a family, and my time was totally devoted to Congress, Betty had assumed a principal role in the day-to-day management of our fledgling family business's investments.

Betty watched markets, studied opportunities for new investments, and decided when it was timely to recommend selling one of our holdings. On her suggestion we sold four of my original publicly traded stocks after a few years at the most propitious time, recouping for our little company about three times their appraised value as of the day we incorporated in 1979. Betty also argued George and me out of investing in the movie *Annie*, which turned out to be a financial loser. "I just don't think we know enough about that business," she stressed. She also conducted a financial analysis that wisely kept us out of an investment in a proposed winery. These judgment calls, along with others she made, netted the two-family enterprise at least four times the token salary of $18,000 a year that the corporation paid her as its only employee.

Now, however, charges leveled by my political opposition in Congress and fanned into the public dialogue by news accounts alleged that Betty really didn't do anything for the corporation. The $18,000 salary, less than half what she had earned before our marriage, was now portrayed as a subterfuge by which businessman Mallick funneled unearned money to me. Never mind that the $18,000 was half Betty's and mine anyway as equal owners of the corporation.

Newsmen began to hound George Mallick, as a consequence of which he had to spend days in Washington answering questions for the House Ethics Committee. "Just what are your legislative interests?" outside counsel Richard Phelan demanded. He would ask the same questions again and again as though interrogating a criminal in a police court. Truth was that George Mallick's business enterprises never depended upon the government in any way whatever. In all the years I had known him, never once had George asked me to vote for or against a piece of legislation or to intercede on his behalf with any

federal agency. Of Lebanese ancestry, my friend now was being portrayed as some sort of Mafia character.

One of the few tangible assets of the corporation was a 1979 car.
The Mallicks and Betty alternated in driving the car and looking after
its upkeep. Now the critics were in full voice, claiming that Mallick
had given Betty an automobile. The implications were demeaning. In
exasperation, I wrote a personal check to the corporation, buying the
nine-year-old corporate car at its book value and giving it to Betty.
What hurt was that my wife, through no error of her own, had been
dragged so pointlessly and personally into the political debate. At
one point things reached the absurd level in which *Star-Telegram*
reporter David Montgomery insisted to my top aide Marshall Lynam
that I must give Montgomery an interview to answer a charge that
Betty actually was illiterate. "Tell him," I said, "that Betty is trilin-
gual. She's fluent in three written languages—English, Spanish, and
shorthand."

Once my sister Mary said, "Do you remember, Jim, that time
about forty years ago in Weatherford when that big tough guy called
you a '*commie sonavabitch*' and you decked him on the spot?"

"You mean Dub Tucker. Of course I remember!"

"Wouldn't you like to do that to some of these sniveling rats who
are insulting your honor now?"

"Of course I would," I laughed. "But the Speaker of the United
States House of Representatives must not do that kind of thing. It
wouldn't be dignified. Besides, I'm sixty-six. Had you forgotten?"

"I know," she said. "I know."

On the afternoon of March 2, 1989, new Secretary of State Jim
Baker came by my office in the Capitol to explore prospects for a
bipartisan approach to Central America. He had been working on
some thoughts but had nothing in writing. Baker's basic idea was a
one-year humanitarian-aid plan for the Contras.

"We want to wind this thing down. We're willing to substitute
negotiations for military action," Baker stated. "But the president is
getting some flak from the right wing. They're already accusing him
of *abandoning* the Contras. That's the one thing he promised in the
campaign never to do."

One of the first things I noticed was that the new secretary, at least
in our private discussion, was using the same vocabulary the media

and most of the public used. Emissaries in the Reagan administration had religiously referred to the Contras as the freedom fighters and the democratic resistance.

Jim Baker, as I had observed when he served President Reagan as White House chief of staff, was an adroit bargainer. He had already spent two days talking with Republican members in the House and Senate before his first conversation with me. This was to be the pattern of his diplomacy during the next few weeks. He would meet with each faction privately, hear its complaints, weigh its demands. Then he would go to the other side and present the opposition's wish as its "bottom line." Baker would tell Democrats how intractable Republicans were being. I had no doubt he was telling them how unreasonably we were behaving.

In this exploratory conversation, the secretary had wanted to talk with me alone. He had not even wanted task force Chairman David Bonior present.

"If we'll drop every reference to a military escrow fund or any money of any kind for arms," Jim Baker asked, "can you agree to go along with a one-year guarantee of continued humanitarian aid—food, clothing, and shelter—for the Contras and their families?"

"If we believe the peace process is going to work, Mr. Secretary, it won't be necessary to keep them in their camps in Honduras for a whole year. In fact, proposing to do so could fly in the face of the agreements which are being worked out right now between the five presidents," I pointed out.

"I've talked with President Azcona," Baker replied, "and I feel sure if we pressed him he would agree to letting the Contras remain in Honduras for another year."

"What I'm suggesting is that it might run afoul of an agreement that seems to be in the making among all the presidents," I explained. "I have been talking at some length, only today, with President Cerezo of Guatemala. He says the Sandinistas are expressing a willingness to release all the prisoners they've been holding for the past ten years, some of them old Somoza national guardsmen. That will set in motion some dynamics among the other presidents. Cerezo believes Ortega is actually going to announce such a plan. If he does it ought to trigger a positive response on our side. Don't we have to hold out some carrots, as well as sticks?"

"You've given me an idea," said Baker. "Carrots as well as sticks!

Maybe we could have a selective menu of carrots. A careful balance of carrots and sticks. Maybe we can work that into our draft. A carrot for each good-faith performance on the part of the Sandinistas."

Baker asked if I would arrange a meeting with key House Democrats. I said I would. "The leadership, of course," he suggested, "and be sure to include some moderates—people like Lee Hamilton and Dave McCurdy." I nodded.

President Marco Vinicio Cerezo of Guatemala occupied an increasingly strong position. In the past year his country's economy had grown by 6 percent. He was steadily restoring respect in that strife-torn land for the rule of law. Cerezo had told me that all five presidents of the region were united. All of them were convinced that domestic economic prospects in their respective countries depended on the success of the regional peace plan. Cerezo's idea of humanitarian aid for the Contras was help for their demobilization, repatriation, and resettlement, either in their Nicaraguan homeland or in some other country of their choosing. "Anything else would go against the grain of our agreement," he insisted. "And it ought not to take a year to carry this out—six months at the most."

On Thursday, March 9, 1989, I received a warm letter of departure from Costa Rica's Ambassador Guido Fernández which described well the difficult path we had walked together (the complete original letter can be found in the appendix). Other good news arrived when James Baker came by with a small retinue of State Department people and a two-page, single-spaced document with the word SECRET stamped in bold letters at the top. (He gathered any spare copies of the document at the end of the meeting, leaving only one copy in my safekeeping.) In addition to Majority Leader Tom Foley and task force Chairman David Bonior, I had invited David Obey, Dante Fascell, and Lee Hamilton. Fascell was chairman and Hamilton the ranking Democratic member on the House Foreign Affairs Committee. Obey, the Wisconsin Democrat, was chairman of the appropriations subcommittee that funds foreign activities.

This was the first in a series of meetings in which Baker practiced shuttle diplomacy between Democratic and Republican leaders. The effort culminated in a bipartisan plan designed to mark a new beginning in our relations with Central America.

The centerpiece of the agreement was an unequivocal commitment to the peace process. The statement upon which we finally agreed proclaimed that the United States was ready to work "in good faith with the democratic leaders of Central America and Latin America to translate the bright promises of Esquipulas II and its successor agreements" into concrete realities.

The United States would "fully support" the Esquipulas accord, including reintegration of insurgent forces "into their homeland under safe, democratic conditions as the peace process evolves." The "humanitarian assistance" provided by Congress would be available to support "voluntary reintegration" by the Nicaraguan resistance "in a manner supportive of the goals of the Central American nations, as expressed in the Esquipulas II agreement and the El Salvador accord."

Senators David Boren and Chris Dodd, along with House Democrats who participated in the discussions, emphasized the sticks-and-carrots theme. The words were refined to "incentives and disincentives." While Baker firmly resisted spelling out the nature of planned incentives and rewards in the published document, the concept drew a great deal of discussion.

Once, as we walked verbally through a series of hypothetical actions, Baker revealed that he was contemplating what he called a "menu" of measured responses. If the Sandinista government, for example, were to release the two thousand prisoners, Baker might show his pleasure by restoring recognition to the Nicaraguan ambassador in Washington and asking to return our official emissary to Managua. If Nicaragua should in fact revise its electoral laws in the way it had indicated, then our government might demonstrate approval by restoring the visa agreement and scheduling a courtesy meeting between our secretary of state and the Nicaraguan ambassador. Assuming Nicaragua permitted the effective political organization of its internal opposition and conducted an unbiased voter-registration program, then our government could tone down the clandestine radio broadcasts it had supported in an effort to undermine the credibility of the Nicaraguan government, and simultaneously reduce the degree of military presence in Honduras.

The secretary suggested that, if equal political opportunity and free speech for all parties were being honored, as the election date of February 25, 1990, drew near, we might want to modify the trade embargo to permit a freer flow of commerce beneficial to the Nicaraguan economy. Finally, Baker suggested that if the election were conducted in a free and fair manner, regardless of the outcome, we would lift the trade embargo, restore the sugar quota, and allow International Monetary Fund, International Development Bank, and World Bank projects to be resumed in Nicaragua. (All such loans had been shut off for several years under U.S. pressure.) And we would make Nicaragua eligible for the benefits enjoyed by other countries in the Caribbean Basin Initiative.

I had a strong feeling that all of this would come about.

One major problem remained. Baker wanted a full year's authorization of humanitarian aid. "Not that we expect actually to need it for a full year," he said. "But we don't want to have to reopen the issue on the House floor every three or four months and crank up a new legislative battle every time we turn around, as we've been doing for the past two or three years."

That made sense to a lot of people on both sides. If this was to be an agreement, then we wanted to agree on a plan once and for all and not tempt fate with a series of recurring votes. But the idea of a full year of maintaining the Contras in military units in Honduras rankled many. It ran counter to the accord reached among the five Central American presidents on February 14 at Tesoro Beach, El Salvador. They had made a commitment to come up with a joint plan in ninety days to demobilize the resistance units. This pledge to demobilize was tied to Ortega's commitment to conduct unquestionably free and fair national elections, with international observers, on February 25 of 1990.

The dilemma was resolved by David Obey. Obey knew that Democrats on his foreign affairs appropriations subcommittee, suspicious of White House pledges, would not support a full year's appropriation unless they kept some strings to pull. They wanted to be able to rein in the money if the Contras misused it to start hostilities anew. Obey proposed a private agreement. While the appropriations bill would cover the full year, there would be a personal understanding between him and the White House. The administrator would not actually release all the money. He would return to Obey's subcommittee periodically through the year, reviewing the situation in light of developments in Nicaragua.

At first Baker did not want to agree to this. I told him it was a cheap price to pay for David Obey's cooperation and that of his committee. Nothing was said publicly of the agreement, but private written memoranda were exchanged between Baker and Obey.

This last obstacle removed, the agreement was ready for unveiling.

In a formal ceremony at the White House on March 24, Good Friday, we released copies of the new bipartisan accord (the complete original accord can be found in the appendix).

Things were on track. Whatever disagreements would erupt over the domestic agenda, the White House and the Congress were singing from the same hymnal on Central America. For all practical purposes, the U.S.-financed war in Nicaragua was over. There would be elections in due course, and ample time to monitor them.

Now we could turn our attention to other parts of the overall problem—to the shifting situation in El Salvador, where elections had just overturned Duarte's Christian Democrats to install an ARENA government headed by the tall, socially presentable new president Alfredo Christiani, and to the gnawing, pervasive problem of regional debt.

Former President Jimmy Carter asked me to participate with him and a group of Latin American leaders in a symposium on the debt issue at his conference center in Atlanta on March 29 and 30.

There Prime Ministers George Price of Belize and Michael Manley of Jamaica and President Carlos Andrés Pérez of Venezuela underlined the urgent need for relief. The life's blood of the region's economies was hemorrhaging in interest payments required by the massive level of debt that had escalated during the past decade.

Professor Jeffery Sachs of Harvard argued strongly that a plan offered a few days earlier by U.S. Secretary of the Treasury Nicholas Brady provided only a starting point. Brady had suggested deferring payments of principal for a period of time. The situation was much too urgent to talk any longer of debt deferrals, Sachs stressed. Nothing less than substantial debt and interest-rate *reductions* would suffice. Senator Paul Sarbanes of Maryland said the objective must be to let the debt-ridden countries regain stability and public confidence in their capacity to survive. To do this, he stressed, they would have to reduce the annual outflow in interest payments by more than token amounts.

Latin America's foreign debt stood at about $400 billion. Several countries were having to scrounge up more in interest payments each year than the total of their exports returned to them. No other part of the world, except for sub-Saharan Africa, had suffered so disabling a reduction in gross domestic product during the decade of the 1980s. Everyone at the conference agreed that the matter was urgent and that a solution would need to be implemented immediately. Banks and lending institutions would have to be parties to the rescue operation, forgoing some principal and dramatically reducing sometimes exorbitant rates of interest.

James Robinson of American Express spoke up forcefully in favor of a comprehensive plan. Over the past two years, he reported, his company had reduced and written off debts from $2.4 billion in underdeveloped countries to a total of only $900 million. "We're ready to participate in a regional plan," he promised, "and write down the remainder as other banks do likewise." It is better to support a planned recovery, Robinson concluded, than to receive nothing because your customers go broke.

Former President Gerald R. Ford joined President Carter as co-host at a Thursday luncheon, and Secretary of State Baker added the blessing of bipartisanship to the occasion in a well-structured noon speech.

The Atlanta conference, dealing also with the pervasive problem of drug traffic among the nations of the hemisphere, was to set in motion a set of debt-reduction measures. Chile, Costa Rica, and Mexico were among the first to begin serious negotiations.

The impetus for this beneficial change would be another in a growing list of quiet but solid achievements made by President Carter. The unobtrusive, soft-spoken Georgian with the easy smile and manner, perhaps as much as any public person I have ever known, practices the biblical injunction against blowing trumpets in the path of one's good works. More than a decade earlier, Carter had confronted the intractable problem of the Panama Canal Treaty with all its political pitfalls and temptations to demagoguery. Patiently he persisted until an unpopular but necessary treaty recognizing Panama's rightful sovereignty won Senate ratification. Perhaps the outstanding achievement of Carter's presidency was the singular act of personal diplomacy that resulted in the Camp David agreement between Israel and Egypt. Disdaining the lure of television cameras, Carter sat in quiet seclusion with the elected heads of the two historically hostile peoples and persisted for fourteen days until they reached an agreement that a decade later was still observed.

Now, eight years after leaving the White House, Carter had begun the tedious task of wedding international creditors and debtors in a bond of mutual advantage. And within six weeks he and a group of former heads of state would oversee the May election in Panama and blow a shrill whistle on General Manuel Noriega and the military buffoons who physically prevented the rightfully elected civil officials from assuming office. In less than a year, Jimmy Carter and others would oversee an assiduously clean and open election in Nicaragua.

Through the first five months of 1989, I struggled to lead the House effectively. I appeared before the Economics Commission and pleaded for an honest, forthright assault on the deficit. I met with President Bush on the eve of his meeting with Gorbachev at the UN. I managed the congressional side of negotiations with Secretary Jim Baker and helped hammer out the agreement on Central America. I consulted with Treasury Secretary Nicholas Brady and addressed the meeting with Third World leaders at Jimmy Carter's library in Atlanta. I presented to the Senate Public Works Committee a plan for a Build America trust fund to finance needed rehabilitation of America's public infrastructure. I moved through the House a controversial bill to increase the minimum wage. None of these things got much notice in the media. They were preoccupied with the House Ethics Committee's investigation into my personal finances and the daily leaks being orchestrated by those who wanted to bring me down.

A Speaker must be symbol and spokesman of not only his party's interests but those of the institution itself. Even as I helped put the finishing touches on the peace initiative with Jim Baker, I sensed that my moral authority was being eroded. I was having trouble communicating the positive side of our agenda.

Another drama acted out in the glare of congressional spotlights that spring would have its own negative effect upon my ability to assert unifying leadership. On March 9, after several weeks of acrimonious debate, the Senate in a 53 to 47 vote rejected President Bush's nomination of former Senator John Tower to be his secretary of defense. The effect was explosive. It was the first time in history that a cabinet nominee had been turned down at the beginning of a president's first term and only the second time any former senator had been rejected for a cabinet post. Republicans were livid. Some Democratic senators had made damaging public allegations against the Texas Republican—that he had a drinking problem and that he was financially beholden to defense contractors.

I knew John Tower. Although we had been Texas political rivals and were on opposite sides of most domestic issues, I liked John personally and considered him totally trustworthy. During the March 2 Texas Independence Day celebration at the Washington Press Club that year, I proposed a toast to my embattled fellow Texan. But the Senate vote one week later reflected party lines, with only one Republican deserting Tower and all but three Democrats voting to doom his confirmation. That loosed a torrent of anger among House GOP ranks.

Two days after the Senate vote, a Republican colleague who was a longtime personal friend came by for a private visit. "You need to know, Mr. Speaker, that the John Tower rejection has hardened the ranks in my party against you," he told me. "A number of us have always believed in you and some of us will support you come hell or high water, but we're under heavy pressure to make an example of you. The Gingrich crowd is putting Bob Michel and the moderates through a virtual inquisition. They want to make your personal downfall a litmus test of party loyalty. They want to go Hammurabi one better."

"You mean an eye for an eye and a tooth for a tooth?"

"It's an even more perfect symmetry," he said. "They want a Texan for a Texan!"

Ethics Committee Republican Charles Pashayan of California had said privately to a few congressional friends that he considered me innocent of wrongdoing. Suddenly "Chip" Pashayan was bombarded by angry letters from right wing constituents demanding he vote to oust me from the speakership. Conservatives in Pashayan's district were being mobilized by other Republican lawmakers on Capitol Hill to put pressure on Pashayan.

Many months later I would read in John Barry's *The Ambition and the Power* of the systematic orchestration by a busy conservative cabal of a series of attacks and harassments aimed at putting me on the defensive and keeping me off balance. Barry devotes most of the last six chapters of his book—177 printed pages—to a description of the scheme and its execution.

For more than a year, a full-time staffer in Gingrich's office named Karen Van Brocklin had been calling people in my hometown and elsewhere seeking negative information, fact or rumor, of any sort concerning me that could be peddled to a newspaper or converted into some further inquiry by the House Ethics Committee. Gingrich and others in his group, according to Barry, would call newsmen repeatedly, importuning them to use these stories.

Almost daily now, from mid-March through April of 1989, a new story would appear in some news periodical, planted by rumor peddlers and plucked up by an eager journalist. Anxious to beat the

competition, some newsmen began running with stories before check-
ing their veracity. One account said I had failed to report a supposed
ride a year earlier in an aircraft owned by a Texas corporation. I
remembered no such ride. But before I could verify my innocence by
contacting the chief executive of that company, who assured me that
his business didn't even own an airplane, the news cycle had passed.
The newspaper's disclaimer appeared toward the end of an unrelated
story in the next day's edition. On another occasion, a Washington-
based reporter quoted an unnamed "source" that the Internal Revenue Service had me under investigation for income tax fraud. It was
not true, but by the time I got a declaration to this effect from the
agent in charge of the Dallas regional office, the damage had been
done.

Television networks now vied to find new angles. ABC ran with a
prime-time story about a $35,000 investment made by Mallightco a
year or so earlier in a Florida housing development. There was nothing wrong with it, but the news hype made it sound sinister. In 1988
I had dissolved Betty's and my interest in Mallightco and put all of
our financial holdings in a blind trust, prevailing on Thomas H. Law,
one of Fort Worth's most respected lawyers, to serve as trustee. He
was not to discuss any investment or divestment with me. Now,
suddenly, in April of 1989 all three networks reported an interest
taken by my blind trust in an east Texas oil well and traded later for
a profit. Other investors in the well were hauled before the Ethics
Committee for questioning. There was nothing wrong with the actions of my trust or even particularly unusual as it turned out, but
exoneration never quite catches up with accusation.

Nor had my judgment been flawless. The Phelan law firm un-
earthed a few episodes that, while not illegal or immoral, reflected
inattention and insensitivity on my part. In October of 1984, I had
delivered the annual Lyndon B. Johnson lectures at Southwest Texas
State University where my sister, Dr. Betty Lee Wright, was a member
of the faculty. At her request and that of university President Robert
Hardisty, an old friend, I had accepted the invitation and expected no
lecture fee. A few days after the event, my Fort Worth district director
Phil Duncan called to tell me the university had sent a check for
$3,000. "Send it back with my thanks," I instructed.

"I have an idea," Phil said. "Why not give Dr. Hardisty an option?
Let him use the check to buy copies of your book of essays to give
political science and history students?" I liked it. "Fine idea, Phil, if
Bob Hardisty wants to do that. Otherwise just send it back." Har-

disty agreed, and Phil ordered books for his students. That set a pattern. Other friends bought multiple copies for gifts. Insurance executive Bernard Rapoport and former Democratic National Chairman John White mailed copies to politically active people throughout the country. Dr. John Silber of Boston University sent copies to fellow academicians. While I did nothing to promote these sales, I approved heartily. I wanted everyone to read my book!

Political enthusiasts, including some members of my own staff no doubt moved by my enthusiasm for the little volume, had suggested to several program chairmen before whose organizations I was scheduled to speak that listeners would enjoy having copies. I do not believe anyone ever represented a purchase of books as a fee, or a price for my speaking, or suggested that I expected it. I was in fact unaware of most of the purchases. But, learning now as this information dribbled out from the committee, I realized those sales could be subject to that interpretation. Although the sales violated no law and no House rule (book royalties were expressly exempted from the limits on speaking fees and outside earnings), they were being made to look like greedy efforts to skirt those very rules. Anybody smart enough to be Speaker should have had sufficient foresight to anticipate such criticism. In my preoccupation with other matters, I had failed to do so.

Major national journals like *Time* magazine and the *Boston Globe*, joined by talk-show savants on nationwide television, some once supportive, were saying now that I should resign and relieve the Congress of this painful distraction. Meanwhile, each day's mail brought bushels of encouragement from individual citizens from all over the country. Polls taken in my constituency by the Fort Worth *Star-Telegram*, whose publisher by now was writing editorials pleading for me to quit, revealed that in April 78 percent of the local citizens—this would go up to 81 percent in June—were on my side. But polls would not change media fixation. It was as though an invisible screen had been erected to filter out any positive news while letting through all the negative commentary.

The last six weeks of my tenure were agonizing. Throughout most of May, our home in McLean was surrounded morning and night by reporters who shouted questions each time I opened the door. There were photographers who trained zoom lenses on me each time I entered my yard. I learned that in the news business they call this the "death watch."

Finally, toward the end of May, it became clear to me that all six of the Republicans on the Ethics Committee, half of its membership, were intent on dragging the inquiry out. They wanted to expand its scope, look into other allegations that had cropped up in newspapers through right-wing "leaks" since the formal charges had been lodged against me the previous June. I'd had only one chance during the entire year to respond personally to the committee. I had given a full day to this in September of 1988, had offered to return if any other questions arose. I was never called back. All the initial charges were subsequently dropped.

Now, in late May, it appeared that new complaints could make the inquiry last through most of 1989. Phelan, the ambitious outside counsel hired by the committee, boasted that he had the votes in his pocket—all six Republicans and Massachusetts Democrat Chet Atkins—to keep the investigation going. To date, Phelan's firm had reaped nearly $2 million from the government. The only way I could get an exoneration would be to pursue the process to its anguishing end—acquiring perhaps a million-dollar debt in legal fees, which I could not have paid—and then go to the House floor toward the end of the year and ask House members to override the committee.

Three weeks earlier, at the end of April, the votes were in hand to support my position if it came to the House floor. Ninety-five percent of the Democrats were pledged to back me, and several Republicans had told me privately that they would do so as well in spite of internal party pressures.

That was before the sensationalized treatment in the *Washington Post* of the assault upon a young woman by a congressional aide of mine sixteen years earlier, when he was nineteen years of age. That happened before I even knew the young man. I had given him a job at the request of the Fairfax County sheriff and had never regretted having done so. He had rehabilitated himself and become an exemplary employee and the father of two magnificent children. But this was not the thrust of the news treatment that was trumpeting his misdeed of so many years before.

Now I was not certain how many of my colleagues could stand the heat. The need to choose would put everyone on the spot, forcing them to explain why they had bucked the House committee and so many of the newspapers. Beyond that, it was clear that Congress would have an almost impossible task conducting the nation's important business while this distraction cast a pall over its corridors. And I was tired. Dog tired. Mentally and physically fatigued. My duty seemed clear. If I could not be an *effective* Speaker, providing moral leadership, I had no wish to be Speaker.

And so, on May 31, 1989, I stood in the well of the House and proclaimed, "Let me give you back this job . . . as a propitiation for this season of ill-will." I loved my job. I loved the Congress. In the end, I loved it too much to stay (an excerpt from the Resignation Address can be found in the appendix).

A kind, June 6 letter from President Oscar Arias of Costa Rica temporarily buoyed my sagging spirits (the complete original letter can be found in the appendix). But as the world soon saw, things changed dramatically.

On Wednesday morning, December 20, 1989, President George Bush announced to the nation that military forces deployed from the United States had invaded Panama. Panamanian dictator Manuel Noriega, Bush said in defense of his decision, had declared on the previous Friday that "a state of war" existed with the United States. Noriega had "publicly threatened the lives" of U.S. citizens in that country. Forces under that military leader's command had shot and killed an unarmed American serviceman, wounded another, and arrested and brutally beaten a third, threatening his wife with sexual abuse. "That was enough," said Bush. Two days later, the president formally notified Congress of his reasons for the military assault as required by the War Powers Act. He said in a news conference that the operation was not over but "pretty well wrapped up."

Casualty reports varied widely. In Panama, one hospital reported taking in more than a thousand wounded and eighty dead. A woman administrator said, "The morgue is full. We have no place to put the dead." After two days of fighting, twenty U.S. troops and two female dependents were reported killed and slightly more than two hundred wounded.

In the U.S. compound, Guillermo Endara—apparent winner of the truncated May election—was sworn in as president of Panama. That same day the OAS formally condemned the invasion as an unwarranted military intrusion into the territory of another nation. Several foreign policy spokesmen said their countries would not recognize the government of President Endara until U.S. troops were withdrawn. Of these developments President Bush said, "We're a little disappointed."

Fueled by the decisive action against Panama, President Bush's popularity rose like a rocket in the United States. Three weeks after the invasion began, a *New York Times*/CBS News poll recorded the president's approval rating at 76 percent, a level rarely achieved by presidents one year into their first terms. Noriega, former collaborator with the CIA, charged now with drug running and money laundering as well as suppressing the will of his people, had become public enemy number one. In a legally unprecedented action, U.S. troops seized the deposed dictator and brought him back to the United States to stand trial. People at home lapped up George Bush's handling of the affair.

In Latin America, however, the reaction was harshly negative. Even this country's traditional friends condemned the United States. Peru recalled its ambassador from Washington, saying the invasion was "an outrage against Latin America" and evidence of "the most grotesque practice of imperialism." Venezuela, Argentina, Mexico—everywhere were heard cries that it was a breach of the charter of the OAS and of the Rio Treaty to which the United States is signatory.

On January 5, 1990, President Bush announced plans to send Vice President Dan Quayle to several countries in the region for diplomatic mending. Presidents Carlos Salinas de Gortari of Mexico and Carlos Andrés Pérez of Venezuela made it clear to the White House that a visit from Mr. Quayle would not be welcome at that time. Ultimately, the Quayle visit was curtailed to encompass only three countries—Jamaica, Honduras, and Panama itself, countries safely within the American camp.

On February 25, 1990, the most broadly observed and one of the cleanest elections of modern times occurred in Nicaragua, fulfilling the series of Central American accords that began with the Esquipulas meeting in August of 1987.

For a full year Daniel Ortega and the Sandinista government had been moving, step by step and under the watchful eyes of the other Central American presidents, to comply with the agreements he had made in February of 1989. First, at Ortega's invitation, fourteen opposition parties attended a series of talks and recommended changes in Nicaraguan electoral rules. Ortega also asked suggestions from the UN, the OAS, Venezuela, and Costa Rica. Then on April 8, 1989, he recommended legislation incorporating seventeen of the opposition's proposed changes. Ten days later, after debate and ten modifications to Ortega's draft, Nicaragua's national assembly approved an electoral reform law.

In May the UN and the OAS reported favorably on the process. In July, Ortega met with Costa Rican President Oscar Arias and Venezuelan President Carlos Andrés Pérez and with opposition parties. The OAS and the UN both agreed to send observers to judge how well the process fulfilled its pledges.

In early August, a landmark agreement emerged following marathon negotiations involving all the nation's political parties. Most of the opposition parties formed an alliance to work together under the common banner of the United National Opposition (UNO). Thirty-five of the opposition proposals were accepted by the Sandinista government. Some of the key changes were to suspend the draft, reform internal security laws, and free television air time for opposition parties. The UNO agreed that the Contras should be disbanded and that no country should covertly send funds to influence the election. The Central American presidents also voted that the Contras should disband and called upon the UN to oversee the process. They agreed that the disarmed and repatriated forces should be restored to their full civil rights and given material help in rehabilitating themselves.

A nationwide voter registration took place on the first four Sundays in October. Sporadic efforts by small Contra bands to interfere with the registration disrupted activities in a few locations. The process was reopened on following Sundays to accommodate any citizens dissuaded or prevented from registering.

Three international groups monitored the registration process, the campaigning, and the February 1990 election. There was a team from the UN headed by former U.S. Attorney General Elliot Richardson, one from the OAS supervised by João Clemente Baena Soares, and a group of former elected heads of state working together under the general direction of Jimmy Carter.

When the numbers of registered voters were tallied, they came to 1,750,550—almost 90 percent of the total estimated number of Nicaraguans eligible to register.

More than three thousand foreigners, representing a wide assortment of civic organizations and political parties from countries of the Western Hemisphere and most nations of Western Europe, came to Nicaragua during the week of February 25 to see and pass judgment on the highly publicized election. There were at least as many more representing newspapers and periodicals. Along with my former colleague Esteban Torres of California, I spent four days in Nicaragua observing the election on behalf of the Southwest Voter Registration project. Our delegation consisted mostly of elected officials of Hispanic origin from California, Arizona, New Mexico, and Texas.

Everywhere there were banners big and small—red and black for the Sandinistas, blue and white for the UNO candidates. In spite of the rule that commanded a halt to campaigning so that a four-day cooling-off period could take place prior to the election itself, a fiesta atmosphere pervaded the streets. Vendors hawked wares, crowds engaged in animated conversation. Flambé, tulip, and hibiscus trees flaunted their colorful flowers. There was no massing of troops or police such as I had witnessed in 1982. Everything was peaceful.

I walked among the crowds the day before the election and visited ten different polling places on election Sunday, impressed with the easy ambience of the people.

Election fervor had receded. A huge UNO rally on the previous Sunday for the candidacy of Violeta Chamorro, and a mammoth happening on Wednesday for Daniel Ortega and his ticket, had spent their pent-up energy. Now people sighed and talked and waited for the Sunday voting.

As I had been four years earlier in El Salvador, I was impressed with the thirst of the ordinary people for democracy. At one polling place in Managua, a Baptist school, some people told me they had stood for three hours or more because ballots had arrived late. I talked personally with dozens of people in that line. None revealed any anger or disenchantment with the process.

"I've waited more than five years to vote," said one man. "It would be no hardship to wait for five hours."

His brother, too young to have participated in the 1984 balloting, did him one better: "I've waited all my life!"

I asked people how often in their lifetime they had voted. Most who were of an age to vote in 1984 told me they had done so once. Only two people that entire day said they had voted in any Nicaraguan election prior to the 1984 plebiscite. (Ty Fain, an Austin lawyer who had served with the U.S. AID in Nicaragua in 1967, told me he believed the mock election that year had been the only effort in the past two generations to go through even the formalities of balloting.)

During Sunday I talked personally with around two hundred Nicaraguan citizens. With only one exception—a man in his forties who frankly said he did not have any preference—every voter either proudly displayed an ink-stained thumb as evidence of having been to the polls or stoutly avowed the intention to vote before the day ended.

The redundancy of precautions against fraud was an object of pride for both Sandinista and opposition partisans. Cardboard ballot boxes were physically constructed by the election judge, in the presence of opposition observers, on election morning before the polls opened. Each voter's name was checked off the registration list as he or she appeared, in the presence of observers from several political parties. To safeguard against the possibility of an enterprising voter's exercising the franchise more than once, each voter upon casting the ballot would have a thumb dipped into a bottle of indelible ink.

About midmorning, a Nicaraguan recognizing me as an official observer reported to me a rumor that the ink, specially imported from Venezuela, was not really indelible. At the next polling place I stuck my thumb in the bottle. The ink did not come clean, in spite of my best efforts to scrub it off, for two days.

Another discovery impressed me. There was no apparent resentment over the huge cluster of foreigners scrutinizing the Nicaraguans' most sacred process. I had supposed that some might bridle at the spectacle of so many outsiders watching a strictly local ritual. Not so. In fact, several Nicaraguans expressed to me their pleasure that so many people had come from so many countries to observe their elections.

"Now," said one, "everyone will know that Nicaragua is capable of holding a free election."

"Yes, and now maybe the world will respect Nicaragua," commented another. After a pause, she added, "Maybe even the United States will respect Nicaragua."

Confounding most predictions, UNO candidate Violeta Barrios de Chamorro won with a very comfortable margin. All afternoon on Sunday, as I listened to Nicaraguans volunteer their sentiments, I had begun to believe in the possibility of an upset. When it actually happened it was a stunning blow to the Sandinista camp. Daniel Ortega was visibly shaken as he came before the cameras and the waiting throng of observers early Monday morning. In the most gracious speech I have ever heard him make, Ortega surprised some cynics by announcing his acceptance of the will of his people and calling for a period of national reconciliation and for cooperation with his successor, Violeta Chamorro.

On Saturday before the election, I had spoken with Sergio Ramírez, the Nicaraguan vice president with whom I had engaged in a shouting match that day in 1982. "I am very glad that you came, Mr. Speaker," said Sergio. "Except for you these elections would never have occurred."

On Monday, the day after the election, I had a long talk with Alfonso Robelo, who had been a fund-raiser and campaigner for Mrs. Chamorro. "You cannot know how pleased I am to see you here," Alfonso exclaimed. "If it had not been for you, there would not have been any election."

Upon my return to the States, I received a call from Tom Loeffler, my former Republican colleague, who had first come to me with the idea of a joint call for a peaceful settlement. "By God, it worked!" was the way Tom began our conversation.

And then came the brief handwritten note from Secretary of State Jim Baker. "But for you," he wrote, "there would have been no bipartisan accord—without which there would've been no election" (the complete note can be found in the appendix).

He was gracious. They were all gracious. Peace was ample pay for the effort I had made in its behalf.

I am encouraged too about the future of democracy in El Savador. There a formal peace was two years later in coming and attended by even more highly visible atrocities against human rights, approved and covered up for too long by a clique of military commanders. José Napoleón Duarte's dream of a civil society free of armed conflict was still in formation when he died in 1990. But the seeds he planted, watered by the Esquipulas agreement, finally bore fruit. The OAS and the United Nations both played vital roles. Peace was formally proclaimed on New Year's Day 1992.

In March of 1993, a UN study labeled "Commission on the Truth" officially assigned responsibility for the wanton killing of literally thousands of civilians to the guerrillas and "death squads" with identifiable links to the Salvadoran military command. That fourteen-year reign of death-squad terror included such internationally publicized slayings as those of Archbishop Romero, a group of nuns from the United States, a group of Jesuit priests, and all witnesses to their killing. Defense Minister René Emilio Ponce resigned upon the release of the commission's findings. President Christiani removed fifteen high-ranking army officers implicated in the atrocities.

The constitutional forms of El Salvador's democracy have now been ratified in six biennial election cycles and the orderly transfer of power. This closes one sad chapter of Salvadoran history. Now it is time for healing and for thoroughly expunging the lawless elements of the military.

But this is not the end of the story. The struggles of peace are harder sometimes, but potentially more rewarding, than the struggles of war. In Nicaragua it is still too early to know if the *spirit* of mutual toleration—the ability of each, as Benjamin Franklin put it, to "doubt a little his own infallibility"—can take root and thrive in an atmosphere so long abraded by strife and death. I am betting that it can. In Central America and throughout our hemisphere, there is a chance for a new beginning.

CHAPTER 12

Make a New Beginning

From the murmur and subtlety of suspicion
With which we vex one another
Give us rest;
Make a new beginning
And mingle again the kindred of the nations
In the alchemy of love
And with some finer essence of forbearance
Temper our minds.

—Aristophanes

On leaving Congress I returned to Fort Worth, where Betty and I live among the people for whom I worked those thirty-four years. I have been writing, lecturing, and traveling, re-learning the joys of private life. I teach a course at Texas Christian University and write a weekly column for the Fort Worth *Star-Telegram,* sometimes picked up by other newspapers. I have accepted a lot of invitations to lecture at colleges and universities across the country and enjoy business relationships with American Income Life Insurance Company of Waco, Texas, and Arch Petroleum of Fort Worth.

While I do not lobby or serve on corporate boards, I am on the boards of Texas Wesleyan University, First United Methodist Church, and the regional Boy Scouts. I have made a dozen or more trips to Mexico and visit frequently with Mexican government officials. At the invitation of former President Jimmy Carter, I have participated in several sessions with international leaders at the Carter Center in Atlanta and helped monitor elections in Haiti. Back in Washington occasionally, I must sound like a recruiter for Congress Anonymous as I reassure former colleagues that there truly is a life after Congress! I find some time to fish, to play a round of golf now and then, to read some good books I had set aside while in Congress—and to think.

Out of all of this, the thirty-four years in Congress and the three years of reflection, perhaps I have learned a few lessons worth sharing about Latin America, about the United States and our nation's government, and about life.

This personal narrative has dealt almost entirely with U.S. relations in Central America, that intriguing group of tropical nations that lie in a semi-inverted arc between Mexico and the Panama Canal. About 28 million people live in the seven republics, bracketed on the east by the Caribbean Sea and on the west and south by the Pacific Ocean. Much, but not all, of what I have learned about that area and its people over the years is applicable to the whole of Latin America. In the following pages, let me suggest a few ways to improve both our image and our performance in Central America, as well as in Mexico and throughout the region.

The past four decades of hope, disillusionment, and reward have convinced me of two things. On the threshold of a new century, we have a better chance now than ever before to make a new beginning in Latin America. And never in my opinion has a new approach been so important. No other region of the world is so vital to our own future. Both global and domestic considerations dictate a much higher policy priority than we have given in the past to our nearest neighbors.

Closer ties are in our economic self-interest. The nations of Latin American have always been our best trading partners. For most of the twentieth century, they have bought more of our goods than any other region of the world, and they have sold more of theirs to us than to anyone else. They link us to vital petroleum and mineral supplies without which we would be crippled or even more dangerously dependent than we already are on the volatile Middle East. While struggling with balance-of-trade deficits, we have largely ignored a yawning market at our doorstep awaiting development, its potential limited only by the opportunities it gets for economic growth. Most of the imported products Latin Americans buy come from our country, although Europe and Japan are trying hard now to cash in on those markets.

Not just our economy but our quality of life as we approach the next century is linked increasingly to the economic well-being of those countries to our south. Halting the flow of drugs into the United States depends on the stability of governments in Mexico, Colombia, and elsewhere in the region. And the only antidote to a tidal influx of undocumented workers into the United States is the dramatic improvement of job opportunities in Mexico and Central America.

Unless we swiftly develop a hemispheric agenda tailored to the rapidly emerging realities of the post–cold war era, it is virtually certain that some of the fragile democracies newly installed in Latin America will shatter on the hard rocks of joblessness and hopelessness. The sinister drug culture will pose increasing threats to youth throughout the Americas until we develop a better-coordinated hemispheric approach. And the suffocating burden of external debt that today stifles new enterprise throughout Latin America will needlessly dry up markets for U.S. goods.

It does not have to be that way. The dangers on the horizon loom no larger than the opportunities. With the collapse of world communism as a political threat, we can turn our energies and resources to these opportunities. The bipolar world so long dominated by a military-spending competition between the two superpowers has given way to a world in which the problems are more diverse, the real competition is economic, and the solutions are increasingly social. One obvious way for us to counter aggressive economic threats from Japan and the European Common Market is to seek ever-closer trading ties within the Western Hemisphere, particularly with Canada, Mexico, and the Central American and Caribbean nations.

To make the most of such opportunities, we need to understand a few basic facts about our neighbors. Each nation is unique in certain ways, and generalizations are dangerous. But these stand out:

1. Most of the people in Latin America are dreadfully poor by U.S. standards. The average Central American family today earns less in a year than a typical U.S. family will earn in a month.

In wide parts of Latin America, most people go to bed hungry every night. Whole villages exist where nobody has seen a doctor in a year. One child in fifty may get a chance to go to college.

2. But the region has a remarkable capacity for economic growth, if it can get the necessary stimulus. Throughout the 1960s and 1970s, Central American economies actually grew faster than our own did, until that area was smitten in the 1980s by civil wars, falling commodity prices, and skyrocketing interest rates. Annual economic growth ranged from a low of 4.4 percent in Honduras to a high of 6.3 percent in Costa Rica. It averaged just 4.2 percent in the United States. In those years per capita income increased markedly in each of the Central American nations. The number of trained medical doctors grew twice as fast as the general population. The rate of adult literacy almost doubled. The number of young people attending school beyond the eighth grade more than doubled. Manufacturing and other industrial activity grew, expanding employment opportunities. Central America's future sparkled with promise.

Then came the fall. A global economic recession choked off foreign investments. U.S. markets dried up to Central American products as our own economy contracted. World coffee prices fell by 26 percent and cotton prices by 20 percent in the 1980s. Banana and sugar markets declined drastically. But the price of borrowed money, on which Latin American growth depends, skyrocketed. Interest on private U.S. bank loans to Panama and Costa Rica had reached 23 percent in the mid-1980s.

The result was a shocking economic dislocation. Massive amounts of money were drained from farmers, workers, and small business people to pay debt service. The "magic of the market place" that Presidents Reagan and Bush would extol as the ultimate economic virtue brought cruel havoc in those years. By 1981 it took two bags of Central American coffee to buy what one bag did in 1978. By 1989, Costa Rica would have to export three times as much of its goods as twelve years earlier to pay for the same amount of imports.

3. As a result, a terrible burden of debts, both public and private, now bears down so heavily on all Latin American economies that it will take dramatic action for almost any of them to claw a new foothold on the uphill path to economic recovery. Much of the financial stimulus to new growth will have to come from outside the region.

4. The maldistribution of wealth, made worse by recession and debt, continues to be a fertile breeding ground for political dema-

gogues who would turn unrest into revolution. The collapse of ineffectual elected governments could be followed by a return to authoritarian regimes of either the right or the left.

"Throughout four hundred years, this country has struggled merely to survive," José Napoleón Duarte once told me of El Salvador. "Two societies have grown up side by side. One-tenth of the people enjoy great wealth. Nine-tenths exist in abject poverty." In several Latin American nations, more than half the land is owned by 2 percent of the people, and most of them keep their money in foreign banks. It is this that breeds wars and this that needs correcting.

5. But where they have a viable choice, the common people themselves clearly prefer democracy. Throughout the region, they thirst for freedom and will support it with their lives if they can see real hope of gaining a fairer share of life's opportunities within a framework of political liberty.

6. They admire the United States and yearn to be more like us in many ways but have no desire to abandon their own traditions or to become carbon copies of our society. They think that our history has not prepared us to understand their problems, and this is largely true.

Complicating the above realities even further are the destruction and waste wrought by wars in Nicaragua, El Salvador, and Guatemala during the 1980s. Now we begin to see in its broader dimension the legacy of economic devastation and social setback that smolders in the wake of that decade, even as the smoke of battle begins to clear.

These facts are no cause for despondency but rather a cry for action. The United States needs to strive for a new policy based on the realities of the post–cold war era. The United States should:

1. *Support democracy in Latin America consistently, respect its choices cheerfully, and stop trying to force political results by secret intrigues and military actions.*

In the early 1990s, the community of Latin American nations enjoys more popularly elected governments than at any time in history. Heartening change has replaced military and oligarchic regimes with the outward habiliments of democracy. The need now is to consolidate the gain so that freely chosen governments can enjoy stability while they move toward the fruits of political democracy—economic development and social justice.

There are several ways in which U.S. policy can support democratic development in the hemisphere. By diplomatic recognition of governments, by deliberate trade and investment policies, through membership in the OAS and international lending institutions, the United States can come down on the side of democracy. We need to do so consistently.

One important contribution we can make is respecting the choice of a nation when it votes and insisting that the military elements of each country with which we conduct relations subordinate themselves to the popularly elected civil government.

In Latin America "emergencies" have often been invoked and then continued on one pretext or another until they have become the norm. Castro in 1959 promised an electoral system once the perceived external threat to Cuba's sovereignty abated. He may even have intended to turn over the reins in due time, but he has held them in a tight fist for more than three decades. General Augusto Pinochet Ugarte suspended Chile's constitution in 1973 on the specious grounds of emergency and hid behind that ruse for seventeen years, apparently deluding himself into believing that the people were incapable of self-government.

In the case of Nicaragua and its Sandinista government, democracy came as a result of a regional agreement to which Nicaragua's president was a signatory. The pressure on that government to carry out the terms of the accord and its successor agreements in face of numerous obstacles and almost implacable hostility was essentially peer pressure. The agreement worked because it was an agreement among neighbors, who wanted it to work. The negotiating process achieved what six years of U.S.-financed military intervention had failed to achieve. It brought peace and restored democracy.

What, then, is the proper role of the United States? It is not to overthrow governments and install others of our choice but rather to respect in each country a government of its own choice. Whenever we have interfered with the electoral process or failed to trust the people's choice, we have bought trouble. Our interference in the elected civilian government of Guatemala in 1954, our "destabilizing" of Chile's elected government in 1973, and our repeated efforts throughout the 1980s to bring down the Nicaraguan government by force have left a legacy of bad faith. Many throughout Latin America have come to distrust our protestations of supporting democracy. They think we respect it only when it produces a government to our liking. For two generations, our basic policy was seen simply as *anticommunism*. It emphasized what we were against, but not what we were for. Now that the cold war is over and Russian influence is no longer even an imagined threat in Latin America, our policy must be conceived and stated in positive terms. It must be *pro-democracy*.

2. *Treat our neighbors as equals, recognize their lawful sovereignty, and honor their territorial integrity as we expect them to honor ours.*

Each of the great religions has an approximate equivalent of the golden rule: Do unto others as you would have others do unto you. With this in mind, let us mentally switch roles with our Latin American brethren and ask ourselves a question or two. How would we like it, for example, if foreign agents came into the United States at will, kidnapped our citizens on our soil, and whisked them off to another country to stand trial for something those Americans allegedly did here in the United States? Our reaction to that would be swift and unmistakable. The American public would scream foul. Congress would reverberate with indignant oratory. The president might sever diplomatic relations and would threaten retaliation.

This, however, is precisely what the United States has done, not once but several times, to citizens of Latin American nations. In the late 1980s, during a critical moment in the peace process, U.S. agents disrupted relations when they swooped down into Honduras to arrest a Honduran citizen suspected of drug and currency trafficking. International jurists were stunned when the United States invaded Panama, seized and brought Manual Noriega to a Miami trial. Nobody I know has any sympathy for Noriega, but trying him in U.S. courts was against the strongly expressed wishes of the new Panamanian government, which wanted to bring Noriega to justice in Panama where the crimes were committed. In June 1992, relations, which had been soaring between the United States and Mexico, plunged to the lowest level in years when the U.S. Supreme Court ruled that U.S. federal agents could legally send bounty hunters to kidnap a Mexican doctor on Mexican soil and force him to stand trial in the United States for a murder committed in Mexico. The world community was shocked. The Mexican Congress unanimously denounced the official kidnapping as a blatant violation of our extradition treaty and of Mexico's territorial rights. The U.S. trial court later released the doctor for want of any credible evidence against him, but Mexico remained outraged at this U.S. violation of Mexican sovereignty and Mexico's cherished principle of juridical equality among nations.

In 1962, Frank Tannenbaum, the astute observer and professor of Latin America history, wrote that the most serious causes of the

U.S. hemispheric problems are "not merely economic or political. They are moral. We treat Latin Americans as lesser people." It was the widespread resentment of this that gave credence to leftist preachments during the first three quarters of this century and drove Mexico and other republics into shells of restrictive trade and sheltered industries.

Now we may be on the verge of a historic turnabout. Latin American governments are inviting closer business ties. Mexico, which closed its borders to many big private U.S. businesses because of their perceived exploitation of workers and resources, is now opening its arms for the first time in fifty years to U.S. investors. Has the United States matured enough to accept Latin nations as sovereign states entitled to the same consideration we demand for ourselves?

Our continued insistence on the U.S. right to invade Latin American countries or kidnap their citizens indicates that we have not learned enough. Laws, we seem to say, do not apply to us in the way they do to other nations. We called on the World Court for relief when Iranian gangs seized the U.S. embassy in 1979, but we paid no attention when that court ruled that we had violated international law in mining Nicaragua's harbors. We led the world in punishing Iraq because it violated international law when it invaded Kuwait, but we thought it permissible under international law for us to invade Grenada and Panama.

These inconsistencies deeply trouble our friends in the hemisphere. We need to be aware of them. And we must understand that even the Monroe Doctrine, still occasionally invoked to justify various paternalistic practices, never presumed the right to change accepted rules of international behavior just because the United States is bigger.

3. *Encourage all nations in the region to pursue dramatic, simultaneous reductions in the arms burden that has sapped their vital resources as it has our own.*

Whatever influence the United States has in the OAS and other hemispheric forums should come down clearly on the side of reducing military weaponry and expenditures. The real initiative, however, will have to come from Latin Americans themselves. Fortunately, there is precedent.

As we have seen, Costa Rica abolished its army outright on December 1, 1948. By almost everyone's accounting, Costa Rica has become the hemisphere's prime exemplar of civility and enlightened democracy. It ranks highest in literacy and lowest in human-rights violations. The country glorifies education and has a good public-health system. This is not to say that Costa Rica is devoid of problems. It has its share. But it has raised a standard to which other nations understandably aspire. Now, in the early aftermath of the long cold war and the prolonged bloodshed in Nicaragua and El Salvador, statesmen are looking anew to Costa Rica's example. They raise the intriguing possibility that the whole region from the Panama Canal to Mexico might someday become an arms-free zone. Perhaps too good to be true, it is nevertheless an alluring prospect.

There is hardly a limit to the urgent public needs that can be at least partially addressed by a substantial reduction in military outlays. Malnutrition, illiteracy, the need for much broader access to education and primary health care, sanitary water- and waste-treatment systems—all these were highlighted in the January 1984 report of the Kissinger Commission on Central America.

If the Central American nations each halved their military forces, they would free up several hundred million dollars annually to address these problems.

4. *Develop a multinational aid program conditioned on respect for human rights, land tenure, and progressive tax reforms; cooperation in drying up the drug traffic; and a commitment to long-starved needs of the public sector.*

In January 1984, the bipartisan blue-ribbon panel popularly referred to as the Kissinger Commission recommended a five-year, $8 billion U.S. economic-aid commitment to Central America. "Human development" was to be the cornerstone. Beyond badly needed improvements in public works, the bulk of the economic relief the commission sought would have been aimed at a group of "ambitious yet realistic objectives." They included the eradication of malnutrition and illiteracy, universal access to primary education and health care, measurable reductions in infant mortality and population growth rates, and a significant improvement in housing.

The Reagan administration never got around to recommending, or Congress to initiating, the called-for stimulus. Instead of $8 billion in economic aid, our country has poured almost this much into military spending in the region. We gave aid to the armies of three countries, financed the abortive Contra effort, bore the cost of twice moving large U.S. military contingents into Honduras, and invaded Panama. Needless to say, the grandly advertised "social objectives for the 1980s" were never realized.

For too long, we have focused our aid program too narrowly on military security and confined it to a few favorite allies. By 1990, two of every three aid dollars went to just five countries—Egypt, Israel, Turkey, Pakistan, and the Philippines. A comprehensive redirection of focus is timely.

Now there is a natural temptation, with the worldwide Soviet threat a thing of the past, to wash our hands of Central America and turn our attentions elsewhere. To do so would be myopic.

In the aftermath of war's devastation, the region needs assistance to feed and resettle at least one million refugees, mothers with children, and indigent aged. There is need also for some plain old humanitarian aid to abate hunger. Two people out of three in Central America are, to one degree or another, malnourished. But the bigger need is for help to rebuild the damaged public infrastructure and restart the engines of shattered economies. Roads, bridges, dams, and irrigation works destroyed by war and worn away through years of enforced neglect are building blocks on which private investments of all sorts must be based.

Equally essential in preparing a seedbed for investment is the *human* infrastructure emphasized by the Kissinger panel. Education and health are the keys. The most basic lack in Central America is a stable middle class of healthy, educated, gainfully employed families. To build this base is the harder task. It requires sustained effort. The need is for investment and for a fairer distribution of its dividends. In the long run, political democracy and economic sufficiency are interdependent.

Whatever program of aid evolves for the smitten countries of Central America, it must not be just a one-time unilateral shot in the arm. If it is to develop economies capable of self-sustainment in world markets, and capable of entering into a mature, continuing trade relationship with the United States, the aid program must embody several characteristics. First, there must be a sustained commitment over a period of years, not subject to fits and starts. Second, it must be based on a long-term plan developed by the Central American countries themselves. Third, the effort should be a coordinated program, not a spasmodic proliferation of unrelated initiatives by a lot of different agencies. Fourth, it should ideally be multinational in conception and in administration. Fifth, its benefits could be conditioned on the performance of recipient countries.

Such an effort would be maximally effective only to the degree that those countries had a voice in establishing the program's objectives and the conditions of the aid. A consortium of the United States, other Western democracies, and possibly Japan could endow a fund to be administered by some authentic Central American instrumentality. That entity would see that the money was fairly parceled out among the seven recipient nations, including Panama and Belize, based on certain conditions. Those conditions might include a commitment to respect human rights, move toward a fairer distribution of land, establish an equitable taxing system that does not invite public contempt by exempting a class of oligarchs, revitalize the public infrastructure of the region, and protect the common environment. One other condition should involve a cooperative commitment to eradicate the deadly traffic in drugs. At a meeting of Latin American leaders at the Carter Center in Atlanta, I became convinced that elected officials are universally opposed to the menace of the drug cartels. Law enforcement arms of all the nations in the hemisphere must form a compact and closely coordinate their efforts to interdict illicit shipments and eradicate drug sources. And at some point hemispheric leaders must make an effort to establish genuine economic replacements for traditionally lucrative coca and marijuana crops.

5. *Support regional approaches to trade and economic development and move as rapidly as feasible toward free and fair trade throughout the hemisphere, building on the North American Free Trade Alliance in ways that will help lift wages in Latin America, not lower them in the United States.*

The economic future of Latin America will ultimately depend upon the expansion of trade and private investments. The boldest inter-American idea advanced in a whole generation, since John F. Kennedy inspired short-lived hope with his Alliance for Progress, is the North American Free Trade Alliance (NAFTA). That plan was designed to eliminate over the next fifteen years virtually all export and import barriers among the United States, Canada, and Mexico. Even without a ratified agreement, lanes of commerce have begun to open. Trade between the United States and Mexico expanded rapidly in the first three years of the 1990s. Mexico's economy got a shot of adrenalin, and the United States reaped from increased exports to Mexico a welcome reduction in its foreign trade deficit.

There are good reasons to favor a trade agreement. With tight regional trading blocs developing in Europe and Asia, it makes sense to form closer ties within our own hemisphere. It is economic self-defense. Latin America, not Japan, may hold the biggest part of the solution to persistent U.S. trade deficits. Since roughly seventy cents of every Mexican or Central American dollar spent on manufactured imports pays for U.S.-made goods, a revival of economic growth south of our border would swiftly expand markets for our products.

Mexican President Carlos Salinas de Gortari has pursued the vision of a North American supermarket stretching from the Yukon to the Yucatán, facilitating the flow of goods, services, and investments and stimulating new jobs. A further step toward hemispheric agreement might be to invite participation by Central America, whose countries experimented with a common market in the 1960s and 1970s and are working now to revive that idea.

Stricken by wars and economic crises, Latin America in the 1980s reduced its imports from our country by roughly 60 percent, resulting in the loss of more than one million American jobs. To regain the initiative in world trade we need to form closer trading alliances and promote economic growth within the region.

In spite of this, recent U.S. opinion polls on NAFTA show public sentiment sharply divided. An increasing number of U.S. citizens worry that Mexico's low wage rates would depress wages in our own country and lure U.S. factories across the border. Ross Perot spoke in 1992 of a "huge sucking sound" made by U.S. jobs being pulled out of the country by the agreement.

Critics point to the eighteen hundred *maquiladora* factories that have sprung up, aided by U.S. tariff waivers, along the northern edge of Mexico. These employed a half million Mexican workers by 1993 to turn out parts and other goods for big U.S. corporations. But wages in some plants are merely $35 to $50 a week, saving U.S. companies an average of $16,000 a year per worker in wages alone. The very people whose labor creates these corporate windfalls are denied a fair share in them.

If the net impact of NAFTA were to close factories and decrease wages for U.S. workers, the result would be bad. But specific agreements could be structured to improve wages and conditions of work in Mexico, making Mexican wage earners better customers for their own goods as well as ours. Why not perfect this trade agreement to embrace the twin ideals of free trade *and* fair labor standards? Mexico's steady, planned movement toward the latter would be a mutually agreed condition of the former. The same would apply to Central America if the pact were expanded. In effect, we'd be saying: We don't charge tariffs on your goods; use that money—and the income our trade generates—to pay your workers better wages.

We shouldn't insist that Mexico, or any other Latin American country ultimately embraced in the agreement, adopt our labor standards overnight, but that they improve, that they begin to move consistently in this direction. If a modern Mexican or Central American factory can outproduce and outsell an older U.S.-based company on the strength of more efficient productivity or a better product, all will be richer for the availability of its goods. If it should outsell the U.S. company solely on the strength of reduced labor costs wrung from inadequate wages, however, both societies will lose.

Let us convene a panel of U.S. labor, business, and government experts to sit down with Mexico's leaders and work out a clear plan in the context of the trade agreement to improve pay and conditions for workers in the industries that sell goods to the United States. In recent years our government has applied a labor standard to at least six other major laws governing trade and investment policy.

And why not? In this enlightened age we speak loftily of human rights. Our government conditions foreign aid, trade, and other forms of cooperation with foreign countries upon their respect for "internationally recognized human rights." What right is more basic than a fair return for the labor of a human's hands or back or mind? That's all one has to offer in pursuit of life's necessities. Human labor is not just another commodity, like beans or lumber or chewing gum, to be traded as cheaply as possible on world markets. Labor is life itself, and NAFTA, if implemented well and expanded with vision, could make life in this hemisphere much better for all.

6. *Promote a new philosophy of investment that respects the right of farming and working families to a fairer share of the growth dividend. Leave a legacy of some lasting value to the people whenever we take resources.*

Now that long-closed doors in Latin America are reopening to foreign investment, North American policy makers and investors need to develop a new philosophy aware of past mistakes and sensitive to deeply entrenched sentiments. What we should pursue are mutually beneficial long-term relationships.

David Rockefeller, as president of the Chase Manhattan Bank, was deeply interested and knowledgeable about investing in Latin America. He noted publicly that most Latin Americans felt that U.S. corporations had made exorbitant profits in Latin America while exploiting and impoverishing the host countries. What we must now strive for in the Americas is a socially conscious capitalism with which the average citizens of Latin America can identify, one in which the historically downtrodden can see some realistic hope for an end to their worst miseries and a better future for their families in their lifetimes.

We need to encourage investments like the historic investments in medium-sized American enterprises that were profitable but also expanded the middle classes and led to greater democracy. Until recently, overseas investment practices too often have enriched only the investors and a privileged few in the host countries. This was one of the major causes of the violent revolution in Mexico early in this century that led to the overthrow of dictator Porfirio Diaz, who ruled for thirty-five years, fulsomely flattered by verbal and material tributes from American businessmen but apparently blind to the appalling squalor in which his own people lived. Foreign owners of Mexican mines and oil discoveries flourished, paid low wages and no taxes, and were free to export Mexico's wealth for their own profit. Their government's apparent preference for foreigners became humiliating to the proud Mexican people, who complained that their country was the mother of foreigners and the stepmother of Mexicans.

Variations of this tradition have cropped up elsewhere in Latin America with disturbing frequency throughout this century. A succession of unpopular and undemocratic regimes became associated in the public mind with American business favors. Batista in Cuba, Trujillo in the Dominican Republic, Castillo Armas in Guatemala, Perez-Jimenez in Venezuela, the Somozas in Nicaragua, Pinochet in Chile—all these rulers courted foreign investments, all favored and for a time at least were favored by official U.S. policy, and all are remembered with distaste at home—regarded as either patrons of colonialism or puppets of imperialism. All were forced from office. It is absolutely necessary that we understand this.

Only blind folly would mimic failed practices that, while emphasizing development and industrialization, actually widened the gulf between rich and poor. I feel so strongly about the need to adjust to the realities of this history that I suggest the U.S. government and investors consider some radical rethinking as they plan for the changed world of the future.

There are two innovations that have served America well and might go a long way toward transforming the reality as well as the perception of foreign investment in Latin American business and industry. The first of these ideas is to build a solid local constituency for new business enterprises by developing profit-sharing arrangements with Central American workers. Limited employee stock ownership plans could be incorporated into the charters of companies established by U.S. investment. I cannot imagine anything that would do more to broaden the base of capitalism and enhance its popularity among workers. This might be one of the fastest ways to develop a middle class in countries that have known mainly the extremes of wealth and poverty. If workers and local suppliers were to become participants in company profits, they would identify with, rather than instinctively oppose, management.

To make this suggestion more than an ideal goal, it will have to become official, conscious U.S. government *policy*. For, left to their own devices, even firms whose managers liked the idea would find a multitude of reasons not to do it or not to do it just now. There are several ways to foster this approach: incentives in the U.S. tax code, stipulations attending official U.S. government risk guarantees, and treaties covering the conditions of investment and trade. The important thing is to *want* to do it—and to make it a general format for U.S. investments over a certain size in Mexico and Latin American countries, not just a vague philosophical concept or a rare idealistic experiment.

The second innovation specifically concerns industries that extract resources from a country's natural bounty. What I am about to suggest can even be broadened to cover any number of agricultural commodities on whose fluctuating world-market prices national economies rise and fall. But it would apply with particular force to the extraction of *unrenewable* mineral treasures underlying a nation's soil. I offer this as an ethical axiom: When a U.S. company takes something irreplaceable from a friendly nation's native endowment, we owe something lasting in return. If we take from its capital wealth, we should give in exchange some contribution to its future.

The principle of depletable resources has been recognized in U.S. law for a long time. Private investors in U.S. minerals are compensated in the tax code by varying percentages of presumed depletion. The oil-depletion allowance has been debated repeatedly in the U.S. Congress. Less familiar to most people are depletion allowances of one kind and another for almost every other mineral—coal, copper, zinc, gravel, etc. But there is a remarkable void in our domestic policy. While we indemnify private owners of U.S. mineral properties against the predictable demise of their investments, we have done precious little to indemnify our nation—the people—against the predictable decline in our *national* reserves. The United States has already run out of some minerals. The price to Americans of falling oil and gas reserves is growing dependence on foreign petroleum and vulnerability to foreign oil profiteers and dictators. We fought a war with Iraq over this issue. The United States as a whole has an interest in the depletion of its natural reserves, just as individual drillers and miners have an interest.

If this is true of the United States, how much more true it is of small and impoverished countries where the tempo of life rises and falls with a single crop harvest and the registers of human hope are fluctuating commodity prices. The Mexican and Venezuelan economies have waxed and waned with the price of a barrel of oil. Costa Rica is as sensitive to the world price of coffee as a child to a high fever. To other Latin Americans, a downward turn in tin, sugar, and cocoa prices can mean the difference between enough food on the table and none.

What I propose is that for each natural commodity removed from a host country—for each barrel of oil or ton of copper—the two governments involved jointly establish a minute fraction of the cost to be contributed by the exporter of that commodity into a permanent fund. We might call it the Fund for the Future. The central bank of each country would have the responsibility of investing this capital endowment in certificates of deposit or other insured securities. Only the invested fund's *annual yield* could be spent, and that only for enriching educational opportunities. After twelve or fifteen years, the fund's annual contribution to the schools of a given host country should reach a point where it would equal the annual income from the commodity export levy. In a generation or so it could double the fund's yearly income.

These are a few suggestions for ways in which forward-looking policy might eradicate not only the image but the reality of exploitation. Bold, resolute decisions made now could help guarantee a more democratic, peaceful and prosperous next century for the hemisphere's children. "Where there is no vision, the people perish." May Solomon's words not become an epitaph to neglected opportunities. Opportunities abound at this moment as we examine the horizon for new directions in our relations with Latin America.

A FEW FINAL THOUGHTS

By now, no doubt the reader understands that I am relatively optimistic about the prospects for improvement in our hemisphere and for the future of U.S. relations with our neighbors to the south. For the present, armed conflict and assassination are no longer everyday occurrences in the cities and countryside of Central America. Elected governments, not leftist or rightist military dictatorships, grapple with the problems of peace. Here at home, the U.S. government and people are arguing civilly over deficits, health care, and stimulus packages. There is no longer a divisive war over peace in Washington.

I suspect the reader also senses that I have few regrets about the small role I played in resolving the conflicts, in stopping the killings, in fostering freely elected governments in Central America. Lest any be tempted to waste sympathy over my having left Congress, be assured that my family and I are better off physically, mentally, and financially for having come home. We are busy but no longer harried. There is such an array of interesting things to do that I greet the options of each new dawn with the excited anticipation of a kid in front of a candy store.

If I have a major regret, it is that my talents for leadership were inadequate to the task of uniting and conciliating the harshly divergent factions within our Congress into a reasonably harmonious consensus toward the problems besetting our nation. I resigned as Speaker because it was apparent to me that such leadership was needed and that it had eluded my capacities. Striving for conciliation, I had reaped polarization. It was time for someone else.

Yet in fairness to my efforts, which were only partially successful, I am impelled to put them in perspective, as I have tried to do here. We have seen books written by Elliott Abrams, Colonel North, President Reagan, and George Shultz. Someone had to explain the role of Congress, and my personal role, in this episode of history.

My purpose in recording these events has not been to impute false motives or bad faith to anyone. It is to shed light, not heat. Where President Reagan and I disagreed, I am sure he felt his convictions as strongly as I felt mine. He and his advisers believed we should influence events by military action. I saw the problem from a different perspective. As for those who lied to Congress and otherwise violated the laws of our country to force their preferred solutions on Central America, many thought of themselves as patriots. They saw the basic menace as part of a world Communist conspiracy that could be resisted only by a counterconspiracy, breaking laws passed by a Congress that tied their hands. In their well-meaning fixation, I believe they profoundly misunderstood both the U.S. Constitution and the historical realities of our hemisphere.

During my years in Congress, I served with eight American presidents—Dwight D. Eisenhower through George Bush—and observed several of them at close range in moments of relaxation and in times of crisis. I believe that each of them earnestly wanted to do the right thing for our country. Warm and wonderful stories, funny and poignant personal vignettes plucked from those years could fill several volumes of this length. For the most part, they would be happy stories. But that is for another book.

The events we have recalled here, at least in the broader perspective, led to a happy ending. I hope they prepare the seedbed for a new beginning. As for me, except for some errors in judgment that are clearer now in hindsight, I think I'd do it all again. I look in the mirror every morning, and I smile. Nobody is dying in Central America because of wars over peace in Washington. It was worth it all.

Appendix: Historically Important Documents

PUBLISHER'S NOTE

We are pleased that Jim Wright was thoughtful enough to preserve the following documents and generous enough to share them with us all. We have included them for the benefit of those readers who wish to probe in greater detail the workings of governments at their highest levels. This unique collection makes *Worth It All* distinctly different from almost all political memoirs. Throughout our work on this book, Speaker Wright was sensitive to the need for historical clarity. He thus responded immediately and positively to our idea that these documents would interest many and would be invaluable to scholars seeking the truth about the 1980s and wars for peace in Washington and Central America. Many of these documents would never have surfaced. Now those studying the period will not have to search official records and news reports, or importune the several governments, agencies, and high-level officials involved.

For the reader's benefit we have provided an appendix table of contents, numbered each document, and labeled its purpose and date. We have also added an author's note at the end of each document and a reference back to the main text. Speaker Wright's notes describe each document's place in the history of the period. Not all documents lent themselves to direct reproduction; but wherever possible, we have reproduced the original document, such as a letter from President Reagan or the last handwritten note from Secretary of State James Baker acknowledging Speaker Wright's role in making peace. When a direct reproduction would not have been readable, we have typeset the copy, faithfully recreating the original.

CONTENTS

1. Letter to Daniel Ortega, September 4, 1980

JIM WRIGHT
Texas

$$\mathfrak{Congress\ of\ the\ United\ States}$$
House of Representatibes
Office of the Majority Leader
Washington, D.C. 20515

September 4, 1980

Comandante Daniel Ortega
Managua
Nicaragua

Dear Comandante:

The public statement as quoted in the news to the effect that elections will be postponed for five years in Nicaragua comes as a major disappointment to those of us in the Congress who have held out hope that Nicaragua, with our understanding and help, could move swiftly toward a truly democratic society. We also are deeply disturbed by reports that restrictions are being imposed upon the freedom of the press and other expression necessary to a free society.

As you and other members of the governing junta are aware, we have taken a leading role in the advocacy of a policy of understanding and friendship for Nicaragua's efforts at self-government, believing that your nation is a vital focal point for freedom in our hemisphere.

To be confronted now, after the verbal assurances we thought we had received during our personal visit to Nicaragua in June, with the dismaying announcement that elections will not be held until 1985 is appalling in the extreme. Our people recall with bitter irony the grand promises made by Fidel Castro in Cuba in 1959 that there would be free elections in due course. Twenty one years have passed from that date. No free electoral system has been established. Cuba remains a dictatorship, its leader having crassly betrayed that solemn promise. In my country, people vote today who were not even born when that promise was made in 1959.

Surely you are aware that many in my country are apprehensive lest Nicaragua abandon its splendid ideals of self-government and follow the Cuban example of oppression and rule by terror. The enemies of Nicaragua in the United States have publicly prophesied that course. The friends of Nicaragua, ourselves included, have sought to convey to our nation and our Congress the reassurances which we felt we had received in good faith from yourselves and others.

We have hoped and believed that the Nicaraguan people can find their own destiny, free from outside domination, while fully respecting private property, judicial procedures, free speech and press, and the other necessary habiliments of a free society which cannot exist without an orderly electoral system in which the people themselves are given frequent and regular opportunity to choose those by whom they will be governed. In a civilized world, that choice must be made by ballots and not by bullets.

Those of us in the United States who want so strongly to be friends of the Nicaraguan people and your beautiful country earnestly hope you will share these thoughts with others in the governing junta and that you will reconsider and give to civilized humanity the reassurance that an orderly system of political democracy will be established through free elections in the near future, much nearer than five years hence.

Very best wishes.

Sincerely,

Jim Wright

Bill Alexander

Kent Hance

Stephen Neal

Author's Note: *This letter, signed by the four members of Congress who had gone to Nicaragua as informal emissaries of President Carter in June 1980, was requested by U.S. Ambassador Lawrence Pezzullo. The ambassador told me in a personal conversation that such a message was needed. He read and approved my draft. This document is referred to on page 47.*

2. Letter to Daniel Ortega, March 20, 1984

TEXAS
MAJORITY LEADER

Congress of the United States
House of Representatives
Office of the Majority Leader
Washington, D.C. 20515

March 20, 1984

Commandante Daniel Ortega
Coordinador de la Junta de Gobierno
Case de Gobierno
Managua, NICARAGUA

Dear Commandante:

We address this letter to you in a spirit of hopefulness and good will.

As Members of the U.S. House of Representatives, we regret the fact that better relations do not exist between the United States and your country. We have been, and remain, opposed to U.S. support for military action directed against the people or government of Nicaragua.

We want to commend you and the members of your government for taking steps to open up the political process in your country. The Nicaraguan people have not had the opportunity to participate in a genuinely free election for over fifty years. We support your decision to schedule elections this year, to reduce press censorship, and to allow greater freedom of assembly for political parties. Finally, we recognize that you have taken these steps in the midst of ongoing military hostilities on the borders of Nicaragua.

We write with the hope that the initial steps you have taken will be followed by others designed to guarantee a fully open and democratic electoral process. We note that some who have become exiles from Nicaragua have expressed a willingness to return to participate in the elections, if assurances are provided that their security will be protected, and their political rights recognized. Among these exiles are some who have taken up arms against your government, and who have stated their willingness to lay down those arms to participate in a truly democratic process.

If this were to occur, the prospects for peace and stability throughout Central America would be dramatically enhanced. Those responsible for supporting violence against your government, and for obstructing serious negotiations for broad political participation in El Salvador would have far greater difficulty winning support for their policies than they do today.

We believe that you have it in your power to establish an example for Central America that can be of enormous historical importance. For this to occur, you have only to lend real force and meaning to concepts your leadership has already endorsed concerning the rules by which political parties may compete openly and equitably for political power.

A decision on your part to provide these reasonable assurances and conduct truly free and open elections would significantly improve the prospect of better relations between our two countries and significantly strengthen the hands of those in our country who desire better relations based upon true equality, self-determination and mutual good will.

We re-affirm to you our continuing respect and friendship for the Nicaraguan people, and pledge our willingness to discuss these or other matters of concern with you or officials of your government at any time.

Very sincerely yours,

Jim Wright

Michael D. Barnes

Bill Alexander

Matthew F. McHugh

Robert G. Torricelli

Edward P. Boland

Stephen J. Solarz

David R. Obey

Robert Garcia

Lee H. Hamilton

Author's Note: *This letter, signed by ten members of Congress whose interests and committee assignments had involved them in Central American affairs, was the outgrowth of a meeting with Alfonso Robelo in March 1984. Robelo, by then an opponent of the Sandinista regime, later participated in negotiations as a member of the Contra Directorate and became ambassador to Costa Rica in the Chamorro administration. He urged us to write this letter, believing that a truly free election could lead to both peace and democracy. This document is referred to on pages 66–67.*

3. Wright-Reagan Plan, August 5, 1987

Recognizing that the Central American Presidents are about to meet to discuss the issues involved and seek a peaceful solution to the problems in Central America, the United States desires to make known its views on certain of the basic elements that need to be included.

With respect to Nicaragua, the United States has three legitimate concerns for the well-being of the hemisphere:

1. That there be no Soviet, Cuban or Communist block bases established in Nicaragua that pose a threat to the United States and the other democratic governments in the hemisphere.

2. That Nicaragua pose no military threat to its neighbor countries nor provide a staging ground for subversion or destabilization of duly elected governments in the hemisphere.

3. That the Nicaraguan government respect the basic human rights of its people including political rights guaranteed in the Nicaraguan constitution and pledges made to the OAS—free speech, free press, religious liberty and a regularly established system of free, orderly elections.

Beyond this, the United States has no right to influence or determine the identity of the political leaders of Nicaragua nor the social and economic system of the country. These are matters wholly within the right of the Nicaraguan people. The United States affirms its support for the right of the Nicaraguan people to peaceful, democratic self-determination, free from outside intervention from any source.

In order to bring an immediate end to hostilities and begin a process of reconciliation, we propose the following:

1. An immediate cease-fire in place, on terms acceptable to the parties involved, subject to verification by the OAS or an international group of observers should be negotiated as soon as possible. When the cease-fire is in place, the U.S. will immediately suspend all military aid to the Contras and simultaneously Nicaragua will stop receiving military aid from Cuba, the Soviet Union, and the Communist block countries. Humanitarian aid can be supplied to both groups. The emergency law will be immediately suspended and all civil rights and liberties will be restored. An agreed, independent multi-party electoral commission will be established to assure regular elections open to free participation by all. A timetable and procedures for all elections, including those to be supervised and guaran-

teed by an agreed international body such as the OAS, will be established within 60 days.

2. The withdrawal of foreign military personnel and advisers from Nicaragua and its immediate neighbors that are in excess of the normal and legitimate needs of the region will be subject to negotiations among the countries of the region. The U.S. will suspend combat maneuvers in Honduras as a demonstration of good faith when the cease-fire is in place.

3. After the cease-fire is in place, negotiations among the governments of the United States, Costa Rica, El Salvador, Guatemala, Honduras, and Nicaragua shall begin on reductions in standing armies in the region, withdrawal of foreign military personnel, restoration of regional military balance, security guarantees against outside support for insurgent forces, and verification and enforcement provisions. As part of this negotiating process, the United States shall enter into discussions with the governments of the region—including the government of Nicaragua—concerning security issues. A regional agreement on security issues shall be negotiated within 60 days, unless this period is extended by mutual agreement. The OAS shall be invited to be a signatory to and guarantor of this agreement.

4. A plan of national reconciliation and dialogue among citizens of Nicaragua, including amnesty for former combatants and equal rights to participation in the political process. There shall be a plan of demobilization of both Sandinista and Resistance forces. In accordance with the implementation of this plan, the United States simultaneously shall cease all resupply of Resistance forces. Both the government of Nicaragua and the government of the United States shall encourage and support the reintegration of demobilized forces into Nicaraguan civil and political society on terms guaranteeing their safety. Nicaragua shall at this time become eligible for existing and prospective U.S. assistance programs.

5. A plan of expanded trade and long-range economic assistance for the democratic governments of Central America in which Nicaragua might participate. By the process of democratization and compliance with regional nonaggression agreements, Nicaragua would qualify for participation in the Caribbean Basin Initiative and the U.S. will lift its economic embargo.

6. The negotiating process shall commence immediately and be completed by September 30, 1987. If the Nicaraguan Resistance, or forces under its command, should refuse to engage in this negotiating process, willfully obstruct its progress, or violate its terms, the United

States shall immediately suspend all assistance to the Resistance. If, because of actions taken by the Nicaraguan government or the forces under its command, the negotiating process should not proceed; or its terms, conditions, and deadlines should not be met; the parties to these undertakings would be free to pursue such actions as they deem necessary to protect their national interest.

Author's Note: For the historical record, above is the final peace plan agreed to by President Reagan and me. This is the version that we handed out at the White House. It formed the basis in major part of the Esquipulas accords adopted two days later by the five Central American presidents. I drafted the original version, George Shultz added minor modifications, the bipartisan leaders of the House and Senate gave it their blessings, and then President Reagan and I jointly gave out the statement on August 5, 1987. This document is referred to on pages 103–104, 108.

4. Letter from Carlos Tünnermann, September 24, 1987

Embajada de Nicaragua

WASHINGTON. DC

September 24, 1987

The Honorable
Jim Wright
Speaker of the House
U.S. House of Representatives

Dear Mr. Speaker:

As you are well aware, events have been moving rapidly in Central America, and particularly in Nicaragua. I, like most Central Americans, am encouraged by these developments and share in the optimism that not only will we be able to end the war, but we can also begin to explore jointly new opportunities for development and regional cooperation that peace can offer to all the governments in area.

As you know, my Government has been faithfully complying, even in advance of the stipulated deadlines, with all the commitments contained in the Guatemalan Procedure. On September 22nd President Ortega announced the first steps being taken by our Government to achieve an effective cease fire. These steps include the suspension of offensive campaigns or military operations in designated zones of the country in order to create favorable conditions allowing for representatives of the National Reconciliation Commission and others to visit the areas and inform the population and the contra forces of both the content and scope of the Esquipulas II Accords. President Ortega has asked Cardinal Miguel Obando y Bravo to play a leading role in this initiative.

Before our announcement on the cease fire, the Nicaraguan Government authorized the reopening of La Prensa without prior censorship. This step was further enhanced by subsequent steps authorizing the reopening of "Radio Catolica" and the lifting of all censorship on any media. I have enclosed the english versions of the texts of the official communiques regarding both the cease fire and La Prensa.

I would also like to take this opportunity to send you the texts of the documents signed in Managua this past week by the Executive Commission. As you will note in the texts, significant progress was made during these meetings. Some of the results of these meetings include:

-- Starting from October 1, 1987, each member of the Executive Commission shall report every 15 days to the other members of the Commission and of the International Verification and Follow-up Commission on the progress of the work of the domestic commissions on the implementation of the Accords.

-- The next meeting of the Executive Commission will be held in the city of San Jose, Costa Rica on October 27-28, 1987.

-- The Executive Commission defined its duties and procedures.

Mr. Speaker, in addition to these public documents, I am taking this opportunity to send you a working document of the International Verification and Follow-up Commission and ask that it not be circulated since its ratification by the Foreign Ministers is pending until their next meeting. The document entitled "First Meeting of Ad-Hoc Representatives of the International Verification and Follow-up Commission" states that the Commission may request the services of the United Nations and the Organization of American States, in addition to whatever mechanisms that it deems appropriate, with regards to cease fire, cessation of external support of irregular forces or insurrectionist movements, and the non-use of a State's territory to attack other States. It also expressly states that the CIVS may carry out in fulfillment of its duties on site inspections. The next meeting of the CIVS will be held in Guatemala City on October 8-9, 1987.

Mr. Speaker, once again I wish to thank you for your leading role in seeking a peaceful solution to the conflict in Central America.

Sincerely,

Carlos Tünnermann B.
Ambassador

Author's Note: *Following the historic Esquipulas Agreement of August 7, 1987, active efforts toward peace began in both Nicaragua and El Salvador. The efforts of the Salvadoran government were described to me in person by President José Napoleón Duarte. This letter from Nicaraguan Ambassador Tünnermann describes the initial effort undertaken by the Nicaraguan government. This document is referred to on page 126.*

5. Note to Secretary of State George Shultz, October 15, 1987

The Speaker
United States House of Representatives
Washington, D. C. 20515   10/15/87

Dear George,

In regard to Elliott, I mentioned your interest to one of our chairmen today, and he gave me the enclosed article.

The problem seems to be a persistent impression among chairmen on both sides that Elliott is contemptuous of the Legislative branch. They feel offended at his Testimony about not being frank and Truthful with Congress and say it is like "pouring salt in the wounds," as one put it, to make Congress look to him for official State Department responses. This is the "feedback" I'm getting.

Author's Note: After Assistant Secretary of State Elliott Abrams acknowledged having deliberately lied to Congress concerning U.S. support of efforts to overthrow the Nicaraguan government, several House committees and subcommittees sent word that Abrams would not be welcome to testify except under oath. Secretary Shultz asked me personally to intercede on Abrams's behalf. I attempted to do so, without result. Chairmen of the subcommittees were adamant. By this handwritten personal note, I reported my findings to Secretary Shultz. This episode is referred to on page 151.

6. Shultz-Wright Statement, November 17, 1987

JIM WRIGHT
Texas
SPEAKER

Congress of the United States
House of Representatives
Office of the Speaker
Washington, DC 20515

JOINT STATEMENT
SECRETARY SHULTZ AND SPEAKER WRIGHT
NOVEMBER 17, 1987

1. We want the Guatemala City agreement [Esquipulas II] to succeed in bringing peace and freedom and democracy to Central America.

2. We believe that efforts toward that objective should be concentrated in Central America and continue to be guided primarily by Central Americans.

3. We strongly encourage Cardinal Obando y Bravo to undertake his mission of mediation and peace.

4. The United States has vital interests in this outcome, as was stated in the Reagan-Wright Plan.

5. As the Cardinal's efforts lead to serious negotiations, the United States will be ready to meet directly in a regional setting with representatives of the countries of the region.

6. Neither of us wants to create unnecessary problems. We want to work together to bring about solutions.

Author's Note: On November 17, 1987, Secretary George Shultz and I jointly issued this public statement in an effort to counteract news stories, at least one planted by a lower State Department official, to the effect that we were feuding over the efforts to bring peace to Central America. I had met on the previous Friday with Cardinal Miguel Obando y Bravo, at his request, and had encouraged the cardinal to undertake the role of peace negotiator between the Nicaraguan government and the armed resistance in carrying out the Esquipulas agreements. Secretary Shultz drafted the above statement, which expressed my own convictions precisely and reinforced exactly the principles I had been endeavoring to support. This document is referred to on page 154.

7. Memo for the Record of Phone Conversation with President Ortega, February 4, 1988

Telephone Conversations between Jim Wright and President Ortega and between Richard Peña and President Ortega

It is now 12:30 noon on the fourth day of February, 1988. I am sitting here in my office in H-204 of the Capitol. This is the day following the House vote narrowly rejecting President Reagan's plan for continued military support for the contras in Central America.

This morning I had a telephone call before the House went into session—it was about 10:40—from Daniel Ortega. I took the call. He was speaking in Spanish, and I understood part of what he said, and I tried to give a message to him that our vote yesterday was intended as a step in the direction of peace, that it opened up an avenue for him to do additional things in the direction of peace, that we expected him to come into full compliance with the Guatemala agreements.

He spoke of the upcoming meeting with the contras in Guatemala, I think Wednesday and Thursday of next week. He said something about the fact that we really need a methodology or a mechanism for verification, and he would like for certain things to be said and cooperation had from other presidents in the area in that connection.

At that point I got a bit uncomfortable with my ability in Spanish to translate nuances, and I said to him that I wanted him to understand that we had only a slender majority in the House, that we had won the vote, and had done this as an act of faith in the peace process and that we really are depending upon him to continue acts of good faith, to move in the direction of democratization and of a settlement with the contras and a cease-fire.

Then I said, because I don't really understand Spanish perfectly, that I'd like to have my friend, Richard Peña, call and talk with him or with whomever he would designate. If President Ortega wanted him to talk with Miguel D'Escoto, he would be glad to do that. President Ortega said fine. So I asked Richard. Richard came; he was on the Hill, and it was very fortunate. He made the telephone call, and talked with President Ortega directly. Richard's here, and I just asked him if he would recite for me basically the conversation that he had with Ortega. Richard Peña:

RICHARD PEÑA: (The conversation goes in this form:) This was a vote for peace.

SPEAKER WRIGHT: This is Ortega saying this?

RICHARD PEÑA: Yes, sir.

This is a vote for peace. This vote puts the U.S. on the side of a peaceful solution to a very important problem in Central America. This vote will allow us to move quickly to meet the conditions in the peace accord. One issue that concerns me is on-site verification of the peace accords which is an overall on-site verification of all the points in the accord. We feel that international verification with the U.N., Contradora, the OAS, and European persons involved in this verification would be very important.

He went on to say that Nicaragua will be fully committed to a total and faithful compliance to the cease-fire. They would be meeting in the next couple of days in Guatemala to continue negotiations on the cease-fire. They would be flexible and reasonable during these negotiations and would expect to quickly move forward in these talks. In addition, he said he would call the four other Central American presidents today to ask them to move ahead as soon as possible and for all of them to comply with the peace accord. He again reiterated that verification would be a major issue and that the verification on-site without any limitations would be something that he would demand.

He said that the Verification and Follow-up Commission had issued a good report, but it was not total and that they had discussed this at the San Jose meeting on the 15th and 16th of January. He went on to say that amnesty was deferred due to the simultaneity of the Commission on Verification and Follow-up, also on the concerns of meeting the cease-fire so there wouldn't be an issue of security involved on allowing these people out of the country.

In addition he said that the people who would be able to receive amnesty would not be exiled even though they may be taken by third countries, even though the third countries may accept them into their countries outside of Nicaragua, because, as soon as the cease-fire is negotiated, they would be allowed to return to Nicaragua to reintegrate themselves into the society.

A further problem is that the verification (again he goes back to verification) is an important issue because there is one country (he says especially Honduras) which had problems with on-site inspection and on the issue of non-usive territory that is part of the peace plan. He said that once this issue is met and reconciled that he feels that they can move quickly to fully commit with the peace plan.

He closed with this saying that the positive advancement of the peace plan depended on everyone and that they all have to work together in the next weeks to be able to put this together. And he sent his regards.

SPEAKER WRIGHT: That's good, Richard. I take that as generally a healthy sign. Were you able to convey to him any message for me?

RICHARD PEÑA: Yes, sir. I mentioned your concerns about the vote in Congress being as close as it was, that he would have to demonstrate his willingness to meet totally with the Arias Plan, suggested that he do this as quickly as possible so that he would not be receiving any criticism that he was dragging his feet and was being difficult in achieving this. I mentioned to him that it is extremely important to reach a cease-fire in place as soon as possible because that is one of the keys that is holding up the whole process and that once this was achieved that the reconciliation, amnesty, freedom of the press and the other issues that are involved in the peace process would have to be complied with. I reiterated that he would have to be supportive of the process, that he would have to meet the process fully due to the slim majority in Congress and that that was something he should consider while he is moving ahead. The last word I gave the President was that it was very important to make positive progress as soon as possible.

SPEAKER WRIGHT: Well, that's very good. Did he seem receptive to that message?

RICHARD PEÑA: Yes, sir. Very receptive.

SPEAKER WRIGHT: That's excellent. I'll tell you what I think I am going to do. Since I'm not really the one to negotiate these things, I think I'm going to have a transcript made of this tape and share it with someone in the Administration who may be in a position to follow up and work with him. I wish we had Phil Habib working down there instead of in the Middle East right now. This kind of thing may be useful to someone.
Thank you very much, Richard.

Author's Note: Following the vote of Congress on February 3, 1988, which rejected President Reagan's appeal to revive military aid to the Contras and renew the Nicaraguan war, I received a telephone call from President Daniel Ortega. Believing it important to share the contents of the conversation with Secretary Shultz as well as to preserve them for the record, I wrote the above memorandum and sent a copy of it to the White House and Secretary Shultz. This document is referred to on pages 167–168.

8. Letter to Secretary George Shultz, February 9, 1988

The Speaker's Rooms
U.S. House of Representatives
Washington, DC 20515
February 9, 1988

Hon. George Shultz
Secretary of State
Washington, D. C.

Dear Mr. Secretary:

Enclosed herewith is a letter which the House Democratic Leadership is sending today to President Reagan inviting suggestions from the Administration in drafting our proposal for humanitarian aid to the Contra forces. We solicit your thoughts as to the composition and delivery of this aid both prior to and during a cease-fire, together with such constructive ideas as you may wish to offer for encouraging both sides in the controversy to negotiate in good faith to the end that peace and democracy may return to the region.

As of yesterday, following my conversation with Howard Baker, I sent to the White House a transcript relating to a telephone call from Daniel Ortega. Mr. Ortega expressed a desire to proceed with cease-fire talks scheduled to be held beginning tomorrow, February 10, in Guatemala with leaders of the resistence. I felt that some of the comments concerning his thoughts on a verification process might be of interest and possibly useful to you.

It was disturbing to read an Associated Press account by Richard Cole today, in which Contra leaders have announced they will delay peace talks with the Sandinista government and not follow through with them as previously scheduled.

Since the Contras are seen in some quarters, rightly or wrongly, as the surrogates of Administration policy, their decision in calling off or postponing the peace talks will lead some to the unfortunate impression that the underlying purpose of official U. S. policy is not a negotiated settlement but rather a military solution. I am sure that you are as eager as I to dispell that impression.

If you think it would be helpful, I would be glad to discuss these developments with you along with any others you may wish, and to explore what possibilities may exist for a united front in the pursuit of peace in Central America. I'll await your call. I did want you to understand that we are quite earnest in trying to achieve, if at all possible, a bipartisan approach to this matter which heretofore has been fraught with so much controversy.

Very best personal regards as always.

Sincerely,

Jim Wright
The Speaker

cc: Congressional leaders

Author's Note: The above correspondence is self-explanatory. I wanted Secretary Shultz to know of the call from President Ortega and of our efforts to develop a bipartisan plan for humanitarian aid to the Contra forces during the cease-fire. This document is referred to on page 168.

9. Letter to President Reagan, February 9, 1988

The Speaker's Rooms
U.S. House of Representatives
Washington, DC 20515

February 9, 1988

President Ronald W. Reagan
The White House
1600 Pennsylvania Avenue, N.W.
Washington, D.C. 20500

Dear Mr. President:

We are writing to urge your active participation in the drafting of a humanitarian aid package to further the peace process in Central America.

Although Congress did not support your request for military and logistical aid to the Contras, we believe that some form of strictly humanitarian aid would now be appropriate.   It seems desirable for such a program to take clear form and be acted upon if possible within the next two weeks.

We have invited interested Members of the House, irrespective of party and philosophy, to participate in the drafting of this package, and we urgently seek your participation as well.

Conflicting statements from representatives and spokespersons both in and outside the Administration, since Congress declined to pass H.J.Res. 444, prompt us to ask you directly to help us develop and enact this follow-on legislation.   Rather than preparing for a confrontation at the conclusion of the process, surely it would be much better to work together at the outset in perfecting the program.

To this end, we invite your suggestions for the form and amount such humanitarian aid might take, as well as any other suggestions you may have for encouraging both sides to pursue a cease-fire and a process of democratization which will carry out the accords.

President Ronald W. Reagan
February 9, 1988
page two

   Your willingness to join us in a bi-partisan aid package would
be appreciated by both parties and would help hasten the
establishment of peace in Central America.

Sincerely,

Jim Wright
Speaker

David Bonior
Chief Deputy Whip

Tom Foley
Majority Leader

Tony Coelho
Majority Whip

*Author's Note: Following the failure of the president's request for
renewed military aid for the Contras, I tried to find the basis for a
bipartisan approach to provide humanitarian assistance. With this
letter to President Reagan, we asked for his help and participation in
this endeavor. This document is referred to on page 168.*

10. Letter from President Reagan, February 11, 1988

THE WHITE HOUSE

WASHINGTON

February 11, 1988

Dear Mr. Speaker:

Thank you for the letter sent by you and your colleagues in the leadership concerning U.S. assistance to the Nicaraguan Democratic Resistance.

I had noted earlier reports that you plan to introduce an alternative package, and it is significant that you recognize the urgency of acting upon further aid to the Resistance. As you are aware, on February 29, 1988, all authority to deliver aid to the Resistance will terminate. Without immediate action by the Congress, the freedom fighters will become recklessly exposed, and may soon have to make irreversible decisions about their own future. Even as I write this letter, we have reliable reports of new Soviet military shipments to Nicaragua.

As I said in my radio address last Saturday, I stand ready to work with the Congress on a bipartisan basis to develop a package that does not result in surrender or abandonment of the freedom fighters. It is important for us now to face together hard truths and make stark choices. A strong and viable Resistance remains essential if democracy is to have a chance in Nicaragua.

Therefore, the outlines of an acceptable package must provide sufficient aid to sustain the freedom fighters in order to maintain those pressures that have moved the peace process forward.

- 2 -

I look forward to hearing the details of your aid
package which I trust is being developed on an
urgent basis. With your proposals in hand, I can
assure you of our prompt response.

Sincerely,

Ronald Reagan

Author's Note: *With the above letter, President Reagan responded
to my offer of two days earlier. He ultimately decided not to offer any
specific suggestions, and Republican members of the House refused
to participate in drafting the bill, which was narrowly defeated on
March 3, 1988. This document is referred to on page 168.*

11. Letter to President Reagan, March 30, 1988

The Speaker's Rooms
U.S. House of Representatives
Washington, DC 20515

March 30, 1988

The President
The White House
Washington, D.C.

Dear Mr. President:

As we see progress being made toward peace and Democracy in Nicaragua, we surely hope most earnestly for fulfillment of those goals, and most of us want very much to make what positive contributions we can to the achievement of those ends. Even so, the question has arisen as to what general legislative procedures would be followed in event you as President should determine at a future time that peace efforts had broken down completely and that the national interest required you to request a renewal of some form of military aid.

In that event, which we do not anticipate and which we truly hope does not materialize, the following legislative procedure would be invoked in keeping with the rules and Constitutional rights of the House:

If the President shall determine at any time during the 100th Congress, upon the advice of the Verification Commission and/or such other sources as he may choose to consult, that the Government of Nicaragua is acting in violation of the terms of the cease-fire agreement of March 23 or of any peace agreement flowing therefrom and that the Nicaraguan Resistance are faithfully abiding by such terms or agreement, then the President may submit that finding to the Congress together with such legislative recommendations as he may deem advisable, and the Speaker shall promptly assign such legislative recommendations to the appropriate Committee or Committees of the House, with instructions to report the same back to the House together with the recommendations of said committee or committees, within not more than 10 legislative days following said referral, and the Speaker shall schedule such proposed legislation for consideration of the House under a fair and orderly procedure.

The above procedure is fully in keeping with our precedents. It would preserve both the rights and prerogatives of Congress and the responsible comity between the Executive and Legislative branches of government.

Very best wishes in your undertakings for peace, both in our hemisphere and throughout the world.

Sincerely,

Jim Wright
The Speaker

Author's Note: In drafting another bill for humanitarian assistance, one that was to pass the House easily on March 30, 1988, some in the administration wanted Congress to grant a special procedure whereby the president could draft another bill for renewed military activity and determine the timing for a congressional vote on his proposal without possibility of amendment. This would have violated congressional procedures. In order to assure the president of our willingness to consider any such requests he might have—but under orderly terms that preserved the legislative prerogative for Congress—I wrote him this memorandum, which amounted to my personal pledge as speaker. This document is referred to on page 176.

12. Letter to Meg Greenfield, May 10, 1988

Ms. Meg Greenfield
Editorial Page Editor
The Washington Post
1150 15th Street, N.W.
Washington, D.C. 20071

Dear Meg:

Please do me the very great favor of accepting this letter in the spirit in which I am writing it. I write not to carp and complain and criticize but rather to seek a better understanding. Between people of good will, it surely must be possible to have an understanding based on mutual respect and a willingness to treat one another right and fairly. During the 34 years I've spent in Washington, the *Post* has been my favorite newspaper of all newspapers. I have admired its journalistic legacy, its literary style, and usually its editorial commentary. It is natural that I would seek, and upon finding would cherish, a relationship of mutual trust, respect and even friendship with the *Post*.

Unfortunately, I have not communicated very well. Maybe I just haven't known how to go about it. I am still fairly new in this job, but I truly do want to perform it as well as I am humanly capable of doing. On three occasions now, the *Post* has written a sharp editorial criticism of an unexpected kind, criticism which has been based in each case at least partially upon misunderstanding of my actions and motives. I can't escape the conviction that these misunderstandings could have been avoided by better communication.

You and I verbally discussed the one instance which involved a misinterpretation of my position on a CBO Director. There is no need to go into that matter. I did talk with your editorialist after the fact and he has a better understanding of my position. Thank you for that.

The other two editorials concern Central America and your writer's quite hostile interpretation of what I should, and should not, be doing in that connection. On last November 16 (*What is Jim Wright Doing?*) you upbraided me for talking with Ortega and Cardinal Obando. You suggested that I might be undermining executive power by having personal contact with these people concerning the peace plan. The idea seemed to be that this wasn't my affair.

Then, last Sunday (*Superdiplomat Jim Wright*) your writer suggests that I ought to get more deeply involved, to "enforce (my) will on the regime," to employ "words to the Sandinistas" so as to make them respect peace and democracy. I am condemned for not having shown the "power (or disposition?)" to get this done.

Gee Whiz, Meg. First, I'm criticized for meddling, and then for not meddling enough. First it was none of my business, and now the whole outcome is my personal responsibility. Like Rodney Dangerfield, I don't get no respect.

In fact, both editorials indulge certain presumptions about just what I have and have not been doing. In the first instance, I was trying to carry out what I supposed all of us wanted—to persuade Cardinal Obando to serve as peace talk mediator and help get the talks going. You have to agree that was what the Administration was at least publicly espousing. I didn't invite myself, incidentally. I was asked to come by the Cardinal's representative, the Papal Nuncio.

In the second instance, your writer might have a point if he presumes that it is wrong of me to try to pursue "evenhandedness." But he should not presume that I haven't been trying in every conversation I've ever had with any Sandinista leader to impress upon them the need to respect democracy and individual rights. Sometimes this is much more effectively pursued in earnest private conversation than in public diatribes branding their country as an "evil empire" or publicly browbeating by threats of retribution. Threats of this kind often drive Latin leaders in exactly the opposite direction in their effort to prove to their own people that they are not intimidated by "Yankee Imperialist pressure." If proof of this were required we'd need only to consider the sad case of Noriega and his capacity to rally his people by nationalistic appeals against the U.S. under just such circumstances.

Suffice to say I am doing everything I can in my limited capacity to convince the Sandinistas that it is in their interest, and that of their country, to open up their domestic political procedures to full democracy. Your writer could have known this if only he had asked. I try also to assure them that the U.S. will treat them fairly if they do these things; and that, Meg, is a much harder sale. It really needs the help of our top Administration officials. Unfortunately, those officials will talk to the Nicaraguan government only through the press and then only in terms of repeated public condemnations.

Honestly, now, I don't regard myself as a diplomat. I have no ambition to be a diplomat. There are a lot of other very important legislative objectives which command my time and efforts. Incidentally, I have not initiated the conversations I've had either with the Contras or the Sandinistas. They have come about by people on both sides requesting to see me. This was true last week when members of the Directorate asked me to sit and talk with them. It is true this week when I am told by my staff that Sergio Ramirez, Nicaragua's Vice President, has sought an audience to come by and talk. It would please me very much if the Administration were willing to carry on these conversations. The Administration, for its own reasons, has chosen for some time to deny any audience to the elected officials of that country even though we maintain diplomatic relations and extend recognition to their government. This has created something of a vacuum which I have *not* rushed to fill. Sometimes I seem to be thrust into it by the demands of simple courtesy, by my instinctive and habitual inclination to give everyone a hearing and my personal desire to do whatever I may to be helpful in the search for peace.

Throughout all of this I have endeavored to be considerate of the Administration's wishes and respectful of the Administration's position even though I profoundly question our right to mine another country's harbors or to finance the attempted violent overthrow of another elected government in our hemisphere. I have consulted from time to time with Secretary Shultz and have told him personally of each instance in which I've had any significant conversation with anybody on either side of the Nicaraguan dispute. I do not covet his job, Meg. I would not usurp his responsibilities. The official attitude of the Administration to "freeze out" the Sandinista government from any direct conversation may have made it possible for me to be helpful to George. I have tried to be. I've endeavored in every instance to give him accurate information and sound advice.

Last week when the AID agency people came by to report to a bipartisan group of us their reasons for not having delivered the aid we voted five or six weeks ago, a group of Democratic and Republican leaders met with them and tried to help unsnarl the clogged channels of delivery. AID was trying to give the delivery role to a private organization named Circle G, an enterprise based in Honduras. David Bonior asked if Circle G had been involved in earlier deliveries for the CIA and the AID administrator Ted Morse acknowledged this to be true. Predictably, that choice probably would be doomed to rejection by the Sandinistas and the verification commission as well. The choice of the delivery mode is crucial to performing the necessary and increasingly difficult task of delivering aid to the resistance forces.

It really is too glib and too superficial just to blame the intransigence of the Sandinista officials for non-delivery of the aid package. I have talked with Adolfo Calero, Alfredo Cesar, OAS Secretary General Baena Soares and Ambassador Robert M. Sayre and have read the minutes of the meeting which produced the Sapoa accord. The following emerges:

Ortega suggested the aid be delivered by the International Red Cross. The Contras refused. Pedro Joaquin Chammora tells me they did not want the Red Cross because it would offend the pride of the Contra forces to receive assistance delivered by an organization which usually provides its services for disaster victims and objects of charity. Both sides agree that the aid could be delivered by a "neutral organization." Mr. Calero interpreted this to include a private commercial company. Ortega responded that he had no problem with that, just so long as the company selected was involved in no way with the CIA. It seems plausible that AID should have known this since that agreement took place on March 23, and should have chosen a delivery vehicle that fulfilled the mutual agreement. I have encouraged our AID people to do so expeditiously. Also I have encouraged them to move promptly after five weeks of delay to fund the verification commission, as the law directed.

Meg, I have made no personal attacks upon our Administration. I have tried my darndest to be constructive in all of this. I really, honest to God, do think it is unfair for me to be invited into this matter by the President and then repeatedly singled out for criticism.

Could we maybe just talk in a calm and unhurried way with the editorial writer, and make sure he understands where I'm coming from, *before* he takes word processor in hand to zing me?

Very best regards.

Author's Note: For the historical record, above is my personal letter to the Post *discussing its editorials. I did not receive a reply. The circumstances described in this document are discussed principally in chapters 9 and 10, and this document is referred to on page 210.*

13. Excerpts from Speaker's Daily Press Conference, September 20, 1988

**Press Conference with the
Speaker of the House
September 20, 1988
11:47 A.M.**

Q. Mr. Speaker, several sources who attended the meeting with the House leadership which you attended with the Nicaraguan Resistance Directorate have said you characterized the incarceration of people as "CIA provocation" and said you are not willing to offer assistance to get the opposition leaders out of jail because they may go out and do more agitation. Did you characterize that as a matter of intent?

The Speaker. Would you identify yourself?

Q. Pete La Barbera, *Washington Times.*

The Speaker. The several sources whom you cite were not present at the meeting or else they were not listening. I said I was encouraging the government in Nicaragua to release the prisoners, and anyone who heard anything different than that was not listening or was inventing for purposes of his own ideological inclination. It is a false story. I said that most emphatically.

I did say that we had seen clear testimony from CIA people that they have deliberately done things to provoke overreaction on the part of the government in Nicaragua, and that these things in my judgment had been foolish things to do, and I did not believe that it was a proper role of our government to try to provoke riots or deliberately try to antagonize the governing officials to provoke foolish overreactions, but I thought we should be using the influence of the United States to encourage the peace process, not to discourage it, not to try to create incidents that would be disruptive of the peace process.

That is what I said, and anyone who heard it differently either doesn't understand the English language or is quite inventive in his selective hearing.

Q. Mr. Speaker, the Contras and the Sandinistas apparently, after meeting yesterday, have broken off their discussions trying to get the peace talks back on track. Do you see that as a lost cause at this point?

The Speaker. No, not a lost cause, no. One could have pronounced it a lost cause ten or twelve times in the past year, and yet it still continues to breathe. I am very earnestly hopeful that both sides, as I tried to say earlier, will be sufficiently conciliatory that they can renew the peace talks and pursue them to a logical conclusion that will bring about peace and democracy in Nicaragua.

Author's Note: While speaker, I conducted a daily press conference before the convening of the House. During the course of questions, most of them concerning the schedule of domestic legislation, the above question was asked and the subsequent answer given. The circumstances surrounding this press conference are described on pages 206–208.

14. Speaker's Formal Statement to the Press, September 23, 1988

For information contact:
Charmayne Marsh 225-8040   Wilson Morris 225-2204

Statement by Speaker Jim Wright
September 23, 1988

When I made a personal comment last Friday in a private meeting with leaders of the Nicaraguan contra-movement, I did not intend that comment to become the focal point of a national debate.

Now that others have chosen to make it that, let's go to the heart of the matter.

The question of greatest importance is not what I said and whether I should have said it. The question is what our government has done, and whether we should be doing it.

The CIA was created to gather intelligence, not to make policy. That is the role of Congress.

Congress is not subservient to the CIA or any other agency, nor dependent upon their permission to speak.

It is the responsibility of Congress to speak out whenever it discovers any agency of government, financed by the taxpayer's money, is operating contrary to established public policy.

In the early 1970s the CIA engaged secretly in undermining and destabilizing the elected government of Chile while we publicly maintained friendly relations. Congress was misinformed, and the truth was revealed by Gerald Ford after he became President.

What resulted from the overthrow and assassination of President Allende has been 15 years of oppressive military dictatorship.

In 1984, the CIA, in violation of U.S. law, mined the public harbors of Nicaragua while we were publicly maintaining diplomatic relations with that country and its government.

Former Senator Barry Goldwater, among others, blew the whistle on that sad chapter in American history. The World Court found us guilty of violating international law.

In 1986, operatives in the White House annex, in violation of law and without informing Congress, sold weapons to Iran and diverted the profits to the contras. This action has resulted in enormous public embarrassment for the United States.

If someone had publicly protested these misadventures when they were first contemplated, perhaps great mischief could have been avoided.

It is unfortunately true that while our government has pursued a public policy of supporting the peace talks in Central America, agents of our government have engaged in efforts to destabilize the Nicaraguan government and to produce incidents aimed at provoking an overreaction on the part of that government of a type that is calculated to be disruptive to the peace talks.

This is the continuance of a policy which has been in force for many months. On September 16, 1985, David MacMichael, a senior analyst for the CIA, testified under oath before the World Court. He said:

> the principal actions to be undertaken were paramilitary which hopefully would provoke cross-border attacks by Nicaraguan forces and thus serve to demonstrate Nicaragua's aggressive nature . . . It was hoped that the Nicaraguan Government would clamp down on civil liberties within Nicaragua itself, arresting its opposition . . . and further that there would be reaction against United States citizens, particularly against United States diplomatic personnel within Nicaragua and thus serve to demonstrate the hostility of Nicaragua toward the United States.

It is my contention that this practice is contrary to officially announced public policy and should be discontinued during the period when we are trying to encourage the peace process.

The United States should not say one thing publicly and do another privately. That is unworthy of our nation. We will not be trusted or respected by others if we do.

I have said these things privately to members of the Administration. I regret the necessity to say them publicly. But I believe they need to be said.

Author's Note: Such a storm of protest arose concerning my off-hand comments in response to the question on September 20 that I made the formal statement above in clarification and amplification of my position. This document is referred to on page 213.

15. Letter to Julian Dixon, October 5, 1938

The Speaker's Rooms
U. S. House of Representatives
Washington, D. C. 20515

October 5, 1988

Hon. Julian C. Dixon
Chairman
Committee on Standards of Official Conduct
U. S. House of Representatives
Washington, D. C. 20515

Dear Mr. Chairman:

It will be my pleasure to cooperate with you and your committee in any way you may desire concerning the allegation that I "may have" improperly divulged classified information. The facts are these:

Such information as I divulged in my comments about the CIA was already in the public domain.

When I said there was "clear testimony" regarding CIA efforts to provoke overreaction and arrests on the part of Sandinista officials, I had reference to testimony given under oath to the World Court by CIA personnel.

It is possible in fact that the CIA may never have formally acknowledged this purpose in any of its testimony before the House Intelligence Committee, and it is my distinct impression that Congress has never authorized such activities.

There is additional testimony by Edgar Chamorro, a former Contra leader who worked with the CIA (copy enclosed) concerning the CIA purpose to overthrow the government of Nicaragua at a time when its announced purpose, to the Committee as well as to the public, was only the interdiction of weapons bound for El Salvador.

It was the discovery of this fact, by means other than CIA testimony to the Committee, which led to the Boland amendment forbidding such activity.

The Chamorro statement also provides revelation concerning the mining of the harbors by CIA employees and the effort to attribute the deed publicly (and falsely) to the internal Nicaraguan resistance.

Concerning my statement that the CIA had sought to disrupt the peace process, I am enclosing a news article which appeared on October 22, 1987, in the _Philadelphia Inquirer_. This story discloses that CIA agents attempted by offering financial rewards in the amount of $3,000 a month to prevent Miskito Indian leaders from going to the peace table. The CIA reportedly tried to persuade the Indians to continue the war even though it was official U. S. policy to pursue negotiations.

All of this is, and has been, in the public domain. However one may feel individually concerning the rightness or wrongness of these reported deeds, it surely is the right of a member of Congress to comment upon them.

If you should want me to come and discuss this personally with your committee, I shall be glad to do so.

Sincerely,

Jim Wright
The Speaker

P. S. Also note underlined passages of the enclosed Newsweek article dated July 25, 1988.

Author's Note: When a group of Republican members asked the Committee on Standards of Official Conduct to investigate whether I may have disclosed official secrets, I wrote the above letter to the chairman of the committee, along with news articles and enclosures from transcripts of testimony before the World Court, inviting any investigation his committee might wish to make. The committee did not pursue the inquiry. This document is referred to on page 209.

16. Letter from Costa Rican Ambassador Fernández, March 9, 1989

EMBAJADA DE COSTA RICA
WASHINGTON, D. C. 20009

March 9, 1989

Dear Mr. Speaker:

Thank you for your letter of March 1, 1988. I am deeply touched by your kindness.

A few hours before I depart for San José, if I may temporarily suspend my customary rule requiring short farewells, a few reflections come to mind which I will like to share with you.

It was a true honor and a rare privilege to have known and worked with you and the members of your staff. Even though our meetings were limited by severe demands of agenda strictures, I have learned to appreciate the significant effort and warm sincerity you have shown with respect to advancing the cause of Central America.

Working together in a Peace Plan for Central America, whatever its shortcomings, provided us both with the occasion to get to know each other better and interact in an environment enhanced by our expanded perspectives.

The determined pursuit of an illusive peace is, as many of us know, not without risk. Developing a permanent solution to current problems is so vital that selflessness had to prevail over personal expediency.

Our joint actions have engendered controversy and challenged many a confortable position held in your country as well as in mine. Many in my country felt isolated, none less than I who knew that my small nation was following a path which diverted from that otherwise expected in light of US policies. It was most conforting to realize that we could count on your continuing belief in and support of our efforts in the search for peace. I maintain that my small nation will be a better friend of the United States because it will never fear to express a few simple truths.

Honorable
Jim Wright
Speaker of the House
United States House of Representatives
Washington, D.C.

Honorable Jim Wright

-2-

    Our work has not yet been completed. Perhaps such work,
however humble, in pursuit of a cause so noble can never be.
I am sure that my leavetaking of today will be of short duration,
for I am changing my address and not my convictions or the extent
of my commitment to the goals which we have so resoluted pursued.

    Until I see you again, my distinguished friend, please accept
the assurances of my continuing friendship and personal esteem.

Guido Fernández
Ambassador

Author's Note: *The Costa Rican ambassador, with whom I had
worked closely in connection with the Central American Peace Plan
perfected by President Oscar Arias, returned to Costa Rica as a
member of the Arias cabinet in March 1989. He sent me the letter
above. This document is referred to on page 225.*

17. Bipartisan Accord on Central America, March 24, 1989

Bipartisan Accord on Central America

The Executive and the Congress are united today in support of democracy, peace, and security in Central America. The United States supports the peace and democratization process and the goals of the Central American Presidents embodied in the Esquipulas Accord. The United States is committed to working in good faith with the democratic leaders of Central America and Latin America to translate the bright promises of Esquipulas II into concrete realities on the ground.

With regard to Nicaragua, the United States is united in its goals: democratization; an end to subversion and destabilization of its neighbors; an end to Soviet bloc military ties that threaten U.S. and regional security. Today the Executive and the Congress are united on a policy to achieve those goals.

To be successful the Central American peace process cannot be based on promises alone. It must be based on credible standards of compliance, strict timetables for enforcement, and effective on-going means to verify both the democratic and security requirements of those agreements. We support the use of incentives and disincentives to achieve U.S. policy objectives.

We also endorse an open, consultative process with bipartisanship as the watchword for the development and success of a unified policy towards Central America. The Congress recognizes the need for consistency and continuity in policy and the responsibility of the Executive to administer and carry out that policy, the programs based upon it, and to conduct American diplomacy in the region. The Executive will consult regularly and report to the Congress on progress in meeting the goals of the peace and democratization process, including the use of assistance as outlined in this Accord.

- 2 -

Under Esquipulas II and the El Salvador Accord, insurgent forces are supposed to voluntarily reintegrate into their homeland under safe, democratic conditions. The United States shall encourage the Government of Nicaragua and the Nicaraguan Resistance to continue the cessation of hostilities currently in effect.

To implement our purposes, the Executive will propose and the bipartisan leadership of the Congress will act promptly after the Easter Recess to extend humanitarian assistance at current levels to the Resistance through February 28, 1990, noting that the Government of Nicaragua has agreed to hold new elections under international supervision just prior to that date. Those funds shall also be available to support voluntary reintegration or voluntary regional relocation by the Nicaraguan Resistance. Such voluntary reintegration or voluntary regional relocation assistance shall be provided in a manner supportive of the goals of the Central American nations, as expressed in the Esquipulas II agreement and the El Salvador Accord, including the goal of democratization within Nicaragua, and the reintegration plan to be developed pursuant to those accords.

We believe that democratization should continue throughout Central America in those nations in which it is not yet complete with progress towards strengthening of civilian leadership, the defense of human rights, the rule of law and functioning judicial systems, and consolidation of free, open, safe, political processes in which all groups and individuals can fairly compete for political leadership. We believe that democracy and peace in Central America can create the conditions for economic integration and development that can benefit all the people of the region and pledge ourselves to examine new ideas to further those worthy goals.

While the Soviet Union and Cuba both publicly endorsed the Esquipulas Agreement, their continued aid and support of violence and subversion in Central America is in direct violation of that regional agreement. The United States believes that President Gorbachev's impending visit to Cuba represents an important opportunity for both the Soviet Union and Cuba to end all aid that supports subversion and destabilization in Central America as President Arias has requested and as the Central American peace process demands.

- 3 -

The United States Government retains ultimate responsibility
to define its national interests and foreign policy, and
nothing in this Accord shall be interpreted to infringe on
that responsibility. The United States need not spell out in
advance the nature or type of action that would be undertaken
in response to threats to U.S. national security interests.
Rather it should be sufficient to simply make clear that such
threats will be met by any appropriate Constitutional means.
The spirit of trust, bipartisanship, and common purpose
expressed in this Accord between the Executive and the
Congress shall continue to be the foundation for its full
implementation and the achievement of democracy, security, and
peace in Central America.

_____
President of the United States

_____   _____
James C. Wright, Jr.   Robert Dole
Speaker of the House   Senate Republican Leader

_____   _____
George J. Mitchell   Robert H. Michel
Senate Majority Leader   House Republican Leader

_____
Thomas S. Foley
House Majority Leader

THE WHITE HOUSE,

    March 24, 1989.

*Author's Note: Above is the text of the agreement worked out with
the help of Secretary of State James Baker, endorsed by the Democratic and Republican leaders of both House and Senate, and formally
issued in a ceremony with President Bush at the White House on
March 24, 1989. This document is referred to on page 228.*

18. Excerpts from Speaker's Resignation Address, May 31, 1989

. . . .

MR. WRIGHT. Mr. Speaker, for 34 years I have had the great privilege to be a Member of this institution, the people's House, and I shall forever be grateful for that wondrous privilege. I never cease to be thankful to the people of the 12th District of Texas for their friendship and their understanding and their partiality toward me.

Eighteen times they have voted to permit me the grand privilege of representing them here in this repository of the democratic principles.

Only a few days ago, even in the face of harsh news accounts and bitter criticisms, they indicated in a poll taken by the leading newspaper in the district that 78 percent of them approved of my services, and that includes 73 percent of the Republicans in my district. I am very proud of that.

And you, my colleagues—Democrats and Republicans—I owe a great deal to you. You have given me the greatest gift within your power to give. To be the Speaker of the U.S. House of Representatives is the grandest opportunity that can come to any lawmaker anywhere in the Western World, so I would be deeply remiss if I did not express my sincere appreciation to you for that opportunity.

I would hope that I have reflected credit upon the people of my district who knew me best, perhaps, and upon the people of this House who, next to them, know me best.

I am proud of a number of things that we have done together while you have let me be your Speaker. I am proud of the record of the 100th Congress.

Many people feel that it was the most responsive and productive Congress in perhaps 25 years, and all of you who were here in that Congress had a part in that.

Many of the things we did were truly bipartisan in character. Together we made it possible for great leaps forward to be made in such things as U.S. competitiveness in the world. Together we fashioned the beginnings of a truly effective war on drugs—to stamp out that menace to the streets and schools and homes of our Nation.

We began the effort to help the homeless, and we still have work to do to make housing affordable to low-income Americans so that there will not be any homeless in this country.

We did things to help abate the financial disaster of catastrophic illness, to provide for welfare reform, clean water, and a great many other things that I shall not detail.

For your help, your great work, and for permitting me to be a part of this institution while that was happening, I thank you and I shall forever be grateful for your cooperation.

I love this institution. I want to assure each of you that under no circumstances, having spent more than half my life here, this House being my home, would I ever knowingly or intentionally do or say anything to violate its rules or detract from its standards. All of us are prone to human error.

. . . .

So without any rancor and without any bitterness, without any hard feelings toward anybody, I thank you for indulging me as I answer to you, and to the American people, for my honor, my reputation, and for all the things I have tried to stand for all these years.

. . . .

When vilification becomes an accepted form of political debate, when negative campaigning becomes a full-time occupation, when members of each party become self-appointed vigilantes carrying out personal vendettas against members of the other party, in God's name that is not what this institution is supposed to be all about. When vengeance becomes more desirable than vindication and harsh personal attacks upon one another's motives and one another's character drown out the quiet logic of serious debate on important issues—things that we ought to be involving ourselves in—surely that is unworthy of our institution, unworthy of our American political process.

All of us in both political parties must resolve to bring this period of mindless cannibalism to an end. There has been enough of it.

I pray to God that we will do that and restore the spirit that always existed in this House. When I first came here, all those years ago in 1955, this was a place where a man's word was his bond, and his honor and the truth of what he said to you were assumed. He did not have to prove it.

I remember one time Cleve Bailey of West Virginia in a moment of impassioned concern over a tariff bill jumped up and made an objection to the fact that Chet Holifield had voted. In those days we shouted our answers to the votes, and Mr. Holifield was there in the back, and Bailey said, "I object to the vote of the gentleman from California being counted." He said, "He was not in the Chamber when his name was called and, therefore, he is not entitled to vote."

It was a close vote. Speaker Rayburn grew as red as a tomato, and I thought he was going to break the gavel when he hammered and said, "The Chair always takes the word of a Member," and then because I was sitting over behind Cleve Bailey, I heard other Members come and say, "Cleve, you are wrong. Chet was back there behind the rail. I was standing there by him when he answered. His answer just was not heard." Others said he should not have said that. Cleve Bailey, the crusty old West Virginian, came down and abjectly, literally with tears in his eyes, apologized for having questioned the word of a fellow Member. We need that.

Have I made mistakes? Oh, boy, how many? I have made a lot of mistakes—mistakes in judgment. Oh yes, a lot of them. I will make some more.

. . . .

Have I contributed unwittingly to this manic idea of a frenzy of feeding on other people's reputations? Have I caused a lot of this? Maybe I have. God, I hope I have not, but maybe I have. Have I been too partisan? Too insistent? Too abrasive? Too determined to have my way? Perhaps. Maybe so.

If I have offended anybody in the other party, I am sorry. I never meant to. I would not have done so intentionally. I have always tried to treat all of our colleagues, Democrats and Republicans, with respect.

Are there things I would do differently if I had them to do over again? Oh, boy, how many may I name for you?

Well, I tell you what; I am going to make you a proposition: Let me give you back this job you gave to me as a propitiation for all of this season of bad will that has grown up among us. Let me give it back to you. I will resign as Speaker of the House effective upon the election of my successor, and I will ask that we call a caucus on the Democratic side for next Tuesday to choose a successor.

I do not want to be a party to tearing up this institution. I love it.

To tell you the truth, this year it has been very difficult for me to offer the kind of moral leadership that our institution needs. Because every time I try to talk about the needs of the country, about the needs for affordable homes—both Jack Kemp's idea and the ideas we are developing here—every time I try to talk about the need for minimum wage, about the need for day care centers, embracing ideas on both sides of the aisle, the media have not been interested in that. They wanted to ask me about petty personal finances.

You do not need that for a Speaker. You need somebody else, so I want to give you that back, and will have a caucus on Tuesday.

Then I will offer to resign from the House sometime before the end of June. Let that be a total payment for the anger and hostility we feel toward each other.

Let us not try to get even with each other. Republicans, please, do not get it in your heads you need to get somebody else because of John Tower. Democrats, please, do not feel that you need to get somebody on the other side because of me. We ought to be more mature than that.

Let us restore to this institution the rightful priorities of what is good for this country. Let us all work together to try to achieve them.

The Nation has important business, and it cannot afford these distractions, and that is why I offer to resign.

I have enjoyed these years in Congress. I am grateful, for all of you have taught me things and been patient with me.

Horace Greeley had a quote that Harry Truman used to like:

> Fame is a vapor, popularity an accident. Riches take wings. Those who cheer today may curse tomorrow. Only one thing endures: character.

I am not a bitter man. I am not going to be. I am a lucky man. God has given me the privilege of serving in this, the greatest law making institution on Earth, for a great many years, and I am grateful to the people of my district in Texas and grateful to you, my colleagues, all of you.

God bless this institution. God bless the United States.

Author's Note: On May 31, 1989, I spoke to the House for exactly one hour on a subject of Personal Privilege, the first time in thirty-four years that I had invoked that rule as a member of the House. In the course of these remarks, I replied to various charges that had been made against me and my leadership of the House and announced by decision to resign the speakership as a propitiation for the season of ill will that had arisen and persisted. The above remarks are extracted from that hour-long speech. The circumstances surrounding this speech are referred to on page 235.

19. Letter from President Oscar Arias Sanchez, June 6, 1989

 The Library of Congress

(Translation-Spanish)

Washington, D.C.   20540

June 6, 1989
PR-5175-89

Mr. Jim Wright
Room 1236 Longworth Building
U.S. House of Representatives
Washington, D.C.
U.S.

Dear Mr. Wright:

Your farewell speech on the floor of the House of Representatives confirms for me two of your greatest virtues: your sincerity and your patriotism. I congratulate you for that decision so honest and in keeping with the dignity of the high office in which you served with intelligence and passion. I believe that part of the ordeal to which your adversaries subjected you in recent months was a way of getting back at you for your support of the effort to terminate the violence between brothers which is covering Central America in blood. Those opposed to peace will not forgive you for the fact that thanks to your vision and your deep commitment to the highest ideals of justice, peace, and process, the Esquipulas II process finally moved forward and is showing visible results for 28 million Central Americans.

The Wright-Reagan Plan, the bipartisan agreement between the Congress and the Executive, and finally the change in policy of the Bush Administration toward Central America, are a testimony and confirmation that you were not mistaken. In truth, you did more for us Central Americans than many of those who here call themselves standard bearers of freedom. I feel that it has been a privilege to know you. Count me among your friends.

Cordially,

Oscar Arias Sanchez

Author's Note: A few days after I announced my retirement from Congress, I received the above letter from my friend, President Oscar Arias of Costa Rica. It was translated from the Spanish by the language section at the Library of Congress. This document is referred to on page 235.

20. Memo from Secretary of State James Baker, March 7, 1990

SECRETARY OF STATE

3/7/90

Dear Jim

This is just a belated note to say congratulations and thanks for the important part you played in making it possible for democracy to triumph in Nicaragua. But for you there would have been no bi-partisan accord – without which there wouldn't been no election! all the best – Jim

Author's Note: Shortly after the election of President Violeta Chamorro in Nicaragua on February 25, 1990, I received the above note from Jim Baker. This document is referred to on page 240.

Index